PROVERBIAL
WISDOM:
FOR A FULLY-FUNCTIONING LIFE

PROVERBIAL
WISDOM:
FOR A FULLY-FUNCTIONING LIFE

VOLUME ONE
HOW TO BECOME THE BEST YOU CAN BE.

BY DONN H. POOLE

XULON PRESS

Xulon Press
2301 Lucien Way #415
Maitland, FL 32751
407.339.4217
www.xulonpress.com

Printed in the United States of America.

ISBN-13: 9781545624586

This book is dedicated to:

Dr. David Richo

Dr. M. Scott Peck (In Memoriam)

Dr. Wayne Dyer

Dr. Phil McGraw

Dr. David Grant (In Memoriam)

For Being Terrific Mentors

&

My Beloved Savior, Jesus Christ
For Saving My Life

TABLE OF CONTENTS

PREFACE

The term "self-help", when used to describe a book, implies that that book is intended to help someone who is "stuck" in life and being "stuck" is prohibiting that person from effectively pursuing life's endeavors. Such a person needs the knowledge given in that particular book to become "unstuck". Thousands of self-help books have been written, many by intelligent, educated, and insightful people. More often than not such books can be helpful to those who cannot afford to see a psychotherapist or psychiatrist. Such people, I believe, also had authority figures, from infancy to adulthood, who did not possess the necessary knowledge to help them become fully-functioning.

I happen to be one of those people who did not have the kind of mentors/authority figures that I needed in order to become the best I could possibly be in my developmental years. Unfortunately, most of my mentors were mediocre in regards to possessing effective wisdom and intelligence to help me, as an adolescent. Also, in my case, I believe my parents were neither emotionally nor spiritually qualified to have, much less raise, children. Nonetheless, the older I became the more I realized that my future was in my hands, and I sought mentors who could fill this "vacuum of effective knowledge" in my life. I was fortunate enough to have selected mentors who were truly intelligent. In some cases, my mentors were scary smart. One mentor, Dr. David Grant, not only possessed an indomitable character, but a spirit that exuded loving-kindness.

This book started out to be about thirty chapters long, but when I perused my notes, I realized it would be close to 600-700 pages, if I kept the structure of the chapters as I had originally planned. Most people will not read a book of this length unless it is a novel. A book that is written in a knowledge-sharing fashion is much too lengthy, if it goes past 250-275 pages (such a length would not even include an appendix). Therefore, I decided to divide this exhaustive subject into several volumes, each book between 250-295 pages. A book this size makes, for a much better "read".

Essentially, this first volume will cover what I believe to be the vital areas in all of our lives, the areas that need to be cultivated, strengthened, and permanently entrenched in wisdom, if we are to become fully-functioning. The concepts and wisdom principles which I will share with you have a biblical base and can mostly be traced to the knowledge I have gained from my study in the book of Proverbs and other "wisdom books" from Scripture.

The second volume will cover the cultivation and development of our relationships. That volume will discuss the components of both good and bad relationships, how to know when you are qualified to be in a relationship—whether platonic or romantic; deal-breakers or barriers to cultivating a long-term love-based relationship with someone; the role of sex in a relationship and how sex ought to be handled within a man-woman relationship; relationships with parents; components of a truly loving relationship; remarriage; infidelity; effective leadership; brutal realities about couple-hood; and the causes of conflict, in virtually all relationships.

The final volume will discuss the components of faith and spiritual development. I will talk about simplistic thinking; the occasions when evil "wins"; how moral people can often be the enemy of the truly virtuous; the secular philosophical enemies of Christianity; the greatest obstacle to genuine faith; the role of emotion in a Christian's life; the vicissitudes and universal realities of life; the four stages of faith; and the components of "spiritual elegance". This volume will hopefully be completed by fall of 2016.

Each of these volumes is a *Syllabus for Living Life*. It is my intent in this multi-volume set to encourage, inform, teach, motivate, positively provoke, instill hope, and in some contexts, even anger some readers. Why would I anger some individuals? I believe it is because I may challenge the pride some might have regarding who and what they are, the habits they have cultivated, and their mistaken beliefs regarding the critical contexts of life and living in which they believe they have the proverbial "it" all figured out. Also, I will probably say some things that run contrary to beliefs, points-of-view, and the ways some have been taught by authority figures whom they love very much. All of us understand John 8:32 - *"You shall know the truth and the truth shall set you free."* However, I truly believe that the truth will first make you uncomfortable, if not angry.

I have taken this *less traveled road* of writing because of sheer conviction. When it comes to the church, which Christ established and for which He died, I am deeply convicted that the church is the *only* entity that can make an eternal, vital difference in the direction the world is currently going. As a result of this conviction, I do not believe that this world will turn toward a constructive and righteous direction, not with the church behaving in a business-as-usual fashion. It is my belief that most ministers, who have the ability to accurately perceive reality, should not have a problem with this statement.

Within the context of the church today, I see church leadership conducting itself and its affairs, first from a position of *not to lose*. So afraid, I believe, is church leadership in regards to the making of mistakes, as well as fearing failure, in any ecclesiastical endeavor, that many church leaders project a position that declares they would rather do nothing and succeed, than risk extending of themselves in a worthy endeavor and risk failure.

When I consider this scenario, I am reminded, that the mediocre are always best avoiding risk, i.e., they opt to avoid *putting themselves* on-the-line, and risk failure when in pursuit of their dreams or other worthy endeavors. As a result, they are choosing to be a slave to another's perception of them regarding their successes and failures. Rather than being true to the one who created them, mediocre-thinking church leadership is afraid to risk being the best it can be for the glory of the Heavenly Father. Personally, I would rather do something and fail than do nothing and succeed.

Based on my observation of "media religion," I believe we are hearing from the pulpits of America today too much regarding the minister's opinions regarding what the Bible says, rather than focusing on what the Bible actually says minus man's opinion. As much as I enjoy studying critical historical data regarding the writings and writers of Scripture, I have sought not to lose sight of the purpose of what I am studying. That purpose is four-fold: *to reveal*

God's revelation of Himself to all mankind; to instruct the human race in how to relate to Him and to one another; to guide us in the discovery of our purpose in life, as well as our mission in this world; and to judge as well as convict each one of us in regard to our thoughts, intentions, and actions (See Hebrews 4:12). Today, I am troubled that there are too many Christian ministers and laity judging the Bible instead of letting the Bible judge them.

Staying in the familiar and in what is comfortable is the quickest way to being forgotten. I have learned far too late in my life that the more one focuses on the fear of losing something of significance, the more likely one will suffer from what one fears the most. We will be remembered primarily in this life for three things: the problems we created; the problems we resolved; and our compassion for those in need. God calls us to be *problem-solvers* rather than *problem-creators ... givers* rather than *takers.*

I want to thank Dr. David Richo, Dr. M. Scott Peck, who died in 2005, Dr. Phil McGraw, and Dr. Wayne Dyer, who died in 2015, for being men of courage, discipline; and integrity. These men have shared mightily of their hearts and lives, as well as the wisdom principles they have learned and lived, so that our lives might be more meaningful, purposeful, and filled with grace. I have not met any of these gentlemen, and I will not ever meet Dr. Scott Peck and Dr. Wayne Dyer. However, I love all of them like brothers. I have a special appreciation in my heart for Dr. Peck for the way he poured out his heart to us in his books. I don't know, logistically speaking, how I can be so fond of these people, but I simply know that I am. They are beacons encouraging mankind to a greater calling, a greater mission, and a greater purpose. They are lights shining in the dim *corridors of life* through which we all must walk. They call us to be better people as well as to be better in how we treat one another. They have worked tirelessly to bring the world into being a brotherhood, rather just being a neighborhood. They are my comrades in love.

In my young adult years Dr. David Grant was the greatest pastor I had ever known. As I have grown older, his life has had a marvelous and profound effect on me. He was a marvelously educated man, yet humble. He was not self-promoting in any manner or form. As far as I am concerned, he was the George Buttrick of my generation. You may have never heard of either of these men, but both were special men of God. Dr. Grant was a marvelous and elegant man, yet he was also the epitome of what I believe an exquisite Christian gentleman should be.

Dr. Grant treated all with whom he came in contact with dignity and grace—as if he or she was the most important person in the world. When he spoke to someone, it was as if there were no one else vying for his attention ... his focus stayed on the person speaking to him at that moment. He will always be in my heart and mind. When I get to heaven, I want to give him a hug, kiss him on the cheek, and thank him for being the finest minister I have ever known.

Finally, to my beloved Savior and Lord Jesus Christ—I owe Him my life. I can never repay Him for all that He has done for me, or all He has given me. He is my example. He is my mentor. He is my rabbi. He is my Lord. I thank the Heavenly Father for such a marvelous Savior and Lord.

INTRODUCTION

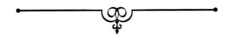

It is not lost on me how fast time flies, nor how stupidity viciously follows just as rapidly, seeking to inflict our lives with its virus. Once it does, it is amazing how we get used to the darkness. That is what I want to write about—our becoming "scary smart" while purging ourselves of stupidity.

There came a time in my life when I grew tired of being stupid—what Proverbs calls "living ineffectively". I wanted to be smart. I was tired of the insanity of doing the same things over and over again ... and always expecting different results. I am surprised God did not come down and hit me on the head and say, *"Hello, Mr. Potato Head. Mr. Potato Head, WAKE UP. Your stupidity is killing you and I love you too much to see you do this to yourself."* I was formally educated but I wasn't wise. I was knowledgeable but I wasn't intelligent. So, the pilgrimage began.

My growing interest in the book of Proverbs and other wisdom writings was, as I came to discover, divinely prodded. I needed a vaccine against my stupidity. I needed to become intelligent. God was not forceful in His prodding for me to give the Book of Proverbs and the book of Ecclesiastes my undivided interest. He was more subtle. He simply impressed on my heart that I should focus on what the wisdom literature of the Bible could teach me. I followed this "intuitive impression" and began to study ... intensely.

As time passed, the book of Proverbs became a part of the growth-study program in my life. Eventually, I categorized every verse in Proverbs according to subject. Although apprehensive that I might not give it due justice, I embraced the task with enthusiasm. The study proved to be a fascinating and illuminating experience and provided inspiration to my soul.

When I considered the task, I actually believed I could finish in a few hours. I finished five days later and began to reflect on what I had just experienced. I found I was grateful for the intuitive conviction from the Heavenly Father regarding the project. The study had truly illuminated my heart and mind beyond measure. God enriched my soul as He had promised! When I was through, I had categorized over 1,000 verses into over 175 subjects. In the appendix, you will find a listing of these subjects and the scriptures that speak to each subject. After the subject heading and before the listing of the scriptures, I give you the number of verses which appropriately belong under the subject listed.

To my surprise, I discovered that Proverbs is primarily a book about relationships. I had thought it was primarily a book of wisdom. Proverbs does speak about wisdom. However, it is wisdom applied to relationships and making decisions regarding those relationships.

Proverbs talks to us and about us as individuals, and about friendships, neighbors, men, women, husbands, wives, fathers, mothers, siblings, the poor, the rich, the righteous, the wicked, and the Lord—the Infinite/Personal God of the Old and New Testament. It also talks about the deceitfulness of the mind and/or the ego. It gives fair warning to not lean on our own knowledge but to put the wisdom of God's Word above our own worldly wisdom. It admonishes us to be prudent about decisions in key areas of life. I speak about these key areas in the chapter on the *Five Critical Lines of Life*.

Proverbs is filled with cautions, admonitions, insight, knowledge, and the illumination of the soul by dealing with the essentials of living each day to the fullest. Proverbs is to the Old Testament what the *Epistle of James* is to the New Testament. It challenges our assumptions, clarifies our purpose, and enlightens our hearts. It gives us a life-map to success in all of our relationships and endeavors. And yes, the life-map of Proverbs does conform to the terrain of life, unlike many maps of so-called reality, which are usually born out of the assumptions, prejudices, and simplistic thinking of most people.

As you peruse the list of subjects, which Proverbs broaches with each accompanying scripture, I believe you will be amazed at the depth of information and insight we are given regarding the components of a fully-functioning life. Please note that there will be a star (*) by scriptures that are key to helping define the subject at hand in a unique way.

Keep in mind that we are to be, as in the words of our Savior, *"wise as serpents and harmless as doves"*. We are to endeavor to develop insightful knowledge in the pivotal areas of life. We are to trust God's ways over our own and give God the benefit-of-the-doubt. We are to acknowledge His paths over the paths we desire to take but that are not in our best interest. We are to be harmless—benign. One of the things that I truly believe is that a consecrated Christian is truly a benign person. Great Christians are not lethal. For Christians, there is no hidden agenda. The terrific people in life are truth-seeking, gentle, graceful, benign, and transparent.

Proverbs tells us the absolute truth about righteousness and evil and about the struggle between what might be "good" in contrast to what is "best". In the words of the Apostle Paul in I Corinthians 10:23, *"I may have the right to do certain things, but doing so may not be within my best interests."* I truly believe that this is what makes *defining moments,* so critical to our lives.

Defining moments often occur when we are struggling to choose between what is good, in contrast to what is best. It is choosing between what is mediocre, in contrast to what is excellent. As is evidenced by the social reality of America, most have not done very well in dealing with such choices.

On one occasion years ago, I was spiritually illuminated in a manner that helped me understand the depth and meaning of certain Old Testament words. I had the pleasure of touring the Holy Land with a multi-denominational group—Catholics, Congregationalists, Church of Christ, Methodists, and Baptists. It was a magnificent experience.

Our guide was an Israeli who had retired from the Israeli Military. He had enormous knowledge of his land and its history. A professing Jew, he gave marvelous insight to the Old Testament events and places. His knowledge of the Hebrew language was marvelous.

One afternoon, we stopped for lunch at a rustic, roadside diner. All of us had ordered and I became acquainted with one particular fellow who was a music minister. I had ordered a wrap sandwich with fried potatoes. My new-found-friend had not ordered potatoes because he did not think of it. He immediately began to help himself to my fried potatoes. Before I knew it, he had eaten over half of my order. I laughed and at the same time turned to our guide and asked, "What is the word in Hebrew, for selfish?" His reply was profound. He said it was virtually the same word for wicked. I then asked, "Well, what is the word for heart?" He said, "The same for the English word ego." He pronounced both of these words for me but I shall not forget, ever, his responses regarding each of these words.

The book of Proverbs speaks a great deal about the heart. For me, seeing the heart as being where the ego also resides, opened the book of Proverbs to me in a way that I know for a fact would have never happened had I not been in Israel at exactly that moment, to hear this man's response. My thoughts moved to I Corinthians 13:12, where Paul says, *"We are looking through a mirror, which is a dark, obscure piece of polished brass."* I marvel at what we know and can know about God's Word, but I marvel more at what we do not know. Such a lack of knowledge humbles me. But greater still is the effect the Word of God has on each of us. It pierces our hearts and illuminates our souls. It has a purging effect when it comes to its conviction of wrongdoing as well as in its conviction of righteousness.

The book of Proverbs helps us see ourselves the way we are. And when we see ourselves accurately, we are often humbled. That is what humility is—seeing ourselves the way we truly are rather than the way we would like/wish to be.

Proverbs is not very politically correct. If anything, it is brutally candid about life. It is also an equal-opportunity offender. Proverbs lets the proverbial dominoes fall where they may and does not apologize for it. As Isaiah stated in chapter five of his self-entitled prophecy, when he found himself in the presence of holiness: *"Woe is me, I am a man with an unclean heart and a man of unclean lips."* In my way, I, too, cry out to God and say *"My Lord and my God! Forgive me for my shortsightedness and my lack of consecration."*

There is no middle ground in Proverbs. We either serve God or we serve our own appetites and selfish desires. We live for God or we live for self. We are either consecrated or uncommitted. Proverbs is explicit, as well as implicit, in its teaching that there is only room for one god in our lives. When the Infinite/Personal God of the Bible is not on the throne of our lives then our ego is. If Jehovah God is not the God of your life, then you are the god of your life. Are you ready for Proverbs?

Proverbs beat me to a pulp and then picked me up and brushed me off. I recall praying to the Lord one evening, *"Lord, I have fallen so far. How can I ever recover?"*

The white-hot flame of His Spirit touched my heart and I sensed these words being spoken to my heart: *"Donn, you fall so you can learn how to get up and get right! Have no apprehension, my son, I never give up on my children!"*

I can only reply, *"Oh, my soul! The love of God is truly greater far than tongue or pen can, as well as will, ever tell."*

I now know why God wept so much for me while I was away from Him. It was because His love went so unloved by me. I can only imagine what I put Him through. God's love leaked from His heart all over me and I could neither see it nor sense it. I had become numb to His love. You have to be hungry for God, as well as close to God, in order to experience His daily loving affirmation. What a promise God gives us! I am thankful that He never gives up on His children. He loves us all. But tragically, His love goes unrecognized and unwanted.

VOLUME ONE: YOU—BECOMING THE BEST YOU CAN BE

"There are two kinds of people in the world: Those, who know and those who think they know … and don't. Those who know often believe they know little. Those, who don't know often think they know more than anyone else."

CHAPTER ONE

THE ESSENTIALS

The Fifteen Universal Principles We Must Know & Embrace

> **Proverbs 3:5-6**: *"Trust in the Lord with all your heart and don't lean on your own intelligence— your own know-it-all-ism. In all your ways give Him the proper credit and the 'benefit of the doubt', and He will take the crooked paths of your life and straighten them out." (DP - Paraphrase)*

o **Wisdom Principle:** *"Not everything that can be counted counts, and not everything that counts can be counted."* —Albert Einstein

In life, we must always be aware that we are constantly making decisions. The populace most often makes decisions impulsively, as well as emotionally, very often without thinking, and with a limited amount of information. Unfortunately, most of the information found or assumed is inaccurate.

Now that I am much older, I look back and ask myself, "What is it that I would like to have known when younger that hurt me as a result of not knowing? If I had known this necessary information, would my life have been richer, more fulfilling, and more effective?"

What I discovered are the following principles. I believe that knowing and respecting them will save you a tremendous amount of heartache, frustration, disappointment, suffering, and pain. These 15 Essentials will be used by God to help keep your paths straight. Memorize these principles. Your life depends on it.

1. Attitude Is More Important Than Facts

It has been said that 80% of the success in one's life is due to attitude while only 20% is due to ability. You may be saying, "You've got to be kidding!", but I'm not. According to William James, the great Harvard professor, you can alter your life by altering your attitude. Life is not primarily what you make it; but how you take it. To be more specific: Life is 10% what you make it and 90% how you take it, and how you take life is rooted in your attitude.

o   **Wisdom Principle:** *We live to our expectations.*

Attitude is partially determined by the experiences life has brought to you, and is ultimately defined by how you have processed those experiences. Further, your attitude is reflected to the world in which you live by what you bring to life as a result of those experiences. Yes, your attitude reflects the perspective you have, of what has happened to you in life, as well as what is happening to you in life.

One of my beloved mentors, Dr. M. Scott Peck said, *"Life is what happens to you when you have planned something else."*

o **Wisdom Principle:** *"Our attitude toward life determines life's attitude toward each of us."*

Victor Frankel was imprisoned in a concentration camp by the Nazis. While millions of his Jewish brothers and sisters were dying in the gas chambers, he experienced something spiritually profound. He discovered what others have that a person can be stripped of everything except choosing the attitude in any given set of circumstances, which he/she is facing.

While in college, I was told by a marvelous man—one of my professors, Francis Marion Warden, that a person's attitude walks three feet in front of him/her. We can often see a person's attitude before he/she even speaks. It is uncanny how true this is when you notice a person's demeanor and look into his/her eyes. Therefore, attitude is more important than even intelligence or talent.

Attitude is more important than fact because among other things, it is an inner magnet. Because of this inner magnet, we attract to our lives, what our attitudes project. In other words, what comes into each of our lives is often the result of the expectations rooted in our attitude. This is precisely why those individuals with similar attitudes as ours gravitate to us; and we to them. I have never seen an individual with a positive attitude attracted to a person with a poor, self-serving attitude.

Attitude is also more important than fact because it is a part of our character. Attitude, within the context of character, I define by another term—worldview. If our worldview is positive, we will project positive expectations, especially when it comes to our experiences. When we project a negative worldview, we find that our life experiences *live down* to those negative expectations. Rooted in a negative worldview is an absence of self-respect and a lack of trust in oneself as well as for God.

In fact, I firmly believe that even death will reflect the attitude and character we have chosen to cultivate throughout our lives. Often in my ministry I have had the privilege of being with individuals who were dying of various diseases, and who still reflected a hope and an outlook that would give anyone reason to pause in awe. At times, I've entered that hospital room at a loss as to what I would say to give hope. But on certain occasions, instead of my cheering up these precious individuals, they have cheered me up. They have taught me, in their terrific attitude, more than I could have ever learned by reading self-help books.

On one occasion when Billy Graham spoke on death, he mentioned how his grandmother, while she lay dying, suddenly sat up and said *"I can see Jesus at the end of the bed."* Then she gently lay herself back down, closed her eyes, and quietly passed. How is this, as proof, of one's attitude?

There is no question but that our death will be a reflection of our attitude—by how we have processed the vicissitudes that have come into our lives. Also, there is no question that a person with a loving heart exudes loving-kindness to those whom they know and meet as well as those who minister to them at a particular time.

Their focus is often on others, rather than themselves. A grateful attitude produces joy, even in the midst of terminal illness.

How do you want to die? What will your death say about your attitude? Better still, how do you believe you will be remembered? If these questions have never crossed your mind, when do you think they will? When you have only a few hours left, before you pass? A little late, don't you think?

Our attitude draws or brings into our lives certain perspectives, experiences, and, even what we choose to remember. I have observed that individuals with a terrific attitude seem to recall the good things of life, as well as experiences which meant the most to them. Challenges in life make these individuals *better* rather than *bitter*.

Our attitude is the root of our expectations, whether *positive* or *negative*. Our expectations are the result of our attitude's approach to life. Even though we will not always get what we expect, we fare much better in life when we have great expectations rather than poor expectations.

Also, our attitude either says, "I am entitled," or "I am responsible." Individuals who consistently possess poor expectations, believe that life just simply isn't fair when it ought to be easy. Individuals with an "entitlement mentality" also believe they are *entitled to happiness*. There is no question that such individuals have, at the root of who and what they are, a bad and bitter attitude. This point-of-view, or worldview, is a "can't-miss predicator" of mediocrity. Individuals who possess this minimalist attitude wait for others to change and adjust toward them before they ever consider the possibility of changing or adjusting toward others.

The idea that we make our own happiness is not embraced by the minimalists among us. Truthfully, we are not *entitled* to a good life … we are *responsible* for making a good life—not something embraced by the mediocre among us. However, positive expectations do set wheels in motion that propel us toward making decisions that move us in a productive and positive direction. There is no question that we will find in life what we are looking for—positive or negative. Life is dull only to the dull among us.

When I was in the 9th grade I transferred to a new school. For a fourteen-year-old, that is an unsettling experience. On my first day, I met a young man who profoundly affected me for the better. Joel Swanson, a young man of medium height and build, was the first person to introduce himself to me.

I knew nothing about the importance of attitude or the definition of character at that time. However, I knew when I met this fellow that I was in the presence of someone quite special. Joel and I graduated high school together, except that he graduated with honors. To be specific, he was our valedictorian. Joel went to the University of Texas, graduated, and was accepted into Harvard Law School. He graduated there as well. I would not be surprised to learn that Joel graduated with honors at both schools. He has been a partner is a prestigious law firm in Houston for years.

What impressed me so much about him was his attitude—one that dripped self-confidence. There was a dignified humility about Joel. He was self-disciplined and pragmatic. In essence, Joel was 15 going on 25. His maturity was a decade beyond his years. Quite frankly, I am not surprised that Joel possessed such unbelievable maturity. I firmly believe that individuals with excellent attitudes mature faster than those who do not.

It has been a long time since I graduated from high school and I still remember Joel Swanson, He had a positive expectation about life, a crystal-clear self-definition. He knew even then who he was and where he wanted to go in life ... that he was going to be a *winner*, as well as an exceptional individual. He has proved the belief I had then to be true and I admire and respect him to this day. He never compromised his commitment, to excellence. **The key to such a commitment is rooted in his attitude**.

Our attitude is a reflection of what we say to ourselves—our self-talk—in the midst of any stress and challenge. Our attitude can be described as our frame of mind—our disposition toward life.

I love the attitude of great hitters in baseball. You see it in their walk and the gleam in their eyes. Great hitters in the major leagues know they will likely be near the top in strikeouts at the end of the season. However, this fact doesn't deter them from believing that the next at bat will be their time to shine. Their expectations produce determination and their determination, in turn, says that even if they don't deliver, they will have given their all. A great attitude disdains fear and has an *assassin's mentality* when facing the fear of losing. Great achievers say, through their attitudes to any fear they face, "Go take a powder, I'm busy!"

o **Wisdom Principle:** *The more one is afraid of losing, the more one loses.*

Finally, our attitude determines our intelligence and insight when it comes to life. Why? Because an individual with a positive attitude is also a terrific listener. Such individuals have open minds. Their minds are like sponges; they have voracious appetites for information and cannot get enough of it. In contrast, individuals with sub-par intelligence are those who possess know-it-all mental attitudes. You can tell them, but, realistically, you cannot tell them very much.

There are 18 references in Proverbs to listening with the intent of doing what one is admonished to do. Nonetheless, most individuals today are poor listeners and this is a direct result of a poor attitude and a lack of self-discipline. In the book of Proverbs, poor listeners are called mockers and fools.

A poor listener learns little, and primarily experiences only disappointment and frustration. *His/her mind is shut down and won't entertain contrary thoughts or new ideas.* The poor listener will develop a bad attitude while ignorantly embracing flawed beliefs and erroneous assumptions about life and people and seek to justify one's performance rather than seek to change it for the better.

o **Wisdom Principle:** *Our attitude is completely self-defined, i.e., we are in charge of the kind of attitude we choose to cultivate, and, as a result, we are also responsible for it!*

So, how do you develop a terrific attitude? How does one turn a sorry, negative attitude around? Here are six points to consider.

First, you must understand that every individual with an "entitlement mentality" has a bad attitude. Trust me on this one ... there are no exceptions. Bad attitudes are *barriers* to excellence and are also *contagious*. People with bad attitudes are *infectors* of a *deadly virus*. They infect everyone around them for the worst. It isn't enough for them to have a bad attitude, they have to bring everyone else down to their level. Individuals with a bad attitude *love to share their misery.*

To change a bad attitude, you must first embrace responsibility. You must immediately stop saying to yourself, "I am entitled and what I have become is everyone else's fault, because they have not accommodated my needs." Instead, you must begin to say to yourself, "I am responsible and what I have become is my fault." Say it over and over again to yourself—24/7/365. *When you realize that you have complete control over your attitude and the definition of your life you will be eager to take responsibility for both.* When you take full responsibility, you will also take appropriate control of your life. When you consistently do this, you will begin to be disciplined, committed, focused, and possessing a sense of personal power to change your life for the better. You then realize that if it is going to happen, it will be up to you to do it.

o   **Wisdom Principle:** *You can change virtually anything that is wrong in your life once you take responsibility for it.*

Also, regarding this point, do not let yourself *skate* on any situation where you are tempted to pass the buck and lay the responsibility for your thoughts, words, or actions on someone else. You need to consistently step-up-to-the-plate and take responsibility. You need to be determined never to relinquish responsibility for your life. This is critical!

Second, you need to have a clear vision (goal) of the person you want to become and begin working to become that person. You must begin becoming that person *within* and, in turn, practice being that person *outwardly*—you must achieve something within yourself before you achieve it without. By without, I mean achieving your desired goal through/by your actions. You must become what you want to achieve. I will say this a great deal throughout this book. There is no question that individuals must achieve any goal within themselves first before that goal can be achieved outside of themselves. Having a great attitude requires that you practice thinking, speaking, and acting as one who possesses such an attitude.

For example, it is believed by the masses that people are successful because they make money. This isn't true. People make money because they are successful! If you are going to make $100,000 dollars a year you had better have a $100,000 attitude as well as a $100,000 self-respect and self-worth.

Brian Tracy and others have told stories of people who set an income goal for a sales year and reached it three to six months earlier than they expected. However, because they had not adjusted their goal as they progressed, they did not sell anything else for the rest of the year. Unbelievable but true. However, my conviction as to why they did not make more money than the goal they had set for themselves was due to their self-respect and self-worth. These two perspectives were not worth more than the income goal they had set for themselves. I believe that an individual is not going to make a million dollars until he/she possess a million-dollar attitude as well as a million-dollar self-worth. You become what you seek to achieve, first. This principle you can take to the bank.

Third, you monitor your environment and relationships. This is pivotal! Our normal reaction to our environment is to think, speak, act, and conduct ourselves like the people with whom we habitually associate. If, according to statistics, only 5% achieve financial independence and live a fulfilling life, then it stands to reason that the 95% who do not achieve financial independence and life-fulfillment, are not doing the things that can help them become the individuals that are reflective of this 5%.

o **Wisdom Principle:** *"Do not be misled. Bad company corrupts good character."* –I Corinthians 15:33

I have already spoken about minimalism and the hordes that have chosen, more often by default, to be so. To avoid the tragedy of becoming a minimalist, you must realize that you are responsible for what you choose to believe, as well as to whom you choose to listen. The information dispensed by others may be flawed, but it is your responsibility to know that it is. Why? Because the ultimate person responsible for what you choose to believe to be true is you!

When a person is *on-top-of-their-game*, other people do not often negatively affect them. Primarily this is due to one's positive attitude, toward others. When you expect positive things from others, it is amazing how such an expectation is reciprocated. You must guard your attitude because it is pivotal to your success. Guard your attitude by being careful of your environment and its influences. If you allow the environment around you to negatively influence whom and what you become, you will ultimately find yourself in a state of discontent. Discontent is always the difference between where you are and where you want/ought to be. Only 5% of the world's population is able to consistently avoid this. Think … only 5%.

It is difficult for the environment in which we find ourselves not to influence whom and what one becomes. This is why 95% of the world becomes just like those with whom it spends its time. Closer scrutiny will also show that the overwhelming majority of the world spends time around minimalists because it chooses to do so. Just as water always seeks its own level, you need to seek to be in environments that are friendly to your dreams and goals, as well as helping you become the best you can be.

Fourth, never have a relationship with an individual who is not committed to your well-being and is also not committed to helping you become the best you can be. I realize that as a rule, individuals do not use such phrases regarding relationships. However, you must realize that individuals who stand in the way of you or anyone becoming the best person possible, disqualify themselves from having a relationship with you. Individuals who do not have your best interests consistently at heart will have no problem asking you to betray yourself, your goals, and your dreams, for their own benefit.

Fifth, never be satisfied with a "that's good enough" effort. Mediocrity is rooted in doing the least for the most reward. The best reward consistently eludes people who embrace minimalism. It's critical that you do not sell yourself to the lowest common denominator in life. Always give the best you have in all of your endeavors. *Perfection is not a human attribute; but excellence is.*

Sixth, seek to consistently treat everyone in your life, and those with whom you come in contact on a daily basis, as if they were the most important people in the world. Everyone wants to be recognized, given consideration, as well as treated graciously. Treat others as if they matter; because they do! When you practice treating others this way, beginning with those closest to you and then working beyond that immediate circle, you will find that they will reciprocate, or mirror back to you, how you have treated them. This is the absolute greatest win-win in life.

There is no question that when it comes to relationships, you will consistently find a person's attitude personified the most. Someone with a marvelous attitude knows that treating others graciously and with importance, will always positively come back to them in ways they cannot imagine.

Remember: Every dollar you will ever make in your life will come from/through people, not primarily from you. Without others paying for the value of your service or product(s), you have no way of becoming financially successful. People are that important to our well-being.

o **Wisdom Principle:** *The motto of individuals with a terrific attitude is: "You do not have to be sick to get better!"*

Individuals who believe that you have to be sick to get better never get better because they never believe they are ever *perfor-mance-sick*. In essence, such people get *stuck* in life. Being *stuck* is an *attitudinal dysfunction*. The only thing that can correct this minimalist point-of-view is to embrace a responsibility-based atti-tude. One's attitude is not another's responsibility; it is the respon-sibility of the person who owns the attitude. When we realize that the attitude we have is our own, we can then take responsi-bility for allowing our attitude to be influenced by others. Once we do this, we can correct the direction in which we are going and change it. I believe, this is—attitudinally speaking—a defining moment for you.

- o **Wisdom Principle:** *"What is occurring within us is often a reflection of what it going on around us."*—Matthew Kelly

2. Life Is a Performance Business

- o **Wisdom Principle:** *Life is a reflection of a self-disciplined life … or lack of it.*

It isn't all about you; it isn't all about me; nor is it personal. Life is simply a performance business. I have always been amazed that we seem to be a society more focused, as a beloved friend says, on "Managing perspectives instead of delivering results." Why do we give excuses and look at the impossibilities, instead of giving reasons for being successful, and choosing to look at the possibilities? It is because we have become an *entitlement society* rather than a *responsibility-oriented society*. Our society is intellectually and task lazy. It has confused wishful thinking with purposeful and goal-oriented thinking and this has reached epidemic proportions.

How has this happened?

First, our society has become one of words rather than actions. We live in a day and time in which when someone says something, it is believed to be a *done deal*. One's words are often equated with accomplishing what has been promised. As a result, whatever has been promised is assumed as having been already accomplished. In other words, that which is "said to be so" equals it "being so".

Unfortunately, this is not how real life works. Saying it, is not the same, as doing it. God may have spoken the world into existence in Genesis, but the speaking of things into existence stops there. In life, we must work hard to bring things into existence. It is not a coincidence, when Dr. Gordon Livingston says: *"That when all is said and done, more is said, than done."*

If you are a person who puts great value in what is said in contrast to what is done, you are, more often than not, off the radar screen when it comes to being dependable and trustworthy. You, like most minimalists, judge yourself by your *intentions* rather than by your *actions*. As a result, how you see yourself will always be *distorted* in contrast to how you actually, truly are. Also, how you see yourself will always be vastly different from how others see you, because, while you judge yourself by your intentions, others judge you by what you do. Big difference, isn't it?

Second, we have become a society that manages perceptions instead of delivering results, because we have created a "Pass Category" for four groups—Athletes, Musicians, Actors, and "The Pretty People".

Athletes, musicians, and actors successful in their careers are recognized by those who have an avid interest in these respective areas.

In three of these four groups are individuals who have honed their certain talents or abilities to the point where they have become valuable and admired. The "pass" we give these three groups occurs when we rationalize and excuse their inappropriate, illegal, or irresponsible behavior, when it occurs, because they are, whom they are.

When the people in one of these three categories "mess up", we perceive them differently than we would someone from our subdivision who might messed up in the same way. However, these celebrities are <u>not</u> different. Our society simply *perceives them differently* and, as a result, treats them this way. Just because these talented people are perceived as "cool," doesn't mean that the irresponsible, narcissistic things they do are cool as well. Right or wrong doesn't change, depending on the individual.

The fourth group mentioned, 'The Pretty People" are unlike the previous three. This group has no talent or ability to offer society, nor is it a group that has earned its "pass". This group is simply made up of "The Media-Defined Beautiful People". To qualify for entrance into this group, one has only to have won the *genetic lotto, i.e.,* one who has "earned" membership through the pro-cess of natural selection. From parental chromosome banks, these "beautiful people" possess certain physical attributes that society and media have determined make them special as well as valuable.

In a pamphlet I wrote years ago, there is a section entitled "The Myths About Media-Defined Beautiful Women" in which I enumerate the reasons why it is a mistake for a man to make physical attraction *the main component* in determining whether to make a relationship with such a woman permanent and I artic-ulated the reasons why this is not wise. As I began, I knew that the reasons men have, as well as the assumptions they make about beautiful women when it comes to long-term relationships, are similar when it comes to determining the value of "pretty people" in general. Realistically, we give "Media-Defined Beautiful People" a pass in society for very shallow reasons.

It has been proven that the giving of such a *pass* has even infected our public educational system. Several years ago, I heard a news story about a survey of teachers across the country showing that better-looking students were consistently given higher grades when their numerical averages were between letter grades. For example, if students had a numerical average between a C and a B and those students happened to be physically attractive, they were given the higher letter grade. If the students were considered average looking by society's standards, those particular students were consistently given the lower letter grade. Unbelievable, isn't it?

Our society behaves as if the more physically attractive men and women, are more pleasant, have better personalities, are nicer, more virtuous, more intelligent, more talented, wittier, more "fun to be with", and are, in general, greater achievers than average-looking people. The truth, in fact, is the total *opposite* of such beliefs and assumptions. *The prettier people in our society are not, in any manner, shape or form, better in these categories than what society calls average-looking people.*

Our society does not judge the pretty people by their behavior, but rather gives them a pass because of how they look. Such is not only immature and *dead wrong*, but ridiculous! *Looks do not define our achievements, actions do.* In the real world where people of integrity reside, people are not given anything. All of us must earn everything. In the integrity-based, real world, there are no passes in regards to performance. We must perform in order to receive a reward.

Make no mistake, regardless of the passes given to those mentioned above, life is a performance business. And, realistically, the most accurate, true, and reliable communication that you can take to the bank every single time is behavior. And, the greatest predictor of future behavior is the same behavior, in the same context that occurred in the past. What people see us do will always speak louder than what we say.

- o **Wisdom Principle:** *"Too many of us are listening to the words being spoken rather than reading the footprints of those doing the talking."*

Third, the reason we have become a society that manages perceptions in contrast to delivering results is that most people have failed to realize that they create their own value. One's value *cannot* be created by *someone else*, or by *an organization working on their behalf*.

Those with an *entitlement mentality* have chosen to depend on something or someone outside of themselves to determine their performance value. For most, that *something* is a person of power and significance in their lives, a parent, the government, or a union. A government or union cannot create your value or mine. Depending on the government to guarantee a value to someone that can only be created by that same individual is nothing less than a failure in progress.

I can tell you most assuredly, that another individual, the government, or even a labor union cannot create a person's *performance value*. This can only be done by oneself. Creating performance value is an intentional, disciplined act that is consistently practiced daily. This is tough to read or hear but you need to make a mental note regarding this: *Each person must understand clearly that effective performance is only possible, when one's per-formance is proportionate to the performance demanded.* If not, then what is required will fail to be achieved.

o **Wisdom Principle:** *Depending on anything outside of one-self to create one's performance value is a prescription for failure.*

Finally, life is a performance business because a person's behavior is the only true barometer of his or her commitments. For those who believe that words, intentions, or physical attrac-tiveness define a person, they need to know that such individuals live in a theoretical world. However, for those who believe that actions define us, such individuals live in the *real* world. Our values are the result of what we believe. Our commitments come from those embraced values.

However, our commitments are still in the theory-stage until we act. *Mental commitment and exemplified commitment are worlds apart.* Remember, the first true barometer of our commit-ments is the intelligence of our choices. Second, our commitments are defined, as well as expressed, in what we do—through our behavior. Others will always determine what we deem important in our lives by and through our behavior, as well as to what we give our time.

Even our Beloved Savior Jesus Christ stated that "By one's fruits" [actions] will one be defined/known." Dr. Wayne Dyer appropriately said, and I'm paraphrasing, *It is only your com-mitments that make a difference in the world. It isn't what you think, but what you do with what you think that makes all of the difference. Our opinions are trivial. It is what our commitments are, that tell-the-tale.*

- o **Wisdom Principle:** *Feelings do NOT produce effective behavior; effective behavior produces positive feelings.*
- o **Wisdom Principle:** *Positive, effective behavior is reflected by a person's willingness to do what they don't feel like doing, in order to create the future they want. Losers, on the other hand, do the things they want to do in order to create what they want in the present-moment, at the expense of their future.*

3. Effective Living Requires Effective Intelligence

The book of *Proverbs* focuses, with great diligence and purpose, on the importance of divine wisdom, what I call spiritual wisdom. There is no question that there are various kinds of intelligence. Where some people do not see the need to categorize intelligence based on the role certain kinds of intelligence play in our lives, I see five distinct kinds of intelligence.

1) **Rote Intelligence:** Rote intelligence is attained from reading books and other materials. This is knowledge primarily gained in the years of our elementary and high school years. Many call this *routine* intelligence, or *mechanical* intelligence. In other words, it is a fixed intelligence that comes from the attainment of knowledge very often without thought to its meaning. I like to think of it as *scholastic* intelligence—the kind of intelligence that provides

the base for developing the tools we need to apply the other intelligences to everyday life.

Contained in rote intelligence is the learning of language, mathematics, geography, the social sciences, etc. Rote intelligence is necessary in order to do well on academic tests. However, attaining rote intelligence does not mean that one is truly intelligent. We want our children to receive solid and meaningful rote intelligence but in no way does such intelligence mean that they are truly intelligent in the logistical and pragmatic matters of life.

2)Task Intelligence: We live in a task-oriented culture. Task intelligence has specifically to do with one's specialization in a certain area of expertise. For example, an accountant has pursued an education specific in nature to assist in the accumulation and maintaining of knowledge. This knowledge is set up in a specific format that can convey financial and/or operational information. Most accounting, if not all of it, focuses on the financial matters of a person, organization, or corporation. A medical doctor, in much the same way, pursues an education in a specific discipline of medical knowledge that will enable him/her to minister to those who are sick or have suffered a trauma from an accident or illness.

Therefore, task intelligence means possessing knowledge to accomplish a particular endeavor. Whether that endeavor is the accomplishment of an immediate goal or a long-term goal does not matter. What does matter is achieving the intended goal.

Not only does task intelligence apply to the pursuit of knowledge to work in a particular profession, but task intelligence also means possessing effective knowledge in order to excel in any endeavor—whether positive or negative. A person, for example, can possess task intelligence to perform a skill in law enforcement, emergency medicine, engineering, teaching, military duties, construction, cooking, or even athletics. When one possesses the required knowledge to accomplish such an endeavor, he / she possesses task intelligence.

It is appropriate to add here that those who excel at task intelligence often do so at the expense of the other intelligences. In fact, the greater one's task intelligence and skill, the more other critical areas of life take second place. Relationships, spiritual development, altruistic works … often these remain neglected and therefore uncultivated at the expense of developing professional expertise to a high level of proficiency.

o **Wisdom Principle:** *You can do anything you wish to do, but you can't do everything you want. You have to give up something to get something. We pay a price for everything we want. The greater the prize, the greater the price.*

3) **Relational (a.k.a. Social) Intelligence**: Relational Intelligence is simply a person's ability to navigate the "social waters" of life in a competent and confident fashion. This requires possessing the knowledge, ability, temperament, and commitment to relate effectively with a spouse,

family, friends, co-workers, neighbors and acquaintances. Many experts in the field of relationship psychology call this social intelligence. For me, relational intelligence is not only having the effective knowledge to maintain positive and fruitful relationships with others, but it is also having the knowledge to accept, understand, and love yourself. You must be comfortable in your own skin before you can reflect these character qualities in other relationships. In fact, how we are with ourselves, is a prelude to how we will be with others.

For example, if we rage with conflict and have unresolved issues churning constantly deep within us, we will transfer that rage and conflict to our relationships with others. Consequently, we will never be able to resolve issues/problems with others until we have resolved those conflicts raging deep within ourselves. Such turmoil will consistently remain in our lives and relationships, until we face our "relational demons" and decide that we will no longer be victimized by such "subconscious compliances". When it is said of someone that they have a high social IQ, it means that a person possesses an above average knowledge and ability in the administration and maintenance of relationships.

o **Wisdom Principle:** *Relational intelligence is in part, reflected by not allowing the friends we know to become the friends we once knew.*

4) **Emotional Intelligence:** Emotional Intelligence is what our world often calls the *Intuitive Intelligence*. The emergence of emotional intelligence is new. Some terrific work has been done in this field by Dr. Daniel Goleman, a professor at Harvard University. His two books *Emotional Intelligence* and *Social Intelligence* are groundbreaking. He is the most knowledgeable individual in these two subjects of anyone I've read or heard. Until Dr. Goleman wrote *Emotional Intelligence*, such intelligence had not been given serious study. Dr. James Dobson's book *Emotions: Can You Trust Them?* emphasizes that emotional intelligence is critical to becoming a disciplined individual.

In fact, key in the pursuit of a virtuous life is the ability to discipline your emotions. I will speak about emotions throughout this book and especially in the chapter on the "Five Critical Lines of Life". No individual reaches a level of living an effective and fully-functioning life by not being emotionally self-disciplined. For most in America, emotions guide decisions rather than the reverse. When a person places their brains in their emotions they are unknowingly placing themselves in the position of living a life that is at best inconsistent and tumultuous. Nonetheless, most people in the United States, and the world for that matter, make their decisions based on feelings rather than facts and do not seem to have a problem doing so.

5) **Spiritual Intelligence:** Spiritual intelligence deals with spiritual insight and wisdom. It is 100% Biblically sourced and based. On the surface, this seems like a rather arrogant statement. However, I have read many of the writings of

26

Buddha, Confucius, as well as other Zen writings. These have, on occasion, provided us good counsel regarding how to be thoughtful and meditative. However, they completely fail in giving wisdom in how to connect with the Infinite/Personal God of the Bible and to understand the *sinful condition* of mankind. Consequently, I am convicted that true spiritual intelligence is having the ability to discern and do God's will on a daily basis. It is possessing illumination in matters which can initially appear nebulous. It is having the skill and ability to allow virtue to be at the core of every decision and action. Spiritual intelligence is possessing profound insight in the discernment of the meaning and motives behind what one thinks, says, and does. It is having the ability to discern what is missing in any idea, proposal, question, or answer.

When Christ was speaking to the woman at the well in the Gospel of John, Chapter 3, He possessed discernment. The woman did not want to confront her relational failures and see them for what they were. She played word games with Christ. He called her on it by stating factually that she did not have one husband, but had three. Our discernment will not reach this kind of depth and profoundness, but it can keep us focused, fully-functioning, and fulfilled.

Proverbs gives us many verses which describe the positive effects of living a righteous life. We will talk about many of those verses in the pages to come. Spiritual intelligence is the least cultivated and the most critical of the five. Why? Paul tells us in I Corinthians 1:25 that the foolishness of God is greater than the wisdom of man. The knowledge which God deems important and necessary is superior to any other knowledge known by, or cultivated by anyone.

Now, it is critical that each of us understand that developing effective intelligence is a life-long pursuit. It isn't simply a parochial endeavor. It is a pilgrimage. I was told by Dr. Warden that if I read one book a month after my college graduation, in thirty years I would accumulate an amount of knowledge that would equal the education of more than a doctor's degree. He said that I may be significantly well on the way to possessing the knowledge sufficient for a second doctorate, if the retention of what I had read stayed at a highly effective level.

I am well into my years of living and to this date I have read close to six hundred books since graduating from college. I have heard of individuals who have read over one thousand books in their lives. George Vanderbilt, the developer, visionary, and builder of the Biltmore estate in Ashville, North Carolina, is purported to have read over 3,000 books.

I simply marvel at such a feat and wonder how such people could have maintained the discipline to accomplish this in spite of all of the distractions with which they must have been confronted. *I also know from experience, as well as observation, that those who read are much more interesting than those who do not.* Those who read have much to talk about. Those who don't read, usually do not. Proof of our intellectual vitality is our interest, as well as our willingness to invest in books.

o **Wisdom Principle:** As Matthew Kelly so aptly says, *"A person who chooses not to read books has no advantage over a person who cannot read them."*

The more knowledge you accumulate in each of these various intelligences, the more balanced you are. By balanced, I mean that your behavior, your language, and your insight into life and living, have a rhythm and balance to it. When such is true, a person is living life well above the norm.

o **Wisdom Principle:** *The narrower your base of knowledge, the narrower your world-view.*

In spite of my conviction regarding reading books, I realize that *intelligence is as intelligence does.* True intelligence is functional and is highly, as well as visually, effective in a person's day-to-day life. There is little theory in true intelligence. True intelligence is logical and pragmatic in its application. Quite frankly, I am of the conviction that whatever knowledge is out there, *if* it cannot be put into shoe leather—that is, put into one's everyday life, as well as be useful in producing positive and effective results in one's life—such knowledge or intelligence is a *waste-of-time*. It is critical that a person continues to grow intellectually and spiritually. Not to do so is to stifle your potential. *Effective intelligence will always translate into effective living.*

Finally, I want to state, without reservation, that in the twenty years I worked with teenagers, I was amazed that one trait, which separated those who excelled from those who possessed a "minimalist" attitude, was the ability to listen in a consistent, disciplined manner. Over the years, I have realized that one unmistakable component of intelligence is the possession of the ability to willingly listen! One individual who stood out in the demonstration of an active listening ability was a young man named Jim Grantham. Conversely, those who are poor listeners, are also pragmatically less intelligent. Such individuals have significant gaps in their "life knowledge", and as a result, struggle consistently in certain critical areas of life.

4. Our Character Is Our Fate

When I was growing up, no one—and I mean no one—ever spoke to me about character by either giving an explanation of it or emphasizing the importance of it. As I have quoted Lamar Henderson, a friend: *"You can't teach what you do not know and you can't lead where you won't go."* This is the main reason why we have such a crisis of leadership in America today. Too many leaders fear the pain and embarrassment of failure. These same leaders also possess a compulsive fear of losing. As a result, I am convicted that we have a generation of leaders who are risk-averse. When we are led by what we fear, we lack courage, and we cannot understand nor define character without courage. Truly, the question still remains: Where have all the real heroes gone? They have gone the way of expediency. The so-called heroes of today are too busy *"Managing perceptions instead of delivering results."*

Character is defined as the reflection of oneself to others. It is a portrait to the world in which we live, of what we believe and to what we are committed inside our mind, heart, and soul. It is also the person we are when no one else is around. Our character is validated as well as reflected in two ways … our *behavior* and in how we *treat* others. Our character is developed from what we have been taught and what we have observed, by what we have experienced and what we believe to be true as a result of those experiences. Our character may be partially developed during the defining moments of life, but it is also revealed, when under duress.

In that pamphlet, I said that there are seven components to character. If one's character consists of these components, which I believe are necessary in living a fully-functioning life, then one's character will reflect the following:

1) Uncompromising Principles of Moral Virtue
2) Pursuit of Truth Which Is Reflected In an Accurate Perception of Reality
3) Personified Wisdom (Having Logistical Common Sense)
4) Emotional Intelligence
5) An Absence of Hypocrisy
6) An Unwavering Commitment to Personal Responsibility
7) A Positive World View (A Superior Attitude)

In that same chapter concerning character, I go through each component of an indomitable character and explain it. I believe, above all, that character is so important, that it has eternal determinations. I may not be intelligent enough to articulate all of these determinations, however, I know that our perspective in virtually every critical area of life is reflected in our character. Also, I know that our character will go with us into eternity. So, when you allow anything to take precedence over your character, you lose—big time!

There are so many, who are obsessed with popularity, looks, fashion, entertainment, cars, homes, and social reputation. They believe that acquiring such things gives meaning and purpose to their lives. They choose to believe that such "acquisitions" are superior to anything else. When this happens, life becomes a rat-race—an endless cycle of satisfying a compulsive need to seek bigger and better things and experiences all the while thinking that such is what one must do to attain happiness. Unfortunately, such is not the case.

Most sacrifice their character for the pursuit of the superficial. But chasing happiness is never going to result in finding happiness. Happiness, more importantly, is a by-product—an effect—of something more profound, and it is not found in the presumptive ways that most people think. It will not be found in acquiring the superficial things of life, because *happiness is not for sale*. It cannot be purchased, manipulated, stolen or given to you by someone else. It does not matter what *People Magazine* says are the real people. And, even if this magazine may implicitly communicate that the way to happiness is by emulating these special people, such magazines are simply dead wrong! If you believe what such publications write and you take what they say seriously, you will find yourself off the radar screen, when it comes to understanding what real life is truly about. The most important reflection of our lives is our character. Our character tells others what we believe, how we perceive truth, of what our commitments consist, and what is important to us. Our character is totally reflected in our *attitude*, and *through our behavior*.

I have found that people who do not value or respect etiquette—either in behavior or dress—as a rule, are often uncouth and tasteless in how they present themselves. Their speech, dress, and behavior are often too casual and rough around the edges. Who would have thought that bra straps and tattoos would ever become fashion statements? Individuals, who approach life in such a manner are not taken very seriously by those who seek excellence in the areas I have just listed. Also, those who take etiquette seriously read about it and cultivate information that improves their understanding and practice of it. Most of all, they reflect the seriousness of their commitment to proper etiquette *through their behavior.*

This may shock you but it is nonetheless true. I have never known a person who was truly spiritual who also was not elegant in his/her social behavior as well. When I say that I have found no exception to this, I mean that I have not experienced, nor seen any exception to this. When it comes to reflecting the components of which our individual character consists, it is no different. Behavior tells the tale.

o   **Wisdom Principle:** *Dana Broadman once said, "Sow an act, reap a habit; sow a habit, reap a character; sow a character, reap a destiny." In other words, we choose our habits, but our habits determine our character as well as our future.*

5. You Are Not Entitled to Receive That Which You Are Not Prepared to Give

In our Entitlement Society, there are millions of citizens who want the reward of toil but do not want to toil. My response to such a perspective is: "Give me a break!" Life doesn't work this way!

I am reminded of the illustration by Earl Nightingale and Matthew Kelly, in which a person is standing in front of a wood-burning stove. When a person says he or she will not commit to do anything, until the other "side" commits first, it is like that same person standing in front of a wood-burning stove saying to the stove, "I will give you wood, if you will first give me heat!" Ridiculous? Yes. Yet when it comes to relationships and other worthy endeavors in life, such thinking occurs more often than not.

Yes, many want the reward of the toil but simply do not want to pay the price to earn the reward. Can you imagine a freshman college student going to the president of a university and saying, "Give me my degree and then I will do the work."? Or can you see someone going to the president of a company and saying, "Give me my paycheck for the month first, then I will do the work."? Of course not. Yet we have raised two generations that, as a whole, have this perspective. Accomplishment and achievement do not work like this.

This essential of life is equally true within the context of rela-tionships. We have all witnessed individuals complaining about their marriage partner, or current significant other. More often than not they are complaining about what their life-partner is or is not doing that is upsetting to them. It is common to hear the complainant say that because the other in the relationship is not doing a certain thing, which is desired, he/she is not going to do what the other wants in the same context either. In other words, he/she is refusing to give to the other what he/she wants. Such a point-of-view does not and will not work ... *ever*. Again, such a person is standing in front of the proverbial wood-burning stove and saying, "Give me heat and I will give you wood".

Many reputable psychologists say that individuals in relationships which are in crisis all seem to want the same things. They want to be respected, listened to, treated kindly, and given the same importance in the life of their "significant other" that the "significant other" has for his/her own self. Either one partner or both believe that giving the other such importance is LOVE exemplified.

However, we find that all relationships that are on "life support" are lacking any of these four virtues. They are individuals standing at a distance saying, "I will give when the other gives". Therefore, the struggle continues. Neither individual, in the end, gets what he/she so desperately wants. And, to make matters worse, they continue to scratch their heads wondering why their relationship isn't getting any better. There is no greater truth than this from Dr. Gordon Livingston: *"The worst deceptions are those we practice on ourselves." An even greater truth is that there is a limit to intelligence but there is obviously no limit to stupidity.*

Such couples are shouting to the world one unmistakable truth—besides being relationally inept—that they are not qualified to be in any kind of romantic relationship. None of us is entitled to receive that which we are not prepared to give. When you shut down and refuse to give that which you desire from another, you immediately disqualify yourself from being in any kind of a relationship and you disqualify yourself from receiving that which you desire from the other person. *Each within a relationship must accept responsibility for nurturing in the other what each wants to receive.* The only way to do so is to give to the other what you desire and to do it consistently as well as willingly.

This is true in any endeavor—whether making money, culti-vating talent or ability, attaining an education, or developing a marvelous relationship. One is not entitled to receive that which he/she is not prepared or refuses to give.

One of the greatest lessons I have learned is that the price of success is always retail and *the price for such success must always be paid in advance*. In my life, I have never seen an exception to this principle.

o **Wisdom Principle:** *We must become that which we want to receive and attract.*

6. The Greatest Pains in Life Are Usually Self-Inflicted

I do not believe people can be successful in life until they realize that the greatest hurts they will experience will be those pains, which they have perpetrated on themselves. As Dr. Gordon Livingston has taught, which is also true, is that *the most secure prisons are always the ones we build for ourselves*.

When I was a young man, I encountered acquaintances, friends and family members who made decisions or did things that brought unbelievable problems into their lives. These included drug addiction, HIV infection, STDs, horrible relationships and DUIs. Also included are bad choices in deciding who and what they become, allowing emotions to primarily be the decision-making component of their lives, and letting their tempers determine what they say and do. As a result, I have come to realize that we humans do not like ourselves very much.

The things that we allow into our lives that are potentially catastrophic to us as individuals, are unbelievable. For example, this is especially true when considering the miniscule criteria we possess when deciding whom we will choose as a partner in marriage. The lack of thought and the carelessness we see from how some people make decisions, as well as conduct themselves and their affairs, is simply "mind-boggling".

Some years ago, I was struck by the importance of this point when I heard, as we all did, about the tragedy of Natalie Holloway—the high school graduate from Birmingham, Alabama, who went to Aruba for her senior trip … a reward for her accomplishments in high school. We all know the details and I don't think any of us denies that Natalie made a decision at some point that turned deadly. In this case the greatest pain in Natalie's life was self-inflicted. Now her family grieves her absence and to this day there has been no resolution to this tragedy. There is no question that our decisions can and will, at times, affect the lives of those we love, very often, forever.

On a personal note, I had a half-brother who contracted HIV. He died a few short months after the person who inflected him had passed. I also heard of numerous instances where "high school acquaintances" had to get shots of penicillin because they had unprotected sexual intercourse with someone who had "been around". I have witnessed teens dealing with drug addiction, as well as alcohol addiction. According to one set of statistics of which I am aware, 45% of 9th graders have drunk an alcoholic beverage and over half of high school students drink occasionally, if not regularly. Over 65% of high school seniors in most states have had sexual intercourse, thinking all of the while that there are no permanent consequences to their heart and soul by having done so.[1]

There is no question that the philosophical basis for such a belief is secular and humanistic at its core. The tragedy of such a belief is the core idea, albeit erroneous, that since we are "our own creators", we can also choose be "our own destroyers".

This is, I believe, becoming quite evident worldwide. One proof of this philosophical belief is how organ transplants are determined. Those who have the power have arbitrarily chosen to declare that younger adults and children are entitled to organ transplant consideration, over senior citizens. There is no question that this is a form of euthanasia. When we treat life disrespectfully—even less valuable than animals—it is no wonder that the un-self-defined among us see themselves as worthless.

Why do we do these things to ourselves? Although it is impossible to list all of the reasons, one that I know for sure is the belief in the "illusion" that bad things happen to others and not to us individually. Not true. Bad things happen to all of us when we do not think clearly and responsibly on a consistent basis. Our self-centeredness—the belief that we are entitled, bullet-proof, invisible and invincible—and the belief that we will "miss out" on something meaningful and "special" if we do not try certain things, are two reasons we do such horrible and stupid things to ourselves. Peer pressure and media influence play an influential role, as well. There is no question that we have, as individuals, *the compulsive tendency to undervalue who and what we are, and overvalue whom and what we are not.*

---

[1]   Current statistics from the last year, where data was available.

More often than not, *we let our insecurities* determine what we do in certain circumstances. Fear of rejection, fear of the pain of loneliness, and fear of ridicule can cause us to do foolish and stupid things. When we limit our options by choosing to see the micro-view rather than the macro-view, we potentially open ourselves to self-destroying experiences.

Men and women in their fifties and sixties have often shared with me that if they could eliminate the pain and suffering in their lives that was self-inflicted, the hardships they experienced, which came from simply living life, would have been a piece of cake compared to what they actually experienced. The problem again is the mistaken belief that bad things happen to others and cannot happen to us—the so-called "special people". We always believe that we will be the exception to the rule when it comes to the law of cause and effect. Truthfully, there are no exceptions. We all pay the dues and sing the proverbial blues for the things we do that are not based on solid, logistical commonsense.

I can speak personally regarding this point. If I were able to eliminate from my life at this very moment all of the self-inflicted pain for which I have been responsible over the years, life for me would have been a "picnic". You might ask, "What was the key to your experiencing those self-inflicted pains?" What happened, in certain instances, is that I did not consider the consequences of my actions prior to my decisions. I was looking at the "micro-view" rather than the "macro-view". I also thought that what happened to others would not happen to me. I believed this because I thought I was too smart for such things to happen to me. All I can tell you is that I was very wrong and naïve about this.

Trust me when I say that self-inflicted pain can kill your relationships, your soul, your life, and in the end, fill you with bitter
memories. *Self-inflicted pain will waste your time, energy, and
money, as well as seriously impede the fulfillment of your potential.* You will accomplish so much more in your life if you will think
through your decisions before you make them, not after. Thinking
about your decisions after you have made them, is to say the least,
too late. Bad memories are mostly, if not all, the direct result of
bad decision-making. It takes a great deal of self-forgiveness and
grace to overcome most of our self-inflicted pains and failures.

o   **Proverbs 18:15:** *"The heart of the discerning person accu-
    mulates wise knowledge and the ears of the wise pursue
    such illumination."*

Remember, you and I are more likely to hurt ourselves more
than others will ever hurt us. *We will limit our potential more than
others will.* We will inflict more pain on our own selves than others
will ever inflict on us.

A couple of points need to be made for your consideration.

**First, you should never cultivate or continue any relationship
in which you are pressured to betray your conscience or character.** This temptation will never leave us. In fact, temptation will
never take a day off from our lives. There will always be those who
will have no problem asking you to betray your character. Such
people live and work among us and we can never totally isolate
ourselves from them.

We must learn to confront and stand firm against any temptation, which threatens our well-being. I don't care how terrific

looking a person is, how high their social I.Q., how much you covet their presence in your life, or how stylish or romantic they may be. *Never allow anyone to talk you into betraying yourself. To do so is to sabotage every meaningful and important component of what makes you special.* To allow yourself to be pressured and "talked into" giving in to any betrayal of yourself, will become a regret that no amount of money or sorrow will ever remove.

Second, stay away from bad people. Bad people are bad news and nothing but trouble. Never cultivate a relationship with people whose lives are unstable and who cannot seem to stay out of trouble. These people will always blame other people and circumstances for their problems. They will also never ever take responsibility for their own lives.

o   **Wisdom Principle:** *Never form a close relationship or even a business relationship with someone who has more problems than you do, or who will cause you to lose the intensity of your focus regarding things that truly matter.*

7. Something for Nothing Equals Nothing. You Have to Give Up Something to Get Something

There is no such thing as a free lunch. The idea that we can get something of significance by doing nothing is a delusion of the highest proportions. For example, I have known scores of bargain shoppers, throughout my life. What they were looking for was the deal of a lifetime. Most are still looking because you cannot get something for nothing.

Like you, I have heard tales of great deals from acquaintances, friends, and relatives. There is something ego boosting about sharing a story of making the deal of a lifetime with others. Implicit in such stories is that others just are not as "sharp" at finding such great deals as the one sharing the story. But upon closer scrutiny, most did not get the deal about which they bragged. If they did, they were very fortunate.

I don't know about everyone's world, but in the world in which I live, a person gets what he/she pays for. There is a reason a Lexus LS460 costs more than a Honda Civic. It isn't because Lexus is trying to take its customers to the cleaners, financially speaking. The Lexus LS460 is simply a better car—light years better. There is also a reason that Calloway, Cleveland, Nike, Ping, and Taylor-Made Golf Clubs cost more than the other, lesser known brands. They are simply designed and made better. You will always pay more for the best-made "whatever" that's available. This principle applies to any product/service we may want to purchase.

If you believe that the "deal of a lifetime" is consistently out there; and you also believe that there is a person who has something of value and is willing to sell it for little or nothing, then you need to put this book down and go find something else to do. This belief is simply not true. If you believe that such is true, you have disqualified yourself from being able to comprehend the wisdom and truth shared in this book. You are a person who refuses to accept the fact that more often than not, you truly get, what you pay for.

Those who believe in getting something for nothing are also people who believe that you do not have to necessarily put significant effort into life in order to get anything meaningful out of it.

Such people believe that life ought to be easy and that attaining significant accomplishments ought to be effortless. These are the same people, who believe in the *Staples "Easy Button"*. For such people, luck is what makes the difference in having a great life in contrast to a mediocre one. However, life is not, nor does not work that way. Luck has nothing to do with whether we have a great life or a mediocre one. However, those who believe that life is a matter of luck and also believe in getting something for nothing are those who also believe that they are entitled to receive greater in life, in contrast to what they have given.

Such people eventually land at the intersection of Disappointment Avenue and Disillusionment Boulevard. When you encounter such people just understand that they are militantly ignorant about this subject, and not smart enough to speak to you or anyone else about it.

In Proverbs, we are consistently admonished about what it costs to be a person of wisdom and sagacity. The answer always comes back the same. It costs everything a person has. The best never comes cheap. Our beloved Savior Jesus Christ said, *"Count the cost."* This brief phrase, within its appropriate context, is speaking of the cost of salvation, as well as what it takes to be a disciple (a dedicated follower). However, its principle is universal. Anything worth having has a price. Usually it is a big price. An extraordinary life requires an extraordinary commitment!

o **Wisdom Principle:** *Looking for something for nothing will have you believing that doing nothing can result in getting something. Not true!*

The second part of this point is that you have to give up something to get something. The "nirvana illusion" that we can have it all is just that, an illusion. To get anything worthwhile in life or to accomplish anything worthwhile in life, costs you and me a very significant something. That something usually means having to give up something we want, or wish to do, in order to obtain what we know is best for each of us.

For instance, if I want a college degree, it is going to require significant effort. On a consistent basis, that effort is going to mean that I need to give up something I may prefer to do in order to study, go to the library, or prepare for a test. Any extraordinary accomplishment requires an extraordinary effort. It is the law of cause and effect. You cannot get something of significant value, without a proportionate effort being made. It is simply required.

Again, you may want to buy a car or a home. In order to do either, or both, you will have to give up several things you want to purchase or wish to do, in order to "sock" the money away for that purchase. This remains true for everyone, unless one has a trust fund or a sympathetic "Sugar Mom" or "Sugar Dad" who will provide the needed funds. From my experience, such is extremely rare.

And if you want to be the best you can be in anything—golf, basketball, baseball, music, art, or theatre—you have to give everything you have. All know the story of Tiger Woods. His father began teaching him how to play golf when he was barely out of diapers. Tiger was performing at an unbelievable level of excellence when he was in his teens. He won the United States Amateur Golf Championship three straight years—1994-1996. It was predicted that Tiger Woods was going to be unbelievable when he became a professional. The person who made that prediction knew what he/she was saying.

However, it is appropriate to remember that while Tiger's friends were out partying, going to the beach, playing video games, and in general, just hanging out, he was hitting golf balls at the driving range and studying the game of golf. Tiger Woods is one of the best things that has happened to golf since Bobby Jones, Ben Hogan, Jack Nicklaus, Arnold Palmer, and Gary Player. All golfers are richer for his sacrifices. The popularity of golf is soaring and golf courses are sprouting up all over the world. Tiger's success is one of the main reasons. He has shown us a part of this game that is not only beautiful to see, but elegant as well. Yes, Tiger had to give up many things to get where he is today. He couldn't have honed his golf skills to a level of extraordinary excellence if he hadn't been willing to sacrifice.

I also realize that some years ago Tiger Woods became embroiled in a sex scandal that ruined his marriage and cost him a very significant portion of his wealth. If you recall, when I was writing about the five kinds of intelligences, I mentioned that those individuals who possess exceptional "task intelligence" and perform at an optimum level often do so at the expense of emotional, relational, and spiritual intelligence. Tiger Wood's over-focus on golf caused him to neglect his character development and his knowledge and understanding of relationships.

The minimalists in our society, those into "instant gratification", believe they are entitled to receive significant things (like an extraordinary ability, wealth, an expensive car or home) with little effort on their part. This is neither possible nor true. We must earn virtually everything we get in life and we usually have to work extremely hard for all that we earn. I always heard growing up that there was no such thing as a free lunch. Let me add here that there is also no such thing as a free ride.

For example, over a decade ago we became involved, as a nation, in a conflict in the Middle East that ended up costing us at least three trillion dollars. I do acknowledge that the President who got us into this conflict was given very bad information regarding the presence of WMDs (weapons of mass destruction) in Iraq. The absolute truth is that more than one major intelligence agency reported the same thing. Acting, I believe, primarily on that information, our country's military invaded Iraq.

Over the years, we have come to realize that, as a rule, it has not been, nor will it ever be, a good idea to fight for someone else's freedom, when they are not willing to fight for it themselves. They will not respect the cost paid by someone else for that freedom. No one can understand or respect the cost of freedom for which they have not extended themselves to earn. It is impossible!

This, to me, is the greatest tragedy of the Iraqi Conflict, as well as the Vietnam Conflict. It is unfortunate that we did not learn from the horrific tragedy of Vietnam. Our military leadership, which in certain contexts is extraordinary, seems to have one flaw. When it does something that does not work—like fighting for the freedom of the South Vietnamese—it doubles the effort, i.e., in Iraq, rather than discarding such an action. Freedom, like anything worthwhile in life, is not free!

We have been a free nation for over two hundred years. I believe one of the reasons we are free is because our forefathers fought for our freedom and many among us continue to fight in order to keep it. No one fought on our behalf for our freedom, nor gave our freedom to us. The bloodshed and sacrifices made by our forefathers made this marvelous country possible.

It is difficult for any of us to fully comprehend the sacrifices that were made for our freedom and for the freedom of generations to come. Even now, millions of people in the United States do not respect this great country; nor do they respect the sacrifices made in the past for the freedom they enjoy and take for granted. I believe this is true because they cannot comprehend the sacrifices made. Neither do they know much about the world's various governments and the flaws of the political philosophies they embrace. If they did, I'm confident they would see the U.S. in a much more positive light.

However, for the moment, they display an attitudinal disrespect for our past and our present as a nation. They are also incapable of comprehending the significance of the sacrifices made for our freedom because they are shallow, as well as possess an entitlement mentality.

Minimalism is a pervasive attitude that infects those who believe that extraordinary things can be accomplished without having to give up anything, as well as not having to significantly extend themselves to get what they want. Such is not true, but significant numbers among us continue to believe it is. Thanks to the media, this minimalist attitude will continue to be perpetuated. Something for nothing equals nothing because one must give up something to get something. Learn it and live it, because it is true.

8. Happiness Is an Effect Rather Than a Cause

In one of his speaking engagements Dr. Wayne Dyer told a story about two cats. The older cat was an "alley cat". The younger cat had gone to "Cat Philosophy School" and really felt like he was smarter than the cats that had not studied at such a school.

The old "alley cat", strolling down the alley one day, saw the young cat running around in circles trying to catch his tail. He asked, "What in the world are you doing?"

The young cat said he had just been to *Cat Philosophy School* and learned that happiness was in his tail. Then he explained that in order to be happy, he had to constantly be chasing his tail. If he were fortunate and caught his tale, then he would find happiness.

The older cat patiently listened and when the young cat was finished, the old cat quietly said, "Well, I haven't been to Cat Philosophy School like you have, but I was also told that happiness was to be found in my tail. However, the harder and faster I chased my tail, the more happiness eluded me. Until one day I realized that if I quit chasing my tail and went about my daily business that happiness would follow me everywhere I went.

When I heard this story, I thought, *"Now, that is a great story!"*

Happiness is the most elusive desire for the overwhelming majority of this world. When people seek happiness for its own sake, it consistently eludes them. Also, this is so because most mistakenly believe that happiness is a conclusion—a *destination* in life—rather than a *condition* of life. *Happiness is something we are, not something we get*. I believe most of us know the things which will truly make us happy, we just won't do them for various unacceptable reasons.

Most people in this world also believe that happiness is found by satisfying their wants and desires. I have known scores of people in my life and many of them well-to-do. The common denominator of most of these individuals has been a life filled with meaninglessness and despair. I learned by observing these individuals that *the road to happiness is not found through the fulfillment of every want and desire.* Consequently, the fulfillment of your wants will not give you meaning. Only the fulfillment of your deepest *legitimate needs* and desires will do so. The urge to fulfill your illegitimate wants is nothing less than selfish. All selfish desires cannot nor will they ever be able to give you lasting meaning, either today or tomorrow.

Why not? The answer is that the byproduct of the fulfillment of a want is to want more. Having what you want will never be enough. The only way to fulfill a want is getting more of that particular want. There is no such thing as enough when it comes to either wants or instant gratification. Also, if a person is honest, he or she would admit that wants are primarily ego-driven. And, if one's wants are ego-driven, *emotion is the fuel for getting what the ego wants.*

- o **Wisdom Principle:** *A component of happiness is not having what you desire, but rather desiring what you have.*

- o **Ecclesiastes 2:26a:** *"To the person who pleases Him, God will give wisdom, knowledge, and the wisdom to find happiness."*

I believe that happiness has many components. For our purposes here, I want to focus on the pragmatic aspects of happiness. These components are reflected in people I have met and come to know throughout my life. They were positive, caring, kind, and virtuous. They were, and are, truly special people, as well as inspirational!

The first pragmatic component of happiness is that the happiest people I have known are also the most intelligent. True intelligence, as stated earlier, is functional rather than theoretical. If effective intelligence results in an effective life, then it stands to reason that happiness is a by-product of living effectively. However, unintelligent people are overwhelmingly unhappy people, because they are usually *militantly ignorant* and *lazy*. Such individuals want happiness but are unwilling to do what it takes to have it. They believe happiness is an *entitlement* and, as a result, *will often struggle with certain elementary issues of life over their lifetime.*

The second pragmatic component of happiness is the possession of a vibrant spiritual life. This point is not part of the "happiness components" purveyed by the popular "psychological gurus" of our day. The reason is that psychology is a secular science. It has no spiritual foundation to which its beliefs and principles can be linked. In fact, I unequivocally believe, with all that I am that psychology cannot motivate a person spiritually or morally.

A person who is spiritually in tune is one who has had a personal encounter with the Infinite/Personal God of this universe. Happiness cannot nor will not be found without this component being part of one's life. We come alive to the Spirit of God when we embrace salvation through God's grace. *When one is spiritually healthy, one is experiencing happiness—yes, even in the midst of struggle, suffering or loss.*

A third pragmatic component of happiness is having something purposeful and meaningful to do in life. Purpose and meaning occur when one is truly aware of the meaning of the phrase *being of service to others*. Whatever our professional and personal endeavors are, those who approach them *altruistically* find that they thrive in what they do on a daily basis.

This is the "giving" component. Happiness, the basis of it, lies not in the getting but rather in the giving. Individuals who are willing to give before being rewarded are those who understand the Law of Cause and Effect and respect it. In contrast, individuals who do anything and everything for selfish reasons are doomed to frustration and disillusionment. They get caught in what Dr. Wendell Johnson calls the IFD Syndrome.

Such people begin by *idealizing*. They say to themselves, "When such-and-such happens, then I will be happy". So, they put all of their hope, expectations, and emotional energy into this "ideal" coming to pass. When it does, it will rarely give them the fulfillment that they believed it would and they go to the second level of the IFD Syndrome, which is *frustration*. They have difficulty believing they could have miscalculated the perceived fulfillment they had imagined such an experience would bring. Once they accept that they indeed miscalculated the fulfillment they had expected, they become *disillusioned*. To get out of their disillusionment, after they have remained at that level for a period of time, they begin to *idealize* once again. Hence, the term IFD Syndrome. It is a vicious cycle that continues unabated in the lives of the self-centered and self-absorbed. What the unintelligent consistently do is continue doing something that clearly does not work. Rather than abandon such an endeavor, they simply double the effort to produce the desired fulfillment. Proverbs calls such thinking and behavior foolish.

   o **Proverbs 23:9:** *"Do not speak to a fool for he will scorn the wisdom of your words."*

The fourth pragmatic component of happiness is having someone to love, someone with whom to share life's road. I will talk more about love and marriage in the second volume of this series. For now, let me state unequivocally that finding someone to love is not as easy as many make it out to be. If it were, we wouldn't have 57% of marriages ending in divorce and we wouldn't have a substantial number of the X Generation and Millennials living together rather than getting married. One reason cohabitation is preferred by a number of individuals of these generations is the fear of eventually winding up divorced. Such fear seems to paralyze them, in the making of a marriage commitment. Also, being unwilling to pay the price to get anything of significance such as a loving relationship, is another reason these generations prefer living together rather than getting married. Shallow people seem to be very comfortable living a shallow existence and being involved in shallow relationships.

Such markers mentioned above are drop-dead signs for laziness, insecurity, and confusion regarding the understanding of successful romantic relationships. So, these two generations, due to their ignorance, selfishness, and lack of knowledge regarding the dynamics of romantic love and the dynamics of relationships, take the path of least resistance and choose to live together without the benefit of marriage. The paralyzing fear of failure, which can result in experiencing pain and the possibility of personal loss, keeps them from making such a significant commitment.

In the end, the path of least resistance gets the least results. Finding someone to love is challenging to the intelligent among us and virtually impossible to find for the militantly ignorant among us. I do not see how a person can experience true happiness when his/her life is not shared with a special someone.

I am deeply convicted that when we focus on becoming someone special, finding someone special becomes much easier. *Too many people are too focused on finding someone special instead of being someone special.* Love is a marvelous thing. It is wonderful to behold. The incredible power of genuine, meaningfulness occurs when love is shared!

The fifth and final pragmatic component to happiness is having something you look forward to doing every day. When you do not have something to look forward to, you have difficulty getting up in the morning. Your energy is depleted and you are in a "survival mode". I know, because I've been there! One thing that I learned from Dr. Scott Peck's writings is that depressed individuals have lost that something to look forward to. More than likely they had it at one time. Or, they thought they had it. However, that something got away from them. What often follows is depression, which is the result of a loss of hope.

To get out of a state of depression, one must first just get active—do something! Ride a bike, throw a ball with someone, or take a walk in the park. Do something! What I love about Dr. Dyer, as well as Dr. Gordon Livingston, is that their first option with their patients was not to recommend some kind of medication, which would have put them in a responsibility-relieving state. Neither of these men are proponents of the belief that the proverbial *"pill kills all ills".*

When we have something to look forward to that something will have three critical components. First, it must be something about which we are passionate. Second, it is an endeavor through which we serve others—in other words, we win but others do, too. Third, it has a relaxing and restful aspect to it.

There are many people who get into a volunteer service and their experience is tense, stressful, and tiring. That is not a good kind of "something" in which such an individual should get involved. One must get involved in something that fuels their passion, serves others, and is an energizing activity. Without these three components, that "something" we all need in our daily lives in order to be pragmatically happy, will never materialize.

Happiness is truly an inside-out job. Having large sums of money will not make you happy. If it did, then those involved in organized crime, or terrorism would be our models for happiness and fulfillment. Such individuals usually have more money than anyone else, however, they are not happy in the truest sense. And, if Proverbs is right, their "enjoyment", which is the result of their evil intents and actions, will be short-lived.

Remember, happiness is not achieved through the accumulation of material possessions. Christ stated that our lives *do not consist of what we possess*. Yet, we consistently see the majority of those among us believing what that once-famous bumper sticker said: *"The one with the most toys wins".* No, he or she does not win. Possessions and riches may make your life more comfortable physically, but they will not make you happy. There is no shortcut to happiness and, as I stated earlier, happiness is not for sale!

9. Watch Your Relationships as You Do Your Money—Like a Hawk!

I have always been amazed at how people seem to love things and use people rather than the reverse. As a rule, I do not believe that all individuals value relationships the same. I have unfortunately encountered people who, unbelievably as well as unfortunately, do not like people. As a consequence, they also do not value relationships. However, I happen to believe that relationships are critically important. If we want people to come to our funeral, we had better see relationships as being very important. I am so convicted about this that those who don't agree, I believe, are not thinking clearly or objectively.

First, relationships, metaphorically speaking, make the world go around. Our lives would be empty, lonely, and meaningless without other people. I know there are large numbers of people who do not agree with me. However, for the relationally healthy among us, when people are part of our lives we find that our existence more meaningful, fulfilling, and enriching. In fact, a perusal of our past will show that our lives have been meaningful and fulfilling in direct proportion to the meaningful relationships we have cultivated over the years. The best of memories for a huge majority of us involves the good times we had with others—others for whom we cared deeply.

Second, we all must understand that relationships are critical to our economic well-being. Few people ever think about this!

However, if you want to know how critical to our well-being relationships truly are, then keep in mind that every dollar we will ever make comes through people. It is impossible to be paid for what we do by avoiding having anything to do with people. As I stated earlier, the people who buy our services and/or our products are the reason we make any money at all. Now, having written what I just have, let me ask you: "How critical are relationships to your well-being and mine?"

If you are a person who does not like people and does not value the cultivation of relationships you need to give the following your undivided attention. You need to know that there is a much better than average chance, as you grow older, that you will grow to be more alone. You, more likely than not, will become embittered as a consequence of this aloneness.

You will likely tell yourself that others are just selfish, mean, and self-centered because if they were not they would drop by, check up on you, and see how you are doing. Also, you will tend to forget all of the years that you made light of the cultivation of relationships, as well as your refusal to get off of your proverbial "duff" and develop some quality friendships. In the end, you will become bitter and you will likely die alone, while blaming others for the primary reason that you have no friends or acquaintances.

It takes enormous self-honesty for one to admit, as well as understand, that the person primarily responsible for your loneliness, is you. You must also recognize that if you were a person who was difficult to get to know for most of your life, and if you were also intuitively distrusting of others, that such traits will have contributed mightily to your being alone. There is no question that the person who will be primarily responsible for your aloneness, when such a time comes, will be no one else but you.

Third, our relationships will always reflect our definition of what we believe being successful is. I have observed over my life that the old adage of "birds of a feather flock together", is true, more often than not. We attract what we are and are becoming. Our commitments in life, consciously or unconsciously, define the kinds of relationships we develop. If, for example, we value *substance over pretense* and *character over coolness*, we will attract to us those kinds of individuals who reflect these same values.[2] Remember that as a rule, successful individuals intuitively seek the company of other individuals who are often equally as successful in their respective endeavors.

This can be easily illustrated by observation. Actors and actresses associate with one another on a social basis. Athletes associate in the same way. It is also likely that famous athletes have each other's home and cell phone numbers. I don't have the personal contact information of any famous athletes. Why not? I am not a world-class athlete, nor am I world renown. Our relationships are a reflection of who we are, no question about it.

A further example: I have never seen a partner in a law firm develop a close relationship with an associate just out of law school unless that associate is a relative. I believe this principle, to be consistent, with only one exception—*the continuous association with those with whom we grew up.* Bill O'Reilly, the successful radio and television social commentator, grew up in Germantown, one of the blue-collar areas of New York City. On occasion, he has

---

[2] There's only one exception to this principle. I will share with you that one exception in a moment.

mentioned on his show that he still has relationships/friendships that began when he was a child and carried those relationships through high school. I believe such relationships keep us grounded.

o **Wisdom Principle:** *There is a huge difference in thinking you are better than others and just simply realizing that you are better off than others.*

Fourth, relationships are critical to our happiness and ful-fillment because we live in a day and time when we cannot be successful on our own. Remember when it was said that a self-made individual became so by "pulling themselves up by their own bootstraps"? I do not believe this to be true anymore. We must learn how to succeed by being a part of a team. We cannot be successful, well-rounded, fulfilled, and happy without the assistance of others. Relationships remind us that we are social beings. We were meant to connect with one another—to relate. When we do not, we die—socially, spiritually, and emotionally.

o **Wisdom Principle:** *Total self-sufficiency is a myth!*

Several years ago, I read a profound story about a king who commissioned an experiment regarding the need for children to be given nurturing, love, and attention. The nurses caring for the new born children who were part of this experiment, were instructed not to hold the babies for long periods of time. They were not to talk to them, sing to them, or be affectionate with them. I do not remember the exact number of babies in this experiment, but these children were bathed, changed, and fed—period.

Within a short period of time, all of the babies died. The lesson to be learned in this illustration is that we are created to be loved, held, spoken to, and valued. Relationships make the fulfillment of these needs possible.

You must guard and nurture your relationships. *You become open to doing so when you realize how valuable relationships are to your personal refinement, development, and maturity.*

Here are some key insights, I call them "value markers" that will keep you from ruining your relationships and underestimating the importance of them. If you do not embrace them, you will likely miss opportunities to cultivate terrific relationships. You could also disrespect the importance of relationships and, as a result, possibly be guilty of abusing them.

Value Marker 1: *You need to view relationships as necessary for your refinement and development as a person.*

If we will allow them to, relationships will reveal our fears, flaws, and frustrations. Relationships can help us learn of our weaknesses, which in turn will help us turn such weaknesses into strengths. Relationships can also help us remove the "blind spots" that hold us back, keeping us from becoming the best we can be in our social and spiritual development. They are invaluable when we let them fix us rather than arrogantly trying to fix them. The winds of relational adversity will teach us where we are flawed in being compassionate and empathic, as well as showing us where we need to focus in our personal development.

Value Marker 2: *You need to view relationships as an opportunity to learn.*

You would be surprised how much you can learn from other people. Simply put, we cannot read every book, see every continent, or experience every legitimate "high" in life. However, through our relationships, we can learn—from what others have experienced, where they have been, and in listening to what they have learned in their life-endeavors and in the making of their own mistakes.

George Strait, the well-known country singer, has a song in one of his "Greatest Hits" CDs entitled "I Hate Every Thing". It is about a man who, at a bar, meets another man who is brooding over "lost love". The man is getting drunker as he talks about hating his job, his life, colors, seasons, and everything else he can think of. His wife left him for another man and he cannot let the bitterness of that pain go[3]. In fact, in the song he says that if it were not for his children, he would hate his ex-wife. She, as well as the experience itself, is "stuck in his craw". The song ends, with the one listening to this bitter man getting on his cell phone and calling his wife. He tells her that he is coming over and that they are going to, as they say in the country, "work this out". The "this" in the context of this song is his relationship with his wife. The song concludes with the man who did the listening, paying for the bitter man's drinks and thanking him—for everything!

Throughout this book, I am sharing with you what I have learned from my mistakes, experiences, and observations. I am motivated to do so because I do not want you to experience

---

[3] Based on how he was handling it, I can't really blame her.

unnecessary pain and hurt from your relationships. I also want you to learn what I have learned and what I needed to know, but do so much earlier than I did. We are all passengers on this "Good Ship Mother Earth", and we can learn from one another what positively works and what doesn't.

We can learn _four_ ways—from *books*, from *experience*, from *observation*, and from *mentors*. Learning from books, by necessity, is a long-term process. It takes time to read books. They are also a cash expense, albeit a worthy one. Experience takes the longest and it is also the costliest. Learning from observation can take more time than one is often prepared to give. Also, one can miss the needed life-lessons they should be getting from their observation. But, it must be remembered that observation is useless unless the correct lesson is learned. *Learning from a mentor is the best way to learn, as well as the least painful way.* Within this context I am your mentor. I am helping you learn the better way, instead of from ways that are time consuming and, within certain contexts, flawed.

o **Wisdom Principle:** *Experience is different than education. When it comes to experience, the test comes before the lesson!*

Value Marker 3: *You need to view relationships as an opportunity to develop courage.*

To extend oneself in a relationship, and to reveal who one truly is to another takes courage. Courage is not the absence of fear but rather the mastery of it. All of us know that the greatest wager in life is the one we will make with our heart. The true blessing and enrichment of relationships will never be known by those who are risk-averse. To take the risk necessary to gain true intimacy with someone else, is absolutely nothing less than an act of raw courage.

> o **Wisdom Principle:** *We gain knowledge from books but we gain wisdom through relationships.*

Relationships will not always be easy and enjoyable, but they will challenge us to grow. They will also be enriching. The only way to find fulfilling and enriching relationships is by putting ourselves on the line. Only the wise know that the one security in this earthly life is that there is no security and that the one guarantee in this earthly life is that there is no guarantee. It is absolutely necessary for all of us to learn this lesson in order to understand the price we must pay to grow and mature. Also, our character is developed and crystallized by how we process our experiences in our relationships with one another.

Value Marker 4: *Relationships offer us the opportunity to experience a critical component to happiness.*

In fact, we need to view relationships as a component to being happy. How? *Relationships give us the opportunity to <u>give</u>.* Happiness is found in *giving of* ourselves in contrast to *getting for* ourselves. *Through relationships, we have an opportunity to make a positive difference in someone's life. There is no greater payoff than that.* Relationships help us give to others. By giving, we resolve problems through meeting the needs of someone else. And the common denominator, for all of us, is that we have legitimate needs which need to be met, as well. A significant number of those legitimate needs can only be filled through our relationships.

Someone very close to me has, as one of his/her "life assignments," the helping of those who have been suffering from illness, misfortune and/or broken-heartedness. A few Christmases ago, this person was told of a young woman whose husband left her for another woman. This happened right before Christmas, and the young wife had no money and no means to purchase gifts for her two children. This woman in need was not a Christian nor did she attend church.

Upon hearing of this tragedy, my friend made it his/her mission to do all that could be done to make sure her two young children had a Christmas. Without fanfare, my friend bought a carload of presents and arranged to leave the gifts with the woman who was kind of enough to tell my friend about this tragedy. The woman, in turn, made sure the young woman received these gifts.

My friend found out sometime later that the young woman was surprised, cried with joy, and was very appreciative. This news set my friend aglow that particular Christmas and I can tell you, unequivocally, it was not because of all the gifts, which received from his/her own family. This person had the opportunity to give of him/herself and from his/her own resources. I know my friend considered it an honor to have given, and it was a marvelous act of kindness.

I find it more than coincidence that we are not complete without the development of a personal relationship with the Infinite and Personal God revealed in the Bible. In turn, we will not experience human completeness in this life without the development of integrity-based relationships with others.

How do you cultivate long-lasting and meaningful relationships? Here are five ways to help you do this.

First, we must like who we are and what we are becoming. To like ourselves—a lot—we must first be self-honest. How? We are self-honest when we are truthful *about* ourselves and *to* ourselves regarding who and what we truly are, as a person. Self-honesty is critical because the more self-honest people are, the more transparent they will be.

When we are transparent we have the ability to be non-verbally *understood* by others. Also, it is being *visible* to others as well as being *easy* to read. When we are around people who are difficult to understand and perceive we are often uneasy in their presence. It is difficult to tell whether such a person has won the lotto or lost a loved one. When individuals are this difficult to read most people will pass on making the effort to get to know such individuals, because getting to know them will likely be a difficult and arduous process. Few—specifically, merciful, mature Christians—have the time or energy to commit to developing a meaningful relationship with someone, when he or she is not transparent and, as a consequence, difficult to read.

Transparency is critical to developing meaningful and life-long relationships, but it's not easy. However, if you truly like yourself you will be transparent. I am not speaking of conceit or arrogance here. I am talking about knowing yourself and genuinely liking who you are and having positive expectations regarding the person you are becoming. *Liking yourself is critical to transparency*.

Second, we must be positive in attitude and expectations. I cover this thoroughly in my first essential. Let me add here that you need to guard yourself and stay away from cynical and negative individuals. If you allow such people to become part of your life-environments, you will become more like them rather than the reverse. You need to respect what is important in becoming a person of excellence.

o **Wisdom Principal:** *One's life is a reflection of the values, beliefs and priorities embraced. Such is reflected by into what, as well as how we invest our time, energy, and resources.*

Third, we must be productive. Moving professionally and personally in a positive direction is a must when attracting positive and enriching individuals with whom to form relationships. It is not lost on me how terrific people build relationships with other terrific people. This is not an accident. You must understand that you protect yourself in the cultivation of your relationships by being productive. How? *Your productivity will repel unproductive individuals from your life.* Unproductive individuals are militantly lazy, obstinately ignorant, and acutely insecure. The last thing such individuals will do is to seek to cultivate relationships with individuals who are the antithesis of who and what they are.

Fourth, we need to be good listeners. Listening is hard work. This is why most people are poor listeners. We learn a tremendous amount from others about what they are like, what they like, and what they dislike when we encourage them to talk about themselves. We help people become at ease when we ask them about themselves, because if individuals are experts about any-thing, they should be experts about themselves.

Letting others talk about their lives shows that we are inter-ested in them. We also convey enormous value to people when we ask them questions about their lives and listen as they talk about what is important to them. Therefore, be a good listener! Look a person right in their right eye when they are speaking and quietly listen. When you give someone such rapt attention, they know you are listening to them. You are making a "fan" when another person speaks to you knowing you are giving them your undivided attention.[4]

Fifth, we must be authentic. To be authentic means to be genuine. Genuine individuals are truthful in projecting, who and what they are. Individuals who are authentic are easy to read as well as believe. Genuineness is a component of such a person's character. Such a "character component" is respected by those who have an indomitable character. Authenticity is the opposite of being fraudulent. To be authentic is to be truthful, honest, as well as transparent. Pretentiousness is completely absent in the life of an authentic individual.

Sixth, we must be an integrity-based individual. How do you do this? By doing what you say you are going to do and by not doing what you say you will not do. It is that simple! To be trust-worthy, your words and your behavior, are complimentary to one another. *You are what you say you are, because you define yourself, mostly, by what you do.* It is not complicated. If it is complicated

---

[4] I will talk more about being a terrific listener in the chapter about likeable people.

to someone, then such a person is confused. Complexity is usually the result of confusion, ignorance, as well as a lack of clarity.

Seventh, we must be gracious! Gracious individuals are joyful and caring. Not only that, but they also genuinely care for others. Everyone likes to be around joyful people, because in virtually every circumstance, joyful people can be counted on to treat others with grace and consideration. To be gracious is to be kind, patient, and considerate. It is a byproduct of an individual having a high social I.Q. I truly believe that although the social etiquette of our nation is in the proverbial "dumpster", people respond positively to being treated with graciousness and kindness. When you are a gracious and kind individual, you do not have to worry about the negative of wisdom principle #10.

10. Knowledge Teaches You How to Make a Living—Wisdom Teaches You How to Make a Life

All of us must decide what is most important to us, *a great living* or *a great life*. By default, one must take precedence over the other. You cannot give equal importance to both. Try as you may to give each equal respect, but you will not succeed. Most of the individuals I have known who made a terrific living did not necessarily have a terrific life. A terrific life was not automatic in such a context.

One reason for this was that relationships were neither cultivated, nor well maintained. Because of this, dreams went unfulfilled and the cultivation of a vibrant spiritual life was ignored, and all for the purpose of making more money. As a consequence, self-nurturing, which involves people taking respectful care of their lives, was totally ignored. Most of these people were task intelligent, yet they were relationally and spiritually clumsy.

This point is a fact, not a feeling or a fantasy. Knowledge cannot help you make a life, because most knowledge is *secular* at its core. Wisdom can help you make a life because it is *spiritual* at its core. This brings me to the remarkable truth that I learned. That truth, if you recall, is that psychology cannot motivate a person morally. Moral sensitivity, as well as the cultivation of component virtues, is spiritually-based.

The Apostle John wrote in his first letter that we are to be "in the world", but not "of the world". In other words, we are not to embrace the values and superficialities of this world at the expense of our souls. "Living the tension" requires self-discipline and wisdom.

At the core of an indomitable character lies wisdom. It is through wisdom that we develop sagacity and insight into solid, virtue-based decision-making. Additionally, the making of wise decisions is a byproduct, of a *virtuous heart*. Proverbs 3:16-21 states that if we make the cultivation of wisdom our priority we will gain discretion. We will experience the energizing of our souls, as well as see our lives reflect the wisdom we are cultivating. This wisdom will clearly reflect itself in our character.

In this passage Proverbs continues to describe a life immersed in the cultivation of wisdom. It says that we will walk securely (with confidence), our foot will not stumble—*we will not be susceptible to the same mistakes to which others, who do not respect wisdom, are susceptible*. In other words, self-destructive mistakes will not consistently, or even occasionally, be part of the "lot" of those who respect and cultivate wisdom. Proverbs continues this thought by saying that when we sleep, our slumber will be sweet—peaceful. A person of wisdom will not fear "fear" itself. Why is this so?

Proverbs concludes this passage by saying that such is possible because God is our confidence and He will enlighten and encourage us to keep our feet on the right path. As a result, even when false accusations come about, in time, they will be proved false. I'm a firm believer that God lifts up those individuals about whom false accusations are made. God is faithful, and in due time He will make those guilty of making false accusations look like fools.

A person who lives a life of wisdom enriches others. One does not regret knowing, relating to, and having in his/her life, someone who is committed to being a person who possesses virtue-based wisdom. People of wisdom are a magnet for others. People want to be like them and they hunger to know what the wise person knows.

11. Don't Bother Defending Yourself—Your Friends Don't Need It and Your Enemies Won't Believe It

One thing I know when reviewing my life. You can be right on target on any particular issue, but if you are with a group that does not care about you, nor about hearing the truth and the accuracy of your position, you are wasting your time explaining yourself. Just be wise enough to know that sometimes it does not pay to stand up for yourself or your opinions because it would be a complete waste of your time and energy to do so. You must realize that such a context might very likely have been orchestrated behind the scene by others, and that it is possibly an *intentional attack on you*. In that case "fairness" is not part of the situation. The best you can do is fasten your seatbelt and ride out the storm.

I have known of individuals, who have stood up for themselves in what I would consider to be a kangaroo-court atmosphere, only to be shot down by unsympathetic, non-truth-seeking, unfair, and prejudiced individuals. Such scenarios are truly no-win situations. Sometimes bad people win. You simply have to let people believe what they choose to believe, because no defense of any repute will do any good, especially when you are dealing with those who have other than noble intentions and motivations regarding your well-being.

I will talk more about "evil winning" in the third volume of this series. *Suffice it to say, you usually wind up in huge trouble, unintentionally, when you work in an organization, and with people who do not share the same values and ethics you believe in and practice.* The best advice I can give you in this case is to stay true to your sense of justice, be noble, and conduct yourself and your affairs far above the riffraff that are out to get you. Walk away; don't burn any bridges; know that when you are treated this way, your vindication will come. Also remember one super-universal reality: people are not always loving and loyal.

o **Wisdom Principle:** *You can control where you work, but you cannot control with whom you work. Those with whom you work are the consequences of business decisions made by the leaders, of the company.*

Be patient. Those who have treated you this way will eventually pay the price. Inevitably such individuals will find themselves in a similar situation—all alone and the target of a kangaroo court, which is out to get them. Almost 100% of the time, such a scenario is *of that person's own making.*

When someone is experiencing this, *take time to pray for him or her.* For most, this suggestion seems outlandish. However, it isn't. This is an opportunity to extend your growth and cultivate further the virtuous part of your character. It is an exercise in truly becoming a benign person. This spiritual exercise is overwhelmingly for your benefit and not primarily for the benefit of the person for whom you are praying. Your relationship with God will never be the best it can be when you have an ambivalent attitude toward others; even those who are self-serving and have wounded your spirit through their dishonesty and mistreatment.

Also, do your best to make yourself available for assistance. A phone call, for example, asking the individual if there is anything you can do to help, would do wonders for you. You can let this person know, through your act of kindness, that you harbor no ill will toward them. Such a gesture is nothing less than taking the high road. Just remember, the conversations people have about you are not nearly as important as the conversations you are having with yourself about yourself.

o **Wisdom Principle:** *You cannot control what people think of you, therefore you must let people believe what they choose to believe. This is pivotal in your being able to live without the good opinion of others.*

o **Wisdom Principle:** *Because of the universal truth that people are not always loving and loyal, the brutal reality* *is that people believe what they do about others because they choose to do so.*

12. Failures Are Stepping Stones, Which Point Toward Success

Fully-functioning people are motivated, rather than demotivated, by failure.

Failure is looked upon in this society—even among Christians—as a self-diminishing experience. Those with this perspective act as if perfection is achievable. It isn't. You cannot afford to allow the illusions of the minimalists in this world to affect your life in any manner, especially when it comes to their perspective of failure. *Minimalists have been victims of self-inflicted hopelessness.* This is why you cannot afford to allow your life to be defined by those who insist on living life by doing the minimum required.

Failure is seen by the minimalists in this world as an opportunity to see you and others suffer. They rejoice over the failures of others. They revel in the pain and suffering of those who have experienced failure, because their own mediocrity does not look so bad in contrast to the failure(s) of those with whom they are comparing themselves.

Not only do minimalists most often behave in this manner, but so do shallow and immature Christians. During my life, I have been in the presence of more than one professing Christian who smiled while describing the failure(s) of another Christian. It was evident that this particular professing Christian was getting a kick out of the embarrassment, suffering, and pain that another Christian was experiencing. Can you imagine anything as horrible as this? I cannot. Such people think the failures of others is a self-diminishing act. Note that the critics of those who have failed believe that their own stature is increased as a result. This is because they have not failed like the person they are criticizing has. This is a "lunch" that will never sell in the "court of integrity".

How in heaven's name can individuals claim to be successful if they have never risked anything significant? How can individuals claim to be righteous if they have never been truly tempted to be unrighteous (see Matthew 4:1-11)? How can people claim to be faithful when they have never been tempted to be unfaithful? There isn't anyone sane and truthful who is willing to make such claims. I truly believe what our beloved Savior said about having hate in your heart—that if you hate, you are just as guilty in God's eyes as if you had murdered. He was speaking of situations like those I have just described.

The truth is that all successful people have failed at something.

As stated earlier, I would rather do something and fail than do nothing and succeed. Most minimalists are risk-averse. They are frightened, almost to death, of failing at something and possibly having others make fun of them, criticize them, or gossip about them because of their failures. Minimalists are frightened of the negative opinions of other people. By playing it safe in life, they hope they will receive the affirmation of others, for not failing like those whom they have criticized.

Minimalists receive meaning and purpose for their existence through the baseless affirmation of others. As many who have been willing victims of such a compulsive need for such bogus affirmation can testify, needing such false affirmation always calls for a betrayal of self. When you casually peruse the words of Christ in the New Testament, you will find no reference of a person needing to be conscious and concerned about the opinions of others. In fact, in Luke 6:26 Christ says, *"Beware when everyone thinks well of you and thinks that you are the coolest thing since sliced bread."*[5] Conforming to the opinions of others is a life-long compulsion of the minimalists among us.

If someone looks me in the eye and tells me that he/she has never failed at anything attempted, my response would be that he/she has not tried to achieve anything of any significance. Such a person has not extended him/herself very much.

I believe these individuals want to be able, at the end of their lives, to stand up and not see anyone pointing a finger and saying that they have seen them fail at something, or seen them make a mistake. *Such individuals believe that not being criticized by anyone, at the end of life, is the truest measure of success.*

People who believe this do not know what they are saying. All you have to do is to look at the life of Christ, the perfect person. He was brutally criticized. However, He was not deterred in the least from the fulfillment of His destiny as a result of other's perception of Him as a failure. He truly was a peaceful person. Our Lord had truly learned, humanly speaking, how to live without the good opinion of others.

o **Wisdom Principle:** *Failure, more often than not, is simply a matter of opinion!*

---

[5] My modernized version.

You have likely heard the illustration regarding Thomas Edison, one of America's greatest inventors, if not the greatest. He had been working for years to develop a long-lasting light bulb. He conducted thousands of experiments before he was successful. Some estimates regarding the number of experiments he tried number from 7,000 to as many as 25,000. At a news conference, he was asked what it was like to have failed 7,000 times. *"Failure!"* he responded. *"I know 7,000 ways how not to make a light bulb. What do you know?"*

Failures are not self-defining unless you allow them to be. They are simply events in a person's life. An often-used example of failure is when Babe Ruth hit 60 home runs in 1927 and set the major league record. In that same year, the Babe struck out more times than anyone else in the majors. When you work at anything and seek to be the best you can be at it, you will experience occasional failure.

The difference between the mediocre and the fully-functioning person is that failure demotivates the mediocre and failure motivates the fully-functioning person. The difference lies in how each views failure. One takes failure personally, seeing it as a commentary on their intelligence, ability, and performance, while another sees it as an opportunity to reassess, learn, and get their bearings. Failures are signs that you need to alter your direction, reassess your information, and possibly consider new ideas. We then take the next step: get up and move forward.

o **Wisdom Principle:** *Our purpose can and will be divinely refined, but our purpose will never be discarded!*

o   **Wisdom Principle:** *The true definition of failure is quitting!*

13. You Cannot Criticize a Person to Excellence

Criticism is a death-knell to relationships and to achievement. It is one of the *four poisons* that kill relationships. One of the major weaknesses of mothers and fathers is the belief that criticizing their children and diminishing their children's dignity as a human being, is part of the duties of parenting. This belief is unfortunate, for it is not so. Parents who live their lives vicariously through their children are the world's worst when it comes to constantly criticizing their children. Such parents see everything their children do as a commentary on them. Parents who are this sensitive will always be over-scrutinizing and overbearing with their children.

I've never witnessed one instance where criticizing a person resulted in higher levels of achievement or effectiveness. I find people who are consistently guilty of such criticism to be idiots of the highest order, and do not deserve to be taken seriously when they have put themselves in this criticizer mode.

One question that needs answering is whether there is such a thing as constructive criticism. The answer is no! There is no such thing. The two words, "constructive" and "criticism", are on opposite ends of the spectrum. Individuals who are consistently critical of others are willingly and militantly ignorant. They believe they are smarter than others especially the people they are criticizing.

However, possessing such superiority on the part of compulsive criticizers is rarely ever the case. Most criticizers are often sub-par in intelligence and try to compensate, for this inherent deficiency through arrogance and the use of criticism. Arrogance and criticism are often mechanisms for controlling others. In essence, as Matthew Kelly says, they are, *"Self-appointed kings and queens of non-existent kingdoms."*[6]

Criticism, if it remains constant and consistent, will kill any friendship, parent-child relationship, or marriage. Life is tough enough on its own. To be criticized constantly is a horrible thing to endure. Criticism wears a person down and it communicates that the person being criticized is unacceptable, as well as less than the person doing the criticizing. Criticizers are nothing more than arrogant troublemakers who are committed to conflict instead of closeness. Overwhelmingly, such criticizers are only into control— of others and of the environments they are a part of.

A significant number of children who grow up in such a life-environment often leave home and never return, not even for a brief visit. In the majority of homes where seeking to "criticize individuals toward excellence" occurs, you will find the parents have to constantly call their children and almost beg them to come by to visit. It is amazing to me that in most cases the parents have no idea why their children will not come visit them. If you are such a parent, you need to re-evaluate your perspectives and think seriously about what you are doing, because you are killing your relationship(s) with your children, and likely others, as well.

Also, unless you want people, including family, to cut a wide swath between you and them, you need to change your demeanor and re-evaluate the commitments you obviously have to conflict and to being in control. Your children's or spouse's failure and performance are not about you. Quit being so self-centered in your perspective about their failure or performance. Just because you

---

[6] The Rhythm of Life by Matthew Kelly.

are obsessed about being afraid of being criticized and/or losing "face" with others, does not mean that everyone, especially those whom you constantly criticize, should be like you and have the same concerns as you do.

If we were all like the criticizers of our day we would still be living in the Stone Age. Nothing worthy would have ever been accomplished. This is because criticizers are primarily sub-par in character and look for limitations rather than possibilities. Criticizers also instill through their constant criticism the fear of failure in the minds and hearts of those over whom they have authority.

Having the perspectives and attitudes of a criticizer is at the heart of mediocrity. Criticizers, ultimately, are losers because all such individuals, whom I have ever known, who made it their mission in life to use criticism as a tool in order to influence and control others, were unhappy and unfulfilled people. They all lived purposeless and dispassionate lives.

Another failure of criticizers is that they neglect the "cultivation of their own garden", yet they are self-appointed experts of other's lives. While their own garden is going to the weeds, they are out and about telling others how to live their lives and what they should do or not do in regards to their lives and the lives of their family members. Criticizers are not qualified to be giving advice to others while their own gardens are in shambles. There is no greater hypocrisy than this. Make no mistake. We will *never* be able to criticize *anyone* to excellence. It is impossible! Only the mentally challenged believe criticizing one to excellence is possible. When you are standing in front of someone who believes such, my advice is to not say a word. Just turn and walk away.

o   **Wisdom Principle:** *Why is it that those who are so quick to give advice are the last ones to take it?*

14. The Illogical is the Enemy of the Logical

I do not know how many times I have heard people admit they have compulsive habits that never fail to create problems and conflicts in their relationships with family and friends, yet they continue to be guilty of such relationship-destroying habits. These people know that behaving in destructive ways will create problems yet, I have noticed that they have this glazed look in their eyes indicating they do not understand why they do such things. Many self-destructive and relationship-destructive actions are seldom the result of rational thought.

Cognitive individuals eventually become aware that most people live their lives on autopilot and as such, they rarely think of what they are doing when they are doing it. They live life unconsciously. Therefore, they are genuinely stumped when they do the same things over and over again with the same negative results. They refuse to believe that for just this once, it did not turn out differently. Realistically, it never does.

o   **Wisdom Principle**: *Insanity is doing what has never worked over and over again and expecting different results each time.*

Why do people continue to be guilty of actions after history has shown time and again that such actions do not and will not work? The answer is in two parts. First, such individuals want to control rather than cooperate and second, they believe the world is obligated to adjust to their desires and perceived needs. Such individuals are also illogical. They do not know how to think logically through such dilemmas. I will even go so far as to say that such individuals do not know how to think. They allow their emotions—how they feel—determine what they do. Thoughtful people act and emotionally-driven individuals re-act.

The brains of some individuals primarily reside in their emotions. When emotions determine what a person does, his/her brain isn't functioning effectively. Time and again such people are shown that what they are doing isn't working, and that the consequences will always be negative and self-defeating. Yet they continue to force the square peg into the round hole, thinking that this time it is going to work. It never does.

o   **Wisdom Principle:** *Learning that is often emotionally-based will perpetuate feelings as the basis of what one chooses to believe and do.*

This is why "you can tell such people, but you cannot tell them much"! Their minds do not know how to think logically. To such individuals, 2 + 2 is 14. What makes it even more amazing is that they think this answer is just fine. You can't talk to someone, who processes reality in such a fashion. Sadly, such individuals are clueless. Most people, who use the I-go-with-what-I-feel mantra, as the means of deciding what to do or not do in any given circumstance, often lead tumultuous lives and have a very difficult time, maintaining positive and meaningful relationships. Their relationships go as their emotions go—up and down. This is the definition of inconsistency!

One strata of our society that lives life on an emotional plain is the Hollywood crowd. As a rule, well-known actors have a plethora of the opposite sex coming in and out of their lives. Their romantic relationships are a revolving door and their lives are often personifications of the term "serial monogamy", primarily because they allow their feelings to determine what they do or don't do in romantic relationships. Do you see the consequences of such an approach to living life? If you don't, then you need to close this book and find something else to do because I cannot help you, and likely, neither can anyone else.

Until you do what the prodigal son did in Luke 15, and "come to your senses", you will never be able to live a responsible, consistent, and peaceful life. "Coming to your senses" means stopping how you are living and deciding to change how you make decisions. Unless you are making your life decisions from a base of logistical common-sense, you are likely finding yourself to be in an emotional, spiritual, psychological mess. You need a spiritual encounter with the Living Christ. You need to understand: Feelings are not facts, and facts are not feelings. Feelings are not and never will be the basis of knowing truth. I know that there are people who believe they can know truth based on feelings. But such people are not thinking clearly. Solid decisions are based on truth and facts, not feelings. More often than not, people who live life based on feelings let how they feel define what truth is, instead of letting truth defining their feelings.

There is no question that the illogical is the enemy of the logical, because when individuals choose to go with how they feel in contrast to going with logical common-sense as the basis of how their choices are made in life, rhyme and reason are completely absent from their daily lives. An integrity-based life can only be lived according to what is true, not according to how one feels.

o **Wisdom Principle:** *The mediocre among us allow their emotionally-driven beliefs to determine what is true. Truth does not define their beliefs.*

I have read a few books by psychologists who talk about feelings and how feelings are important. Within a certain context, feelings are important, but feelings are not meant to be the basis of how we make decisions. Feelings are our response to our thoughts and about what we have experienced; and they add power to our abilities to be sympathetic and compassionate with others. However, feelings are rarely based on what is true and factual. Feelings are our emotional reaction to what we experience—nothing more and nothing less. Too many people rely on their "feelings" to give them some "special illumination" into problems and dilemmas, which they are facing. The only thing that can give insight to your problems and dilemmas, is wisdom—spiritual intelligence. Spiritual intelligence is virtue-based and truth-based rather than being emotionally-based.

Every person I have ever known who lived their lives based on feelings, as well as, whose learning curve was emotionally-driven, was below average in their life-performance. Also, their insight into living life and solving everyday challenges was sub-par at best. If you want to live your life based on the illogical, get ready for a tough life. You may be living the life you want when you go with how you feel, but you will pay an unbelievable price for doing so. Such a price will always be more than you would have wanted to pay. It will also be too high a price in comparison to what you received. Life will never be what you want it to be, because you have thrown truth and facts to the wind. Solid decision-making is a byproduct of gathering facts and knowing what is true, then having the courage to do the right thing in contrast to wanting to get your own way.

15. Never Allow Your Well-Being or the Well-Being of Your Family to Fall into the Hands of Those Who Do Not Care

Life has taught me many things, but this one has been the toughest to get right. I cannot begin to tell you the pain, suffering, and humiliation one suffers, when the well-being of one's own life, the life of one's spouse, and the lives of their children fall into the hands of people who couldn't care less about what happens to them. One of the reasons I am a proponent for self-employment is that an individual is in complete charge of his or her own success. When you go to work for yourself, it is funny how you will immediately notice that politics goes right out the window. What you find yourself doing is dealing with reality as it is, rather than dealing with a perception of reality, which others will often admonish you to cultivate. You actually go from managing perspectives to delivering results. Big difference!

   o   **Wisdom Principle:** *You don't know that God is all you need, until He is all you have.* –Rick Warren

When you allow the wellbeing of you and your loved ones to fall into the hands of those who do not care, you have lost self-determination and you are at the mercy of the character or, more often, the lack of character of the ones in whom you have put your trust. The stability of your life and the lives of your loved ones is paramount. So, because such is so, you need to know the following.

1) **You and your spouse must work to build a loving bond within your family.**

 Make faith in God your foundation. Teach your children to pray and to believe in God. Practice your faith in front of your children—every single day. Let them see God work in your life on a daily basis. Let them see you pray—daily! Let them see you continually cultivate an indomitable character. If you and I consistently do these things, our children will truly believe that God is greater than any challenge that you and your family will ever face.

2) **Live your life in such a manner that your spouse and children never suffer because of your selfishness, irresponsibility, or ignorance.**

 You are responsible for the safety and nurturing of your children. They did not ask to be born. You and your spouse chose to bring them into this world.

 Implied in such an act is a commitment to procure the necessary knowledge to help them become the best they can be. You also need to realize that you must protect them from harmful people and harmful environments. You are responsible for providing for them. This involves the provision of the necessary tangibles of life—shelter, clothes, food, and health services. Finally, you are to prepare them for this world by teaching them wisdom principles and the proper application of such principles. Your responsible behavior, demonstrated consistently for them to see, will give them a sense of security. Your children will trust and respect you when you put them at the top of your list of priorities. Ultimately, they will follow your lead, and will do so, confidently.

3) Be resourceful.

Never allow yourself to be professionally competent at only one thing. Be good at several things, if possible. I remember, years ago, an electrical engineer, who was a member of the same church I was, lose his job. He tried for four months to get another job. There were none to be found at that time that required his expertise. He'd had a double major in college, engineering and history. He loved to read history books and he decided to major in history just for the sheer joy of it. He also, intuitively, thought it would be good to get a teacher's certificate. He spent an extra year in school to get his teacher's certification.

In June, when his employment drought continued, he applied to teach in the school district of the county where he lived. He was hired to teach history and on the side, began consulting in electrical engineering. His wife got a job as well. He taught for a full year before a job in his chosen field opened up. Because he had a job teaching, he was not forced to take the first job that came along. He had the option to wait for the right one. Sure enough, in time, the right job came around and he was ready to take it. Because he could do more than one thing well, his wellbeing and the wellbeing of his family did not fall into the hands of those who did not care. This, for me, was a lesson well-learned.

I have many other stories I could tell you of individuals who applied themselves to do more than one thing well. Eventually one of the other things they could do well came in handy. Individuals, who understand this principle do the necessary preparation. I have known of individuals who not only earned one doctorate, but two. I met a woman in the early 90s who was a licensed social worker as well as an attorney. She told me she had never been unemployed.

There are seminaries in our country who train ministers to be educated to do more than just pastor a church. One seminary in the Atlanta area requires their ministerial students, who majored in theology in college, to cultivate another professional option in case it is needed.

If you do not prepare to protect you and your loved ones, there will come a time when your wellbeing and the wellbeing of your loved ones will fall into the hands of an individual or individuals who do not care about what happens to any of you. When this happens, gird yourself up. You and your loved ones are in for a period of tough and uncertain times.

It is in such times that you learn that people are not always loving or loyal. People are inherently selfish and lazy. They do not care to cultivate the compassion and love to care for others. We must care enough for ourselves and the wellbeing of our families, not to allow such people to determine what happens to us.

CHAPTER TWO

THE SIXTEENTH ESSENTIAL

One of the social markers that I have observed over the decades is how each generation intuitively defines itself. Each seems to make sure that the definition of themselves is clearly different from any previous generation. All generations, therefore, are arrogant in the sense that each sees itself as superior to previous generations. Also, each succeeding generation often sees itself as more intelligent, more enlightened, more stylish, and more in the know than others. There is no question that each in the prime of its youth believes it is invincible and invisible. Also, while in the midst of this euphoric invincibility, each generation inherently becomes chronically deaf to any advice, wisdom, or illumination given to them by the previous generations. This is a dangerous position in which to be ... attitudinally, psychologically, and spiritually.

o **Wisdom Principle:** *To the truly intelligent, a generation's superiority is always determined by the contribution it makes to community and country, not primarily by its own opinion of itself.*

How do I know this? For the simple reason that I was part of one of the generations I have just described. My generation produced some of the greatest actors, musicians, and athletes in history. This same generation also gave us the demand for legal abortions, a higher use of drugs, the belief that love was a feeling in contrast to a commitment, and an excessive emphasis on sexual fulfillment as an entitlement rather than a responsibility. My generation took the "sex angle" in male-female relationships to a level not known in our social history, before.

It was this generation that moved us more toward the secularization of society—especially in the area of moral decision-making. This is the baby-boomer generation—those individuals born in 1945 and afterward.

During the decade of 1960-70, our nation, due to the decisions of the Kennedy Administration, became involved in one of the costliest and most fruitless military conflicts in our history—The Vietnam War. It eventually cost us over 58,000 of our beloved sons and daughters. To this day I am sure many parents are asking, in spite of their patriotism, what for? They will never receive a satisfactory answer, because those responsible for leading us into this conflict do not know, and have never known, the answer themselves. Moreover, I do not believe they are smart enough to give a satisfactory answer, nor do I believe they care to give one.

In the midst of that conflict, our sons and daughters—many of them in college—took to the streets to protest this war. I believe that what they did was correct, necessary, and courageous. However, the methods that many of them used to force the government to get out of that conflict were off the radar screen. These young people essentially and eventually, questioned all of our values—socially and spiritually. They began tearing down our culture and our traditions. I agree that some parts of our culture at that time needed to be honed, remodeled, and in some cases eradicated. The same could be said about some of our social values and traditions. However, once the baby boomers did this they put nothing back in the place of those things which they destroyed or discarded.

What my generation managed to do was create a larger problem than what originally existed. Many will disagree with this, but all you have to do is look at what we have become socially and spiritually since the late 60s. *Behavior does not lie*. We have become more immoral, more selfish, more self-centered, more shallow, and in some cases, more narcissistic than any time in history. However, even more tragic is that we took individuality to the extreme, to the point that such self-centeredness initiated the fragmentation of the concept of teamwork, confused cooperation with conformity, and destroyed the meaning of mutual respect. Consequently, we have also become dumber! The children born to these rebellious baby boomers are the most spoiled, self-centered, unspiritual generation in the history of this country—which leads me to the sixteenth essential. I have put it in the form of a wisdom principle.

o **Wisdom Principle**: *The more casual you are with your dress, behavior, and language, the less seriously you will be taken by those who make important decisions in the direction of your life—both socially and professionally.*[7]

Just because one may think he/she is OK does not mean he/she is. This is the "Achilles heel" of the X and Millennial generations that followed the baby boomers. There is a young man that I describe in the next chapter on self-definition, whom I saw at Dollywood. I could tell that he thought he was really cool with all of his tattoos and his mutilated clothing. He probably also thought he possessed an insight above most of those who were in the theme park that day. I could see this attitude in his walk and in his eyes when he looked at other people.

Self-awareness was evidently absent from his life. Such a lack of self-awareness is also reflected in the lives of those of the next two generations who were also in that theme park that day in great numbers. A significant percentage of these people

---

[7] **Writer's Note:** I am aware that many will disagree with point two of my discourse in this chapter. However, I truly believe that if we are reasonably cognizant of the environments in which we find ourselves, we will know exactly what will be the appropriate dress in any given context. As far as business dress is concerned, one needs to be aware as to whether their work environment would be classified as professionally formal, i.e., IBM or other Fortune 100 companies; professional dress-casual, i.e., retail sales, fashion designers or interior designers; professionally casual, i.e., Home Depot, ACE Hardware, construction, creative arts careers. Most of all, if one is physically clean and his/her clothes are clean, that means more to most people than anything else. There is no question that how you present yourself tells others how disciplined you are, how well you take care of yourself and the effectiveness of your judgment in determining what is appropriate or inappropriate when it comes to how you present yourself to others. There's no question that individuals will take care of their professional responsibilities, about as well as they personally take care of themselves. —DP

possessed an unbridled narcissism in their youth. Unfortunately, there isn't much evidence that it has changed significantly over the succeeding years. This makes those who possess such a perspective, psychologically and spiritually off the radar screen.

A person will rarely succeed in having access to the CEO while looking like a reject from the Salvation Army. This is not a put down but simply one of life's brutal realities. The failure of the boomer generation, to put something in place of what it discarded in the arena of social protocol, has left a huge vacuum and now we do not have any social norms or even a standard social etiquette, which we can justifiably expect others to follow. In essence, we have nothing! When this happens, we have social, professional, and spiritual anarchy.

Because of this failure to the void left in place of the social norms discarded in the 60s and 70s, the boomer generation was left empty and unfulfilled. *Having the heart of a rebel was simply not enough to give meaning and purpose to their lives.* Discarding the culture created by their grandparents and perpetuated by their parents did not give the rebels of this generation the sense of fulfillment and meaning they thought they would get. They were just not intelligent enough to have something more significant, meaningful, and superior with which to replace the old culture left behind. This is an incredible lesson*: the destruction of something makes no sense when you do not have something more significant to put in its place.*

Proof of this was the boomer generation's unbridled search for meaning and fulfillment, through the use of drugs. Mistakenly, those of this generation also thought that an uninhibited and insatiable desire for sex, coupled with taking psychedelic drugs, would provide the necessary components to fill the incredible void in the center of their beings. This alone proves that destruction without contribution is unmistakably narcissistic, short-sighted, and unintelligent.

o **Wisdom Principle:** *Be careful what you want! Authentic meaning in life comes from the fulfillment of your deepest desires, not your illegitimate wants.*

o **Wisdom Principle:** *The ultimate fulfillment of narcissistic desires leads to despair and, ultimately, self-loathing.*

The parents of the past two generations are not something to write home about either. Therefore, un-self-defined have the last two generations of parents been that we see a significant percentage of these parents seeking to dress, speak, and behave in such a manner, as to resemble their children. They want to be more like their children rather than the reverse.

There is no question in my mind that when a parent imitates a child, such a parent is communicating that he/she does not have a clear self-definition and has not formulated any significant standards of behavior, dress, and social etiquette for his/her own life. This violates virtually all manner of parental responsibility toward a child, because parents are obligated by the position they hold to be role models for their children, not an imitator of them.

o **Wisdom Principle:** *A lack of self-definition is always linked to a life that has conformed to the social secular-humanist philosophy of our day.*

Children have no business being a role model for their parents, whether in behavior, dress, and social protocol. They barely are able to understand the rudimentary principles of life and living. Most teenagers have not been able to digest even these basics. But when you have parents (authority figures), who are as spaced out as their children, what you get is parents who desire to look like children, behave like children and talk cool like children at the expense of their dignity and their appropriate roles.

I never thought that I would see parents afraid of upsetting their children at the expense of doing what is best for their children. Unfortunately, this is occurring all over our country. Aren't you impressed? I am not! Such an approach has not worked, is not working, and will not work. It is too shallow, too nebulous, and too irresponsible.

What the boomer generation and the X and Millennial generations have failed to comprehend is that if you are going to make changes, if you are going to bring about progress, you must conduct yourself and your affairs in a manner that reflects responsibility and which also makes sense. By making sense I mean implementing something that brings clarity rather than confusion. What we have now as "sense" is no sense. When everyone does what is right in their own eyes, you have social, spiritual, and familial anarchy, i.e., a breakdown of cultural norms. At this time, we don't have any new and more workable norms for the X and Millennial generations. Long term, making it up as you go along will never "get it".

We must have something clearer, character-based, and virtuous. What we have currently, is a society that has become increasingly obscure in identity; irresponsible when it comes to social norms; dumber when it comes to being able to think analytically; and "out-to-lunch" when it comes to understanding the meaning of excellence.

There are three specific areas, in which this obscurity has been reflected. Those areas include how we behave, dress, and speak. In all three areas, our society has "dumbed" itself down. Now anything goes. Let's look at these three areas one at a time.

The first social determinate in the United States is how one behaves. In the area of behavior, our society—especially the Boomer, X, and Millennial generations—has become completely obtuse when it comes to defining cultural norms, in which case, there are no cultural norms today. The inconsiderateness, rudeness, and hostility that is consistent within families and society proves this to be true. Members of the X and Millennial generations are rarely polite when waiting on me in a retail establishment. I seek to treat everyone as respectfully as is humanly possible. I live by the behavioral principle that I am to treat people in a manner that gives them a terrific role model to which they can aspire. I do this especially with those who serve me—from janitors, to waiters/waitresses in restaurants. I am truly thankful for what anyone does for me even though it is rare that anyone does it with a positive attitude.

This inconsiderateness, rudeness, and even hostility is due to unbridled narcissism, and our society as a whole embracing an "entitlement mentality". The X and Millennial generations are particularly consumed with this. Such narcissism is so pervasive that I choose to believe these generations have to know, deep within, that they are compulsively selfish. As a result, I also believe they intuitively know they do not deserve respect from others and that, justifiably, they should not be surprised when they cannot consistently be trusted to do the right thing in the defining moments in life.

What produces such narcissism and selfishness is a belief of entitlement. This is very often the result of experiencing the gamut of extremes from a childhood filled with emotional pain and being unacceptable to parents and peers, to being a child who was given virtually everything he/she wanted. The "I-deserve-to-get-my-way" mentality is entrenched in these two generations as a result. However, one comeback these generations will have is that they were taught well, by the boomer generation. Unfortunate, but absolutely true!

Behavior is a manifestation of one's attitude—rebellious or cooperative—one's self-discipline (or lack of it), knowledge (or ignorance), and one's graciousness/kindness (or self-centered-ness). Also, it is a manifestation of one's self-respect or lack of it. No one who truly respects himself or herself would ever treat family, as well as non-family, with the rudeness, inconsiderateness, and hostility that I have witnessed from these two generations. There is no question, at least to me, that self-respect is nonexistent in the life of such narcissistic and self-centered generations.

- o **Wisdom Principle:** *You cannot give away anything to others that you first have not given to yourself. It is impossible!*

How a person behaves is also a commentary on their self-definition, the environment in which they grew up, their values, their commitments, their tastes, their self-respect (or lack thereof), and their intelligence. Behavior is so critical to one's life that it has become one of the social determinates by which a person is judged competent, self-disciplined, gracious, and trustworthy.

Therefore, when someone ridicules and derides the importance of behavior, they are indeed revealing to those who are socially cognitive that they believe a person ought to be believed for what they say, not for what they do; and that *intention* is just as valid as *behavior*. The only reply I can give to such a perspective is "Baloney". Behavior matters. It is pivotal in determining one's graciousness, dependability, character, and trustworthiness. As stated in Chapter 1, the greatest predictor of future behavior is pertinent past behavior. One's behavior gives the observer more intimate insight and more accurate information, than any other knowledge that would be considered dependable.

- o **Wisdom Principle:** *Behavior permitted is behavior perpetuated!*

- o **Wisdom Principle:** *The mature primarily define themselves by their* <u>competence</u>. *The immature primarily define themselves by their* <u>appearance</u>.

The second social determinate in the United States is how one dresses. A person's self-perception and how he/she wants to be perceived is communicated by how he/she dresses. Now I am acutely aware that dress being a social determinate has not existed since the mid-eighties. *However, among those who create jobs, place significant investments in companies which employ hundreds, if not thousands of people, and who pay most of the income taxes in this country, how one dresses matters.* Why?

Because much can be determined by how one chooses to dress. A person's self-respect, self-perception, and the kind of environment in which he/she grew up, as well as what kind of environment with which one prefers to be identified, is often communicated by how one dresses. This is equally true for men and women.

Many working in the human resources division of corporations have said to me, *"When I have someone of the X and Millennial generations come into my office for an interview, I can tell by their dress what they think of themselves, as well as what their attitude is toward those of us who make the determination as to whether they will or will not work for us."*

Fashion and style are two entirely different things. Just because you dress fashionably, which in today's society means looking motley and/or "grungy", does not mean that you know anything about style. What is fashionable today is not fashion in the truest sense, and what is stylish today is not style. We have come full circle in our culture and we now can say that we truly personify bad taste by how we dress. Whatever fashion was considered to be in the 60s, 70s, and 80s is on the opposite side of the spectrum today. Now bra straps, tattoos, and rubber-thong footwear are considered a fashion statement.

Anyone, who believes that the fashions ushered in by the X and Millennial generations are a step forward in contrast to the past, has lost his/her mind. When I recall the elegance of Jackie Kennedy, the dresses she wore, the taste and dignity of her wardrobe, I am appalled that designers of the X and Millennial generations believe their fashions are just as terrific and elegant.

Because of these tasteless designers, we now have, in certain pockets of our society, a standard for formal wear consisting of jeans, tee-shirt, tennis shoes, and a double-breasted blue blazer. Coinciding with this definition of style in current fashion trends we now have "for sure", "cool", "totally", "awesome", "dude", "whatever", and "you know" as the nucleus of our verbal expression, which supposedly reflects "coolness". Add to this rudeness and a lack of graciousness as the means of proving one's own individuality. "Popping off"—saying or doing something to embarrass those of the older generations—seems to be the "in vogue" way to show one is cool. Forgive me if I don't "feel the love" in these displays of so-called "authenticity" and "coolness".

In behavior and dress, the destruction of our major cultural norms since the mid-60s has made it impossible for many adults to know just how to behave socially or professionally. I recall an article in *The Journal-Constitution* in Atlanta, speaking about the "grunge look" being "in fashion". The article, from the late 80s if my memory serves me correctly, showed a photo of a mother and her child walking down a sidewalk in a tee-shirt, jeans, and black & white sneakers. She was an adult imitating a teenager. I did not catch it then, but as I chose to contemplate this scene, I realized that there are significant numbers of adults that have become imitators rather than pace-setters for our younger generations. When this kind of thing occurs, I guarantee that many significant facets of our lives, especially the social and familial, will begin to move into obscurity. Those who cannot see this, disqualify themselves from joining the conversation of the subject-at-hand.

I have surmised from my research, that the grunge look was ushered in, not only as the result of a lack of taste and class on the part of the generations who have embraced that style of dress, but also as a way to identify with those "less fortunate". Since most of the families that can afford to pay the ridiculous costs for "mutilated clothing" come from the middle and upper-middle classes; looking like those who are poor seems to be their contribution, to helping the poor have a better life. Crazy, isn't it? However well-meaning this desire to identify with the poor may be, it has not nor cannot accomplish the intent desired.

The X and Millennial generations have decided that it is better to look cool than to be competent; that it is better to be popular than to be proficient; that it is better to be a ridiculer than to be respectful. Unbelievable, isn't it? Because of this, we now have young people all over the world looking at U.S. teenagers and college students with disdain, perceiving them as unintelligent and not very serious about anything. We have a public-school system that has *become a social event, instead of an academic event.* Depending on the state, we have an average of 65-74% of our high school students who graduate. Borrowing a term cultivated in my generation, this is <u>not</u> cool.

You would think that if a generation truly wanted to be superior to any previous generation that it would seek to improve over what the previous generations created and produced. However, in many contexts today this has not been the case. I can find only one context where the current young-adult generation has perpetrated something worthwhile—expanding our use of information technology. However, their obsession with technological toys has spawned a problem—technological obsession. The X and Millennial generations did not create the technology we now enjoy. *They are only the perpetuators of it.* And if any generation wants to truly be remembered, it needs to be committed to *resolving problems* in contrast to *creating them.*

The third social determinate in our country is one's use of the English language. It is a reflection of one's self-respect (or lack of it).

I was stunned to hear how thousands of Americans make excellent salaries teaching English to citizens of varying countries. In these countries people pay enormous amounts of money to learn the English language. In fact, English is the world's "common language—the number one spoken language in the world. This is true even in China where most school children and professionals study English.

Yet in our country children get to learn English without having to pay someone to teach it to them privately. *In spite of such a privilege, American children speak worse English than many of the young people who are learning it in other countries.* What a disaster!

Perhaps you can dress the part and you might be able to play (behave) the part, but when you open your mouth to speak, you cannot hide how educated or uneducated you are. You cannot fool anyone when it comes to revealing who and what you are, while you are speaking.

There are scores of individuals who will look at this social standard with disdain. However, it cannot be denied that those who speak the English language with proficiency, achieve high levels professionally, and are seen as more sophisticated and dignified than those who do not speak the English language all that well. I do not doubt that those who speak English well do better and make more money than those who do not. There will always be exceptions to the rule, but such exceptions are extremely rare.

Earl Nightingale, in his speaking engagements, tells of a large university that gave one particular graduating class a vocabulary test. The test scores were categorized in 5% intervals. Periodically, over the next two decades, the members of this graduating class were sent questionnaires and were asked about their professions and their level of achievement—both monetarily and in the position currently held within the company where they work. Without exception, those who scored the highest on that vocabulary test 20 years earlier, made the most money and held higher positions in the corporate structure of their respective companies.

Other surveys have been taken over the years regarding one's ability to speak the English language well and comparing such skill with their station in life. *Each survey confirms that knowing the meaning of a large number of words, and knowing how to use these words, accompanies outstanding success.*

Another example that Earl Nightingale gives comes from Dr. Johnson O'Conner. He researched the vocabulary skills of executive management and supervisory personnel in 39 large manufacturing corporations. He found that all of those individuals researched ranked high in the basic aptitudes relating to leadership skills. However, the differences in their vocabulary aptitude were dramatic and clearly noticeable. The highest score a person could make on the vocabulary test was 272 points. Executives averaged a score of 236. Mid-level managers averaged 168. This is 68 points lower than those who held executive positions. Superintendents averaged 140. Those holding the position of foreman averaged 114. Finally, floor supervisors averaged a score of 86. The difference between the average score of a floor supervisor and an executive was 150 points! Unbelievable! In each case, the use of the English language by individuals correlated with executive levels achieved, as well as income. There is no question to those who are perceptively intelligent that the effective use of the English language determines the extent of one's knowledge ... the two go together.

o **Wisdom Principle:** *Class is an aura of confidence that reflects being sure without being cocky. Class has nothing to do with money. It never runs scared. It is enveloped with self-discipline and self-knowledge. It is the surefootedness that comes with having proved you can meet life.—* Ann Landers

There is no question that a person can "Wow", "Awesome", and "Cool" themselves into poverty. Such verbiage may find you a place among the "clique cool" but will not place you among the elite in effectiveness and excellence, or with those who achieve legitimate financial success as well as success in their personal lives.

Therefore, where will being cool and popular get you long term? Are you becoming a better person because of your coolness? Or are you just simply being cool in order to be acceptable to the clique you want to be part of? Sooner or later you have to get serious about you—who you are, what you have become, and what you will become. The earlier you start on committing yourself to becoming a person of excellence, the less painful, embarrassing, and regretful your life will be when you must face the question: "Do I have what it takes to be very good at what I am seeking to achieve?"

- o **Wisdom Principle:** *Intellectual hunger comes from our desire to be the best we can be.*

- o **Wisdom Principle:** *The more prepared a person becomes, the less fearful he/she is of failing. Being <u>unprepared</u> is at the core of the fear of failure.*

CHAPTER THREE

SELF-DEFINITION: THE INFLUENCES AND COMPONENTS

How we define ourselves is absolutely critical to our happiness, our fulfillment, and the contribution we make to our own life as well as to life in general. Our self-definition determines several things:

1) Our self-definition determines the kind of person we become. This will specifically be shown through the character we have developed and continue to refine as the years go on.

2) Our self-definition will reflect our values—what is important to us—whether such values are selfish or altruistic.

3) Our self-definition will be reflected in how we treat others. This includes just how important other people are to us in our lives, as well as how we treat those who cannot help or hurt us.

4) Our self-definition will reflect how we have learned to handle adversity. The vicissitudes in each of our lives can and will reveal flaws in our character. Through experiencing

adversity, our character is not primarily made but rather revealed.

5) Our self-definition will reflect what we have learned both professionally and personally. The quantity and quality of what we have learned, determine how we have processed these experiences, both mentally and emotionally.

6) Our self-definition will consistently reflect our priorities.

7) Our self-definition will reflect how accomplished our lives are—specifically, if our accomplishments have reflected selfishness or unselfishness.

8) Our self-definition will reflect how effective we have been in discovering the purpose for our lives. How we define ourselves will be reflected in how we understand what our purpose in life is and, as a result of such understanding, whether our lives have positively and effectively reflected this purpose.

9) Our self-definition will be reflected in our attitude—our worldview. Specifically, whether our attitude reflects an "entitlement mentality" or a "responsibility mentality".

Our self-definition also determines whether or not the basic questions of life will be ultimately answered for each of us. For centuries, certain questions have been asked time and time again. For example:

- *Who are we?* Such a question speaks to our personal identity.
- *Why are we here?* This a question speaks to the purpose for which we were created.
- *Where are we going?* This question regards our destiny.

- *What can I do?* This question speaks to our potential and opens the door to our divine assignment.

These are very good questions. Rick Warren, in his book *The Purpose-Driven Life*, answers these questions quite clearly and fully. We are created for God and for His purpose. We are here on this earth to love, worship, glorify and serve Him. We each have an assignment of His choosing, which we are put on this earth to fulfill.

In fact, we are fully-functioning in direct proportion to how close we are to the daily fulfillment of our Godly purpose. The farther away we are in the fulfillment of our Godly purpose, the more dysfunctional we will be. Our joy, meaning, and fulfillment in life are in direct proportion to our willingness to obey our Heavenly Father in the pursuit of that assignment. We are God's handiwork. Before our conception, God knew us and He loved us! Because of God's love and His longsuffering, patience, and mercy toward mankind, there is no question that all of life is implicitly and explicitly declared to be sacred.

We have much more power in determining who and what we become than we will ever realize. We have been divinely given a will. How we use that will in our choices mostly determines who and what we have chosen to become. While most will blame others and circumstances for who and what they have become, Proverbs teaches us that our choices and what we allow to influence us are our responsibility. Such choices significantly determine our self-definition.

o **Wisdom Principle:** *We cannot do what is right, unless we are taught what is right.*

o **Wisdom Principle:** *You must know where you are going. If you do not, you will never get there.*

It is more than a coincidence to me that Proverbs begins in the first chapter by listing several reasons why these proverbs were being written. The reasons given are directly related to one's self-definition.

Among the reasons for Proverbs being written are:

1) The attainment and comprehension of wisdom.
2) The acquisition of a disciplined life, which is defined by possessing a depth of insight regarding life, the decisions it sets before each of us, and applying that insight in the various critical contexts of life.
3) The development of a virtuous character.
4) To develop discretion (sound judgment) in the decisions which are critical to one's stability and fortification of one's character.
5) To be virtuous in our dealings with everyone we come into contact—loved ones, friends, neighbors, acquaintances, and even those whom we do not know.

There are two things clearly evident when a person embarks on a study of Proverbs. This is a book that calls a person to respect the role of parents. And it is a book that calls a person to commit to living a disciplined life. It is a call to being wise in the development of one's self-definition.

It is clear in the first seven verses that there is such a thing as spiritual intelligence. Comprehending the five kinds of intelligence, which I mentioned earlier, helps in being clear regarding the critical decisions we all face, as well as to understand how such decisions affect the various intelligences with which we all wrestle. This understanding is necessary for walking the path of positive effectiveness as well as for living virtuously.

You see, most people focus on one or two kinds of intelligence in their maturation. Individuals who choose to excel in only one or two kinds of intelligence will usually pay a hefty price for not having an effective comprehension of the kinds of intelligence they have neglected. This is one cause that opens the door for dramatic swings in the stability and effectiveness of a person's life.

For example, a person who is quite competent at task intelligence but is abusive at home with his/her family, speaks directly to this point. Another point-specific example is a person who is excellent at rote intelligence but in turn is rather clumsy in their relational intelligence. The lack of effective knowledge in the intelligences, which have either been ignored or neglected, has created this instability. Proverbs teaches us that happy people are consistently spiritually intelligent people. In turn, they are people who live positive and effective lives.

Self-definition is primarily affected by five critical influences. The primary influences that contribute to our self-definition are: our parents, our authority figures, our peers, the social standards—the expectations that our society has of all of us and our life-environments. There are no greater influences in who and what we become. These influences have tremendous power and ability to affect our beliefs and actions.

Our parents and siblings have a tremendous influence on our self-definition, because they are the primary individuals in the beginning of our lives with whom we have the most interaction and communication. Their influence is absolutely unbelievable, as well as incapable of being measured. Such influence is also undeniable. What shocks me is how unwilling we all are to admit just how much we have been influenced by our family regarding who and what we have become. People seem to forget just how much time is spent around family.

As we become older, we also become more mobile and the time we spend with our families obviously becomes less and less. However, in spite of not realizing that as we grow older we spend less time with our families and loved ones, it is foolish to deny the impact their attitudes, beliefs, mannerisms, and behavior have had on each of us. Such family influence is very powerful, an extremely entrenched influence on who and what we have become.

Another factor in our self-definition, for better or worse, is the influence authority figures have on us. How such individuals influence children is important, because if parents are not cognizant of what is being taught to their children by other authority figures, it is possible that their own influence and authority in their children's lives can be sabotaged or usurped by these individuals. Whether this has occurred intentionally or unintentionally isn't primarily the point here. It simply isn't all that uncommon if or when it happens.

Children need to hear the ideas, convictions, and exactly, what is important to their parents regarding their lives and their decisions/choices. When authority figures prove to be untrustworthy, such an experience in the lives of children can be lethal in their willingness to be led in the future by other authority figures.

It is not a mystery, at least to me, why we have rebellion on the part of employees toward corporate leadership in America. Many individuals who have had roles of leadership in our children's lives have often proved to be unreliable, untrustworthy, and, in many cases, hypocritical. As our children have grown older, they have begun to look at the authority of the leaders in their lives with great suspicion and distrust. The lack of competence past leaders have shown, has contributed to this distrust.

When authority figures in business, government, or the military encounter such obstinacy, they should and ought to realize that the lack of appropriate and benevolent leadership that parents and other authority figures have displayed toward America's children, has been one of the principle causes for the lack of respect, the distrust, and the apprehension these adults now have for all authority. Such leadership should be wise enough to realize that the lack of compliance and fulfillment regarding their expectations of those they have under their tutelage and leadership, will not improve until strategies are developed to rebuild the trust and respect, which was lost.

The influence of our peers takes on a more dominant role as we move into pre-adolescence. At this stage of our social development, we usually have less respect for anybody over 30 and we are becoming knowledgeable of our own individuality, as well as the opinions of our peers. When we were children, other children our age may have been a nuisance. Now the opinions of these peers begin to matter, because teens are beginning to wrestle with their own aloneness—their own individualization. There is no question that our self-definition is affected profoundly by our experiences with our peers and the environments in which we find ourselves when we are with them.

The fourth influence in our self-definition is society's standards including the perceived expectations society has of each of us, which in turn are often articulated to us by the media. It is the media that communicates these social expectations and so-called standards.

Most of the influence that the media seeks to have in the lives of Americans, as a rule, is both untrustworthy and shallow. Much of the media is made up of people who, for the most part, are ego-driven, emotionally-driven, shallow, inconsistent, and militantly ignorant of the critical components of what it truly takes to live a life of excellence. It is impossible to teach what you do not know or lead where you will not go.

The American media, for the most part, is un-self-disciplined, self-centered, and arrogant. The media embraces, and is permeated philosophically, by secular-humanism. Rooted in secular-humanism is a pervasive know-it-all attitude by those who believe that man is the center of the universe. Secular-humanism implicitly and explicitly preaches that given time, mankind, on its own, can resolve any problem or dilemma which it faces. Based on the evidence, an appropriate response to such a belief is, "Yea, right! Now, where did I leave my iced tea?" Let's take these one at a time:

For better or worse, our families—both parents and siblings— have a profound effect on who and what we become. And the effect that most families have will be negative. This is partly due to a lack of awareness of the dysfunctional tendencies acquired as a child, regarding the cultivation and management of relationships.

o **Wisdom Principle:** *If an adult primarily depends on the knowledge gained from observing his/her parent's style of leadership, and the life-experiences in their interactions with them, such knowledge will always be an insufficient base upon which to build an effective parenting style.*

Dr. Gordon Livingston, a psychiatrist, has often been asked by parents what they can do to insure their children will become positive and productive individuals. His answer was stunning. He—and I am summarizing—says that, as a rule, parents can do very little to make sure their children turn out well after they reach a certain age. If they can do anything, parents could cut down on the conflict that seems to be a consistent thorn in most families. *He states that parents, more often than not, have a counterproductive influence in their children's lives, especially when their own behavior contradicts what they say to their children.* What adults say isn't even close in importance, in comparison to what their children see them do. This old adage applies here: *"What I see you do speaks so loudly that I cannot hear what you are saying."*

After spending almost two decades as a youth, college, and singles minister, I can comfortably say that in a home where parental control is harsh and uncompromising, you will find a lack of internalized limits in the children who have been the victims of such harsh discipline. The same is true where absolutely no guidelines have been established for children ... what I call an "unconscious home". The extremes on any spectrum are always unproductive.

Such children find themselves having a horrible time finding a comfort zone in which to work and live comfortably with others. You just cannot do what you do not know you ought to do. When

Dr. Livingston says that danger is consistently at the extremes of the spectrum, he is also applying this maxim to parenting.

o **Wisdom Principle:** *"In life, danger exists at the extremes of the behavioral spectrum."*

The most brutal consequence of being a bad parent is the passing on of dysfunctional attitudes, beliefs, and behaviors to children. This happens when children live and grow up in a home that is filled with inconsistency and turmoil. To make matters worse, many parents will reinforce such dysfunctional behaviors in their children by arguing for such limitations, in themselves and their children as well. Parents do this so they will not lose face with others—especially other parents and authority figures. Parents, who would rather argue for the limitations in themselves and in their children, rather than face up to their mistakes and their children's mistakes and take positive action to correct such, are hopeless cases.

They should be disqualified from being parents. They have compounded their children's problems and dysfunctions, as well as lessened the probability that their children will grow up to be positive and effective adults. What such parents end up doing is endangering the possibility that their children will develop the skills and discipline necessary to live in this imperfect world, and face enormous odds when trying to find true happiness.

Such children grow up with what I describe as subconscious compliance. These dysfunctional attitudes, beliefs, and behaviors become embedded deep within their subconscious. These children then grow up saying and doing things that even baffle them.

In many cases, these poor people have no idea why they do such self-destructive things. They have no idea why they sabotage their stability, hopes, and wellbeing. What they are experiencing is often beyond their ability to comprehend. They are unconscious of the fact that they are perpetuating the weaknesses of their parents and will likely pass those weaknesses, without even realizing it, to their own children. This is truly the personification of Progressive Dysfunctional Behavior.

It is my profound conviction that one of the roles a youth minister must do in his professional endeavors is become familiar with dysfunctional behaviors that can sabotage a young person's future. Through the implementation of a psycho-spiritual curriculum, a youth minister can expose such behaviors that can be counter-productive on the low end, and lethal to life on the high end. I can guarantee that due to pride and self-deception, most parents are not going to help their children confront such subconscious compliances. Instead, they will guard their parental pride at the expense of their teenager's future and happiness.

On the other hand, children who grow up in a home that is healthy both psychologically and spiritually live happier and more productive lives. Their maturity skyrockets. Such children are not afflicted with the same struggles as those who are raised in more dysfunctional homes. They get an unbelievable head start in life.[8]

According to Proverbs, Chapter 1, we are to listen with the intent to obey our parents. I have found it interesting that listening to and obeying the counsel that parents give are critical to a child's stability and ability to avoid mistakes, which in some cases can be

---

[8] My reasons as to why this is so will be in the chapters on parenting in the Volume II of this series.

catastrophic and life-changing. Without exception, children and teenagers who talk back to parents giving them unnecessary grief, are compulsively selfish, and in general, turn a deaf ear to their parents' counsel, often turn out living embittered lives, filled with frustrations, disillusionment, and a consistent lack of constructive continuity. The lives of such children do not turn out well.

Such is the payoff of a narcissistic life. Narcissistic children are know-it-alls of the highest order. Narcissistic children are also poor listeners; and are often foolish in both thought and action. Proverbs says that we must listen to our parents, especially when they seek to guide us in the paths of virtue and discipline. I believe it cannot be emphasized enough that being disrespectful of parents not only breaks the fourth commandment, but it is also a sure sign of a child heading for trouble. Any young person who does not get this, is not intelligent enough to be having a conversation about this subject ... with anyone! This sounds strong but it is nonetheless true.

Our authority figures are the second significant influence in our lives that contributes to our self-definition. This could be grandparents, other extended family members, teachers, neighbors, coaches, ministers, or media personalities. Our children will choose which authority figures they will listen to and whose lead they will follow. Such a choice is based on our children's perceived wants, desires, needs, and insecurities. It is critical that you understand this. *We choose, which influences we will allow to mold and define us.* This significant influence deserves serious scrutiny, because our values, desires, beliefs, and our need to abate our own insecurities determine which individuals we will allow to contribute to our self-definition.

The third most significant influence in our self-definition—often not for the better—begins to occur when we start observing and listening to our peers, while at the same time devaluing the counsel and guidance of our parents and other worthy adult authority figures. Our self-definition is on shaky ground, when this begins to occur. Teenagers listening to other teenager's advice about life, love, and the pursuit of happiness is the dumbest move our children will ever make. Most teens who become "Dear Abby" for other teens don't know who they are or where they are going any more than the teens they advise.

Most teens find life confusing at this stage of their lives and they usually have more questions about life and living than they have answers. Some of the things my peers said to me or to a group of us when we were in high school were not only untrue, but bordered on insanity. Most of the advice given was inaccurate, and if acted upon would have put us in difficult, if not dangerous, circumstances.

But as we peruse the landscape a few decades after I graduated high school, the lifestyle of teens has not changed that much. We still see teens bowing to the fear of rejection and going along with the proverbial crowd. While thinking they are playing follow the leader, they are unknowingly following the followers. Proverbs talks about this peer pressure in Chapter 1 where parents are admonishing their teen not to follow bad influences. It is, in fact, our first great defining spiritual moment as a semi-independent person. And by semi-independent, I am describing teens who have the ability to choose and make decisions in their lives, but do not have the resources to embrace total responsibility for the consequences of such decisions.

Do we follow the principles of righteous living? Or, do we lean on the "lack of understanding," of our peers? That is the key defining question that most teens fail to answer correctly. Proverbs says that following those who can negatively influence us is risking the making of mistakes that will, in some cases, lead to losing our lives. "Losing our lives" is a multifaceted phrase and can mean losing our spiritual wellbeing, losing relationships, or even losing our physical life by putting ourselves in dangerous situations.

Here is the kicker. When we allow peers to influence us, we leave ourselves open to being defined from the outside in, rather than inside out. What is going on around us begins to dictate how we feel, think, speak, and behave. This is not good. Teens are not knowledgeable enough to advise other teens in how they ought to conduct themselves and their affairs. Most of the advice dispensed by teens is *mush*. It is media-influenced and often peer-filtered—by what is cool at any given time by one's peer group.

Most advice given by teens to other teens is given with the purpose of redefining the teen to whom the advice is being given. This is critical: Peer pressure, pure and simple, is *seeking the redefinition of another individual for the purpose of becoming what the clique-leaders wants that individual to be.*

There is a sense of *false security* which teens have when *they are like everyone else.* My question to teens, when they are in the midst of being redefined to be just like everybody else is this: *"What do you have to offer, when you are just like everybody else?"* The answer is ... *nothing!* When you are just like everyone else, you have lost your uniqueness–what makes you special.

When it comes to cliques, my research has taught me that such groups exist, and are as influentially powerful as they are, because of the so-called "security" they profess to give those who are a part of it. Cliques are where teens and young adults go *to abate the fear of rejection, to hide their insecurities,* and *to postpone having to wrestle with their own aloneness (individuality).* Some make it a life-long goal never to leave the comfort of a clique.

For example, the *role of gossip in the teen world is to force independent-thinking teens to conform to and join the clique.* The clique then becomes a necessary component to a teen's survival rather than an option. The leaders of cliques are insecure and use their manipulative skills, as well as the fear of rejection of others, to force the insecure to conform and become part of the clique.

Of course, a teen moves up the clique-ladder by kissing up to the leaders. Clique leaders are often narcissistic, ego-centric, shallow, drama kings and queens. They are filled with a false self-assurance, as well as gripped by the fear of rejection and a loss of significance if they should lose control of the clique. Clique leaders are frightened to death of becoming invisible. They are also filled with a kind of pride that none of them can truly afford to embrace. Clique leaders are users of others for their own ends. Such teens cannot get what they want on their own and therefore use others to get what they want and always at the expense of those who are giving them what they want.

On the other hand, true leaders encourage the independence of others, not their dependence on them. When teens are part of a clique, they throw away everything that makes them unique as individuals and become subservient to the fears of rejection and the pressure to conform to the expectations of the clique.

Another horrible consequence of conformity is experiencing the pressure to consistently compromise beliefs, values, and convictions in order to fit in with the clique. I know, from personal experience as a teenager, that once one begins to compromise, the need to do so in order to remain a card-carrying member of the clique never ends or let's up. Only when a teenager becomes a young adult do they realize that they have lost three of the most important things in life: *their uniqueness*, *their identity*, and *their integrity*. Giving in to the desires and wishes of the members of any clique literally destroys everything that makes us special in the eyes of those who love us and care about us, as well as in the eyes of our Heavenly Father.

o **Wisdom Principle:** *You lose your significance when you lose your uniqueness!*

Most teens do not realize the damage they do to themselves by caving in to peer pressure until it is too late. More often than not, some costly mistakes have already been made by most teens by the time they have graduated college. These mistakes may not be recognized by the teens, but eventually they will return to bite the teens when they least expect it.

Mistakes are part of being human and can be a profound teacher in moving a person toward a more constructive direction in life. However, *some mistakes have no business being made, especially when logistical common-sense warns us otherwise.* These mistakes occur because teens have arbitrarily decided to listen to their so-called friends instead of their parents, pastor, youth minister or integrity.

Just remember, the lie in the Garden of Eden is the same lie told to teens today: *"Others have suffered bad consequences from doing what you are thinking of doing, but it will be different for you. The others just weren't careful. If you are careful, nothing will happen to you."* My response to this Is, "Are you kidding me? I am surprised that the evil forces of this world can't come up with anything more original."

So why do teens graduate high school and enter their college years not knowing who they are, how they have become what they are, or where they are going? Why are they so confused? Because they probably had parents who worked with them from a base of parental authority rather than a base of parental responsibility. Also, they chose to listen to the wrong people, were likely task lazy, as well as morally lazy. They let the fear of rejection determine what they chose to do and *went with their feelings* instead of *looking at the facts*.

In Proverbs 1:10-19, the father warns the son to not allow sinners to entice him, to join up with them, and participate in their destructive and selfish lifestyle. It is here that we are confronted with God's main competition, for the eyes, ears, and heart of a person—peers. Media-influenced peer pressure is the number one reason young people stray from the right path—kids listening to kids. When you take a step back and consider this, it is only then that you realize how dumb, ridiculous, and tragic this is. Even more demoralizing is that this is a tragedy that was and is avoidable.

The next significant influence on our self-definition is the media. When I was a teenager, I was deeply affected by the attitude and style of many media personalities. I combed my hair in a manner that was cool for that day and time. When athletes became my heroes, I got a crew-cut and tried to look like King Hill, an All-American quarterback who played at Rice University. I do not deny nor do I underestimate the influence that media and media personalities have had on all of us. I was a willing participant buying into their lines and lies.

The goal of media is to influence for ratings and profit. Media could care less about any of us. Media personalities must believe, while on camera, that their intelligence, insight, and the coolness of their information are superior to what anyone else possesses and that those who do not listen to them are the real dummies. I laugh when I am getting this subliminal message from the media because the complete opposite is true. Many media personalities are intellectually sub-par, often have the personality of a peanut when they don't have their script to help them look cool. They also have puddle-deep characters.

A significant number of television, music, and movie personalities have been scripted—that is, they have been prepared by having their lines fed to them through the use of a teleprompter. Few of the "role models" teens look up to today have graduated college and many others live amoral, narcissistic lives. This is a consequence of having their convictions and beliefs saturated by secular-humanistic or post-modernist philosophy. Such personalities have no objective standard of right or wrong but rather go by how they feel or what the crowd does.

The question stands: "How has this worked for them?"

Answer: Based on the consequences of their behavior, not well. The only word to describe the lives of Millennials is *childish*.

Any person who allows the media to become the dominant influence in who and what they become, is in for a rough life. The media just does not have the character to deliver what you want out of life. If you buy into the bunk they are spewing, you will evolve into a confused, shallow, easily-led, sub-par individual.

If you allow yourself to be defined by the media, you will eventually grow to despise yourself when you see yourself the way you truly are. When this happens, do not count on the media to help you through your disappointment and dilemma. They will not be there because they do not care about you or anyone else. All the media want is to get from you what they want and they do not care if it is at your expense.

The final critical influence on our self-definition are the various life-environments we move in and out of throughout the first twenty-five years of our lives. By the time we are 25-30 years old, our self-definition is virtually crystalized. Your self-definition may not be crystal to you, but *it will be to others*.

I marvel at the various environments in which we, as individuals, find ourselves. Monitoring your life-environments, and staying away from environments that do not contribute to your becoming the best you can be, will be essential to your effectiveness, your character, your life purpose, and your happiness. When you let your guard down, you are opening yourself up to being influenced for the worst, not the better.

I am not recommending that you conduct yourself and your affairs being compulsively distrusting of others. I am advocating that you be a person who knows what kind of person you want to become. Hopefully, that person is an individual with a virtuous indomitable character. Candidly, anything less than this, is second-best.

Any environment that does not contribute to your becoming the best you can be disqualifies itself from being worthy of your presence. Leaving any social gathering where friends and acquaintances are, but which has no true "up-side" for your continuing presence, has nothing to do with your unconditional acceptance of those, who are present for whom you have nothing but fondness. It has to do with who and what you are and what you are becoming. It has nothing to do with your being tolerant of others, who are different from you. It has everything to do with what is best for you.

I might add here that as a teenager, you should never stay past 11:30 P.M. at any function. My grandmother used to say that nothing good happens after midnight. "Be home by twelve o'clock," she used to say. It has been proven time and again that police rev up their presence on the streets and highways of many metropolitan areas after 10:00 P.M. This time of the evening is precisely when the most irresponsible and un-self-disciplined individuals are out on the road.

Environments either decrease you or increase you—lift you up or knock you down. Whatever your peers choose to do, you must have the discipline to walk away when you are in an environment that decreases you. You may be saying to yourself, "I want to be with my friends. If I can't be with my friends, I'll be all alone." Loneliness has absolutely nothing to do with companionship or receiving affection. It has to do with having a lack of purpose in your life. Also keep in mind that this will not be the last time your character will be tested. That will happen every single day of your life in all kinds of ways. If an environment decreases your effectiveness and your ability to be the best you can be, I can assure you that such an environment will do the same thing to your friends. Do you have the courage to do what is best for you? Think about it?

The sad truth is that the self-definition of an individual is not done by the self at all; but is done while living life on autopilot, i.e., without thinking. Most of the time, individuals allow the definition of who and what they are to be done by others. In fact, self-definition created outside the self ought to be called other-defined rather than self-defined. We often allow ourselves to be defined by influences outside of us, but it is still other-defined, as well as outer-defined self-definition. When I said in the first chapter that the greatest pains in life are usually self-inflicted, such pains start here. Here are some questions to ponder as we progress on our journey, on the subject of self-definition:

1) What will be the basis of who and what I choose to become?
2) What values will I choose to embrace and what will determine those choices?
3) What will my beliefs be and how will I determine those beliefs?
4) What will be the basis by which I determine what is true or false?
5) What kind of attitude/world-view will I embrace?
6) What will I decide to allow to influence and determine this critical area of my life?
7) What will determine what and who will influence me?

These are pivotal questions in anyone's life and no one escapes having to wrestle with them. No matter how much one ignores facing them such decisions will be made, either deliberately or by default. Those who allow these decisions to be made by default usually have mediocre lives and become minimalists, both philo-sophically and attitudinally.

As stated earlier, Proverbs begins its wisdom discourse by asking the son to listen to his father's instructions. He is also told to not forsake the teaching of his mother. The Hebrew word for "listen," is a word which means to listen with the intent to obey. This is commonly called receptive listening. Listening to parents and obeying them is a person's *first* exposure to authority.

How children choose to honor and respect this authority in their lives determines how they will respond to the other author-ities. Children who are consistently disobedient to parents will be difficult to discipline as well as difficult to teach in school. Such chil-dren could eventually find themselves in trouble with law enforce-ment. Without exception, every teenager I have known who had conflict with law enforcement was a difficult child to discipline in the home as well as in school. Their life-performance was primarily ego-driven, selfish, and, as a consequence, self-destructive.

The final thirteen verses of the first chapter of Proverbs per-sonify wisdom. We read about wisdom calling out to all to listen to her teachings, and wisdom asks some pointed questions:

➢ How long will you simple (naïve and easily influenced) ones love your ways?

➢ How long will mockers (proud and arrogant individuals who are deliberate troublemakers) delight in derision?

➢ How long will fools (gullible and morally irresponsible) hate knowledge?

The text continues to describe how willingly and devotedly wisdom would have instructed those to whom these questions were asked. It is implied in this text that wisdom is available to all; but *most will refuse* to embrace it. *Here we see that spiritual intelligence is paramount to a fully-functioning life; but few truly believe this is true.* For those who fail to listen to Godly parents, the warning continues.

Wisdom will not hold out its hand forever. There is a window of opportunity to embrace and cultivate what wisdom has to offer. When that window closes—and it is clear in this text that if this window of opportunity is ignored, it will close and much self-inflicted pain will occur in the life of an individual who ignored wisdom's call. We are also told that wisdom will laugh at this disaster and calamity. Wisdom says that when those who ignored her find themselves in the grip of a whirlwind disaster and then will seek to call upon Wisdom for help that she will not answer. These people will also search for wisdom but they will not find her.

You may ask, "What does this text mean?" Let me digress for a few paragraphs from the direct purpose of this chapter to explain.

It means that if you wait to seek God when until you find yourself in a self-made crisis and you really need Him, I can guarantee that you will not find Him because you are guilty of tempting God. On occasion, I have heard about adults who ignored their need for a vital relationship with God, and who, at a particular time in their lives, suddenly found themselves in the midst of a crisis, i.e., a critically ill child. Neither they nor medical science could solve their child's health problems. In many cases, such family members were on death's bed.

When this occurs in the lives of those with family members in crisis, you don't see many of them professing to be atheists. You find them praying—however feeble—to God. In most cases these prayers go unanswered in the sense that those praying do not get the answer, for which they were hoping. When the person for whom they are praying eventually passes away, they usually become bitter and give up or repudiate any professed faith in God, as if they had any faith in God, to begin with. This scenario happens quite often.

    o **Wisdom Principle:** *Miracles rarely happen, in the life of unbelievers, when they are looking for them.*

I firmly believe that God is not some pigmy deity who can be manipulated to one's ends. God hears the prayers of devoted and obedient people. However, many of their prayers did not get answered the way these dedicated souls would have liked. Still they did not repudiate their faith in God, but rather their faith became paradoxically stronger. A supreme example of such faith, shown to us in the Bible, was Job.

In contrast, for those who have cultivated an attitude that at its core is spiritually shallow, it is believed that God, for some unknown reason, is *obligated* to heal the critically ill family member for whom they are praying. At the same time, God is also expected to alleviate their apprehension of the potentially devastating loss of a loved one so they can avoid the experience of the pain and suffering that comes with such a loss.

Years ago, a famous television icon in this country lost a sister to illness. This person prayed for her healing. I understand that this person was thinking of becoming a missionary, when this tragedy occurred. As you know, most of us are more idealistic in our youth than we are in our older years. However, this person renounced faith in God because, from their point-of-view, God refused to answer their prayer. Their anger toward God, because of this loss, was unquenchable.

Dr. Gordon Livingston—one of my favorite writers—lost a son to suicide and another to cancer. He prayed for his younger son to be healed from this wretched disease when a bone marrow transplant failed to arrest his son's leukemia. His son died. He vowed, then and there, that any God who would allow an innocent young boy to die the way he did was not worthy of one more second of his time and energy.

He envied those who could experience such a loss and continue to be faithful. The Bible teaches that God isn't primarily responsible for removing all of the uncertainties of life nor is He obligated to give each of us a 100% guarantee that we will not experience suffering, loss, or anything of significance. We forget that Jesus suffered greatly in His life at the hands of the Pharisees and the Romans. If we want to be more like Christ, we must be willing to suffer as He suffered.

I do not believe that God exists to primarily solve our problems and to bail us out of crises that are very often primarily self-created and/or are part of simply being an imperfect human being living in an imperfect world. He loves us. However, our relationship with Him requires commitment, time, and nurturing. In fact, I John 3:21 tells us: *"If our hearts do not condemn us, we have confidence, before God and receive from Him what we ask, because we obey His commands and we do what pleases him."*

When we have been faithful to God's teachings and live the life we have been taught to live, we find that our prayer life is not as self-serving and self-centered as it is with the spiritually shallow among us. When devout believers pray to God, their prayers are not primarily self-serving. Devout believers want God to answer their prayers but more than anything *they want God to use the circumstances in their lives to aid them in becoming more like Christ.*

This scripture also implies that people who are devoted to God and love Him are prepared people. By prepared people I mean people who know that having confidence in God hearing their prayers comes from their faithfulness in loving God, and being devoted to Him. Remember, people of wisdom do not pray primarily to get their will done but rather to know God's will so that they can do it! Rick Warren teaches us that for people of wisdom the white-hot fire of suffering produces the "gold of godliness".

Exactly how does suffering do this? By producing love, humility, and meekness in our hearts as byproducts of the lessons we have learned. We also come to know the provision of God's nurturing love and presence, through our trials and sufferings, by drawing close to Him in the midst of such pain and suffering.

God will never owe us. However, it is my conviction that we will always have a debt to pay to God. God will always out-give us. He will always love us more than we will ever love Him. Also, I know that He has forgiven us more than we will ever be asked to forgive others.

For those who ignore God and His wisdom principles for living, prayer is a self-serving act. God does not draw near to those who pray for self-serving and self-centered reasons. I think you can count on that. Unspiritual/unbelieving individuals who live secular-humanistic lives do not, and cannot comprehend this.

This is what Proverbs is saying in this context. You cannot expect God to hear your prayers, and be there to bail you out of your problems, when you have ignored Him for most your life while things were going somewhat well. Wisdom teaches us at the conclusion of Proverbs Chapter 1 that the waywardness of the simple (those of nebulous character and nebulous spiritual self-definition) will kill them and the complacency of fools (arrogant, silly, and irresponsible people) will destroy them.

I am reminded of a story told to me by an eastern European gentleman named of Ian. This beloved man died of cancer years ago, but he kept his sense-of-humor until the end. He told the story of a jockey who rode a horse that was currently running last in a race with six other horses. The horses passed the ½ mile marker and the jockey became desperate. He looked up and asked God to help him move up from last to 5th place. The horse moved up to 5th place. The jockey then prayed and asked God to help him move up from 5th to 4th place. The horse moved up to 4th place. This give-and-take with God continued until he reached 2nd place. The jockey prayed one more prayer. He asked God to get him into 1st place. As soon as the horse moved into 1st place, the jockey called out to God and said, "OK, Lord, I'll take it from here."

We are a lot like this jockey. We pray in a crisis, but when the crisis is over, we want to resume control, act as if we were always in command. We think that we did something extraordinary, rather than realizing that it was God's marvelous love, mercy, and grace that made our positive circumstances possible.

In the pilgrimage of self-definition, we find that we have the ability to choose our attitude, as well as to whom we will listen. However, once we do, our habits, our attitudes, and choices will determine the path we take in life. Proverbs tells us that one of the ways we define ourselves is by choosing to whom we will listen.

Will we give our parents, who love us and will be there for us when we fall, our devotion and ear, or will we give our peers, those who want our allegiance and attention for self-serving reasons, our devotion and ear? This choice is a defining moment in one's life. It is a key to one's self-definition. Why? As we learn to trust our parents to lead us in paths for the purpose of helping us become the best son or daughter that we can possibly be, we will more easily learn to trust God in leading us to become the best person we can possibly be.

    o **Wisdom Principle:** *Being obedient to our parents, prepares us for the obedience we will need in order to have a fruitful relationship, with God.*

This leads us to another key to our self-definition. Proverbs 1:7 says that the respectful reverence of the Lord (our Heavenly Father) is the beginning of knowledge. The next defining moment in our lives is answering the question, "What place will God have in my life?" This is a huge question, and it must be answered either deliberately or by default. It is your choice. If you choose wisely, you will say yes to God's call to be a child of His.

People of faith fair much differently in life than those who have no faith at all. This is what wisdom is saying in chapter one. Wisdom is stating with no hesitation that there is essentially no downside, to embracing faith in God, and trusting His leadership. When you chose God over self, you have nailed down the critical component that leads to the opportunity of having a blessed and fulfilling life. Notice I did not say a temporally happy and comfortable life. God did not create us to be comfortable. He created us to be people dedicated to learning, growing, and being of service.

o   **Wisdom Principle:** *The role of the Holy Spirit, in many contexts, is to <u>comfort the afflicted</u>, as well as <u>afflict the comfortable</u>.*

Christ states in Matthew 5:45: *"He causes the sun to rise on the bad and the good and sends rain on the righteous and the unrighteous."* What does this mean? It means that people of faith are not immune from the vicissitudes of life, nor are the unrighteous immune from the "common hand of God's mercy and grace" that God gives to us all. Just like the unrighteous, we are vulnerable to suffering, pain, and loss. However, God promises that He will be with us when we go through such experiences and that He will not leave us. This *silent strength* that God provides for us in such circumstances will sustain us, while those who have chosen not to embrace His wisdom principles will collapse under the strain (see Matthew 7:24-27).

The proof of this collapse will be evident in one's attitude, which more often than not will be saturated with bitterness. This bitter attitude has its root in entitlement mentality. That is, the belief that one is entitled to be rescued from the pain and suffering all of us experience at one time or another in similar situations. God is not our problem solver but rather He is our strength and shield. He is our "very present help in and through trouble".[9]

---

[9]   Psalm 46:1

o **Wisdom Principle:** *A joy that is not cultivated in the 'soil of suffering' is shallow, at best.*

In Joshua 24:15, Joshua said: *"But if serving the Lord seems undesirable to you, then choose for yourselves this day whom you will serve, whether the gods your forefathers served beyond the river, or the gods of the Amorites in whose land you are living. But as for me and my household, we will serve the lord."*

Joshua was a simple man. He was not confused at all. The choice of serving the Lord Most High was not complicated to him. He and his household stood and declared that they would serve the Living Lord, Creator of heaven and earth. What is your decision?

In the beginning of this chapter, I said that we were made for God. We were created by God for God. We have a still-small voice within each one of us confirming that truth. Unfortunately, we are bombarded with a cacophony of sounds that are intended to drown out that small, soft voice and to get us to ignore its intent. That intent is to draw us toward faith in the Living/Infinite/Personal God of scripture.

I also told you about the fall of Adam and Eve in the garden. This fall occurred because Satan told Eve that what she was told regarding the consequences of eating from the tree of the knowledge of good and evil was not true. Satan turned the tables on Eve. Satan got her to focus on the possibility of her being deprived and as a result would miss out on something really special. Satan appealed to her ego, to her sense of entitlement. Satan declared that what God said would happen would not happen, that it would be different with her. She and Adam would be like gods possessing insight into life, living, and the mysteries of the universe. Satan lied. It told a partial truth. The only special knowledge she and Adam received was the meaning of guilt, shame, and failure. Believing partial truths is one of the paths to self-destruction. Eve took something—a knowledge that God did not give her—and God, in return, took something away from Eve that He did give her.

- o **Wisdom Principle:** *The deadliest poisons taste the sweetest!*

- o **Wisdom Principle:** *When you take something that God did not give you, He will take something away from you that He did give you. —Anonymous*

Personally speaking, I can tell you that I was raised to be defined from the inside/out. However, over time, and because of my desire to be accepted by my peers, I changed. I voluntarily, I might add, changed the basis upon which I would define what I became. I truly believe, that if I had had an adult authority figure standing tall and stating without apology that being defined from the outside/in is dangerous and foolish, I would have reconsidered my decision to become just like everyone else.

I must also say that during my adolescence I allowed my emotions—specifically, the fear of rejection—to determine how I would define myself. This was a foolish thing to do. It was a deadly thing to do. I lost, in one fell swoop, my individuality as well as my uniqueness. I also became shallow, just like my peers. I was more desirous of being "cool" than being "competent", being popular instead of being proficient. Even though I became part of the crowd, at times I was very alone in that crowd. I have realized, as the result of such a bitter experience, that *attitudinal conformity* is the death knell to one's uniqueness. Learn from an expert on conformity—me. It is a loser's path. It does not lead to somewhere, but rather to nowhere.

- o **Wisdom Principle:** *Conformity—being like everybody else— is following the followers to nowhere.*

- o **Wisdom Principle:** *Conformity occurs in one's life as the result of a lack of purpose, direction, and goals.*

Now, having discussed the influences that affect our self-definition, let's discuss the by-products of those influences that molded our self-definition. In other words, the its components. The meaning of the word component is something that is part of a larger whole. A component in the area of self-definition, is a clear-cut factor in determining the definition or makeup of who and what we become as individuals. I will use this word "component" to describe each factor that has a direct bearing on how we define ourselves.

A few years ago, I had an experience that contributed greatly to my research on self-definition. I was sitting on a bench at *Dollywood* near Knoxville, Tennessee. It is an enormously successful theme park and the family decided to go and have some fun. After three hours of walking, I needed a break. I sat down on a bench shaded by a large tree. The cool air was refreshing. So, as most of us do in similar situations, for about an hour, I became a people-watcher.

I first noticed a young man in his early twenties wearing a tee-shirt with the sleeves ripped off, cut-off jeans, and rubber-thong flip-flops. He was tattooed from just below his neck, down each arm to his wrists. He also had tattoos on his back, chest, and legs. By my standards, he had severely overdosed on tattoos. However, I could tell from his demeanor that he thought he looked pretty cool.

A few moments later another young man, about the same age, walked by. He was wearing a red Ralph Lauren Polo shirt and his khaki-colored Bermuda shorts were pleated and pressed. He wore Cole-Haan tasseled, soft-soled shoes. His appearance was excellent and he seemed to ooze self-confidence.

Sometime later, a young woman walked by wearing a pair of shorts that revealed more than what most of us would have cared to see. She had on a revealing knit top and rubber-thong flip-flops. Walking next to her was a young woman wearing a worn-out, faded tee-shirt, jeans with holes in them—large holes, and rubber-thong flip-flops. Her jeans, were about 6" longer than they ought to have been so that she walked on the hems which were now frayed.

Finally, a mother and daughter walked by. I could tell they were related because they looked just alike in their facial features. And, you could tell, at least physically, which one was the mother and which was the daughter. Except for the colors they wore, they were dressed alike. Both were blonde, both had their navels pierced, with a dangling "something". They were tanned and dressed in the trendy fashions of the day.

I contemplated, for some time, on the mystery of it all. Here were people who lived in the same country and had been exposed to many of the same social and media influences that all of us are.

Yet, how they each processed this information and applied it to their lives was, for me, interesting, baffling, and unbelievable. I know that God absolutely loves variety but I must say, many of the people I saw during that brief time were pushing the envelope.

They had all made choices in how they had chosen to define who and what they were. By their physical appearance it was obvious that these individuals came from and lived in very different environments.

Some were couth, others uncouth. Some were clean, others dirty—even filthy! Some wore clean and pressed clothes, while others wore clothes that were worn, tattered, and looked like they had been slept in for at least a year. Some were attractive while others were not. Some were well-behaved and some were not. Some you would take seriously, and some you would not. You could tell that only a few of them knew how they projected themselves to others. However, most of these people did not seem to care, or perhaps were not aware that they lived their lives on autopilot—unconsciously.

o **Wisdom Principle:** *There is a difference in being sensitive to the opinions of others and in being cognitive of the non-verbal messages you convey to others, about who and what you are.*

There was no question, at least to me, that only a few bucked the trend of exhibiting the "grunge look" for something more dignified. However, the majority behaved, looked, and spoke similarly. They dressed grungy, therefore looking unkempt. What is even more amazing is that they projected a confidence, however misplaced, that they were "cool" and more "in style" than those who didn't look as they did. This was unbelievable to me.

While considering my experience that day, I also did a mental perusal of my life, remembering the people with whom I went to school, with whom I socialized while growing up, and those with whom I attended church. Many of them ended up in very different situations than I thought they would.

I have marveled at how one person can be raised in a religious home and become an alcoholic. At the same time, I have been amazed at how a person can grow up in an abusive environment, or suffer neglect, and still become an outstanding, loving, and altruistic individual. I have also seen people who have been given every opportunity to succeed but consistently fail. I have also seen people who have had to work very hard for every opportunity and succeeded.

I have seen siblings, raised in the same home, where one becomes a responsible adult and one becomes a minimalist. It is uncanny how the self-definition of individuals differs when most are exposed to many of the same things you and I are. How does this happen? How we choose to define ourselves depends on the life-environments we desire and cultivate, as well as to whom we choose to listen.

o **Wisdom Principle:** *Choices either chain us or free us!*

So, how does self-definition happen? How do we all end up being who we are? Good question. Let's try to answer it.

I am deeply convicted that the components that make up our self-definition are: life-environments, (familial, educational, social, religious); activities (those to which we give our time); relationships (family, friends, authority figures); education (what we have learned and how we have processed such information); experiences; desires; dreams (by-products of our interests and passions); and beliefs—which are the values and convictions developed from all seven of these components. Of these components, only life-environments and relationships carry over from the influences covered in the beginning of this chapter. Let's take these one at a time.

1. Life-Environments

Our life-environments are the first critical component and affect how we define ourselves individually. By life-environments, I mean anywhere we spend or have spent significant time. This could be at home, school, church, work, social events, where we choose to hang out, and even what we watch on television. Where we spend time is where we learn from and experience all we see, hear, taste, touch, or smell. I do not think it is understated to say that home is where we are most profoundly influenced, at least in the first twelve years of our lives. It is the key influencer of all of our life-environments.

o **Wisdom Principle:** *Environments are always a reflection of the people in them.*

I believe in monitoring the home environment. One that positively affects a child's life is safe, clean, comfortable, peaceful, enjoyable, and educational. All of these are equally important, and the parents are responsible for making sure these characteristics of the home environment are reflected by the markers listed.

You and I know that life is not always fair. However, in spite of this reality, there is one place where life ought to be fair, kind, encouraging, and accepting, and that is where we live. Our homes ought to be a shelter from the storms of life as well as be an environment of love and unconditional acceptance for all who occupy it.

But be careful where you spend your leisure time. Don't put yourself on autopilot and "go with the flow", when it comes to "the crowd". Mediocrity—being just like everybody else—is not in your best interest and following the crowd is a prerequisite for mediocrity.

Monitor what you hear, see, and do. If what is happening around you is not going to help or contribute to your becoming the best that you can be, leave that environment immediately! Consistently being in a particular environment that does not help you become the best you can be is lethal to your effectiveness and competency as an individual. The longer you stay in any environment—positive or negative—the more it seeps into your life and begins to have an effect on your self-definition.

Just remember, no matter how enjoyable an environment is, keep in mind that some pleasurable environments are nothing less than sweet poisons. They can and will adversely affect your future. You may not notice the effect immediately, but you will when you least expect it or when it is too late.

- o **Wisdom Principle:** *You become what attracts you, because of the time you dedicate to it.*

I admonish parents or teens to watch what is going on at school. Students should be aware of what your teachers are teaching you. You should be aware of the influences you are facing when interacting with your peers. Be aware of how the activities in which you are involved after school are affecting the quality of who and what you are becoming. Keep in mind that choosing to be cool at the expense of being competent is always a losing choice.

Monitor the pressure your so-called friends are giving you to do or not to do certain things. Responsibility, even at a young age, does not take a vacation. Regardless of where you are or in what circumstance you find yourself, you live a life of your own making. Choices never stop being made. Choosing is the business of life. Especially when you are a teenager and are consistently associating with individuals who are not positively enhancing your life. The same holds true when you are involved in activities that are not helping you become the best you can be. Both will be lethal to your well-being.

> o   **Wisdom Principle:** *To make good decisions you must get the facts, discover what is true, determine whether you will be a better person as a consequence of deciding to do something, or not, then make the decision you are being called on to make and move on!*

Where we worship and cultivate our spiritual life is a huge part of our life-environments. I encourage you to be part of a church that will help you become the best you can be. If it is not, don't leave that church without first doing all you can to make it the kind of church that helps everyone become the best they can be.

We change churches too often in this society because many seek churches that are trendy and primarily entertain. Our assignment and mission within the church is to contribute to making it better and stronger. Your primary role in your church is not to be served but to be of service to others.

Professional environments are a part of our life-environments and are secular by nature. This secular influence is rooted in the corporate culture itself. In many ways our professional environments are also amoral. If there is an environment where an adult can get on the wrong path, it is here. I believe this to be true because we spend so much time at work that our lives can actually take on a completely different perspective if we do not monitor and sift what we are experiencing.

Most adults, if they are not careful, will cultivate their worst habits by being around secular, mediocre, and perspective-managing individuals. Politics, rather than ethics, currently reins in corporate America. You must keep the sixteen essentials at the forefront of your mind when in such an environment.

Finally, our social life is part of our life-environments. We are a social people. We go to movies, concerts, shows, restaurants, and other places for entertainment. Some of these, as all of us know, are best not frequented—bars, gentlemen's clubs (this term is a major joke), etc. Teens must avoid homes where there is little or no adult supervision. It is this part of our life-environment that can get us into problems that can turn into horrible self-made prisons.

No one escapes being tainted by one or more of these life-environments. We may burn our hand on the "stove of life" but you and I know that it is another thing to leave it over the fire until our hand is burned off. Once we find out that we have made a bad decision, we need to vow not to repeat the act or offence, i.e., we must learn from our mistakes.

o **Wisdom Principle:** *Wise individuals rarely cross a bridge more than once.*

What makes us stupid and foolish is that we don't learn from the first time. Many just experience more suffering and pain by going back to the places, or associating with the same people that were the source of their failure and pain to begin with.

o **Wisdom Principle:** *Never share your failures with anyone who is not directly affected by them or who cannot help you through them. You will save yourself a significant amount of judgment and condemnation from others.*

2. Activities

The second component of our self-definition relates to the activities in which we are involved, and to which we choose to give significant time, make up. It is difficult to choose the right activities in a vacuum. You must use logistical common-sense and Christian principles in making wise decisions, as to which activities you will give your time. I believe that activities for which you have an interest and passion are key in determining your choices. The influence of your parents is a key here as well.

For example, if your parents have no interest in music, more than likely they will not encourage your cultivation of a musical talent. If your parents are not interested in athletics, then they will likely not encourage you to become involved in them. Wise parents, however, will listen to their children regarding where their interests lie. Then, they will discuss the up- and downsides of the activity under discussion.

I want to pause here and ask parents to be wary of pushing their children into activities that, as parents, they would prefer them to participate. It is important that children choose to participate in such activities, rather than being pushed by parents. Parents who are concerned for their children's happiness and well-being do not, nor will not live their lives vicariously through their children.

Here are some questions you can ask yourself and that also can be used as guidelines:

1) Do I have an interest or passion in a particular activity?
2) Where do I need to go to cultivate my interest in this?
3) Will my parents need to help me or can I cultivate this passion or interest at school?
4) Can I positively develop my character, while participating in this activity or will the development of my character be inhibited or hindered?
5) How much time and money will need to be given, to develop this interest or passion?
6) Does this interest or passion have a place in my life, for the rest of my life? In other words, will I be able to perform this activity no matter how old I become?

I think this sixth question is critical. Any activity needs to be balanced with other activities in order for a child to grow into a well-rounded person. I would not advise any young person to become so involved in any one activity so much that no time or energy is left for other life-sustaining and skill-building pursuits.

One example of this is sports … certainly an enjoyable activity that can help young people learn team work and individual discipline. A sport might even become a career pursuit, but it is more likely to lead to a lifestyle of self-confidence and accomplishment in other areas of their lives.

But what happens when the parents become too obsessed with their child's talent or prowess in a sport and begin to pressure their children into learning that only winning has value rather than learning that playing well and enjoying the fun is the first order of the game? Imbalance and misdirection.

There are too many children and teens who are giving significant time to activities that they will only be able to enjoy for as long as they are in school or college. When these years are completed, participation in some sports requires far more time that is feasible as an adult with a career and family. Do they lament for the rest of their days "what might have been"? Or have they learned to make right choices that will lead them to other activities that are just as fun and also life affirming?

When I was a child, I cultivated an interest in the three major sports—football, basketball, baseball. I loved all three. My mother put a halt to football because she was convinced I would be injured. She feared my having horrible aches and pains as I became older. Therefore, I focused on basketball and baseball. I went to college on a duel scholarship—playing both sports. These sports were good choices for me if only for that reason. But as I grew older, I had to quit playing both. They were too time consuming and physically demanding. I needed to change my athletic interests. I took up golf instead and have enjoyed that game immensely.

Now, most kids dream of a professional sports career, or becoming a famous musician or hip-hop recording star. But that's not realistic for the majority of us and they come to understand this with time. I sometimes regret that I didn't find golf as a kid. I would be a much better player today if I had. Even now I sometimes daydream that I might have been a golf professional if I had dedicated the time to it that I dedicated to basketball and baseball. Who knows … anything is possible. However, as an adult, I know that golf is a sport I can enjoy the rest of my life. A good lesson to learn.

Therefore, I encourage you, and through you your children, to consider your ability to enjoy, for the rest of your life, whatever activity you give your time and energy to.

7) Will I become a better person as a result of giving my time to this activity?

8) Will my self-discipline be enhanced or hindered, as a result of my being involved in a certain activity?

9) Will my church attendance suffer as a result of this activity? Gauge this by the consistency of your church involvement being hindered, rather than such a hindrance being occasional.

10) Finally, will my parents and siblings support the time and energy this activity will take for me to become good at it?

Frankly, I do not advise any young person to go against their parents' wishes just to be involved in a particular activity. However, if the activity is really important to you, talk with your parents in an ethical and respectful manner about your passion for the activity. Remember, rebellion is a drop-dead sign that the activity you want to be a part of may not be in your or your family's best interest.

The activities we participate in will have an enormous effect on who and what we become. The quality of the relationships we cultivate, within each particular activity, will influence what we become for years to come. Again, you need to choose wisely when it comes to this component.

3. Relationships

The third component is relationships. These define who and what we become. I will speak in the next chapter regarding subconscious compliances. However, for now let me tell you that the stopgap in making sure you do not practice dysfunctional thinking and behavior, is your relationship with the Heavenly Father and your consistent involvement in church, Bible study, and prayer. Meditating on the Word of God, and letting it seep into your heart and life, is pivotal in minimizing the effect of dysfunctional influences from your past and current relationships. The second and third volumes, of this series, will thoroughly discuss the dynamics of relationships and making sure you make good decisions regarding them. Again, please remember that any relationship that does not contribute to helping you become the most effective and competent individual you can possibly be, disqualifies itself from being part of your life.

4. Education

The fourth component in our self-definition is our education (or lack thereof) and it is a profoundly influential one. Whether someone is going work with his/her hands (blue-collar worker), or work primarily with his/her mind, that person will need a solid education in order to function at a level of excellence. An education is paramount to one's success.

I never cease to be amazed how getting a good education affects all areas of a person's life for the better. I have never seen a person get a good education and be hurt by it. I have seen someone with a good education let it go to his head, perceiving himself/herself to be better than others. However, I have never seen a person hurt by getting a good education.

On occasion, I have had people tell me how an education hurt a particular individual's faith. It made faith "irrelevant" to his/her life. This person had developed a cockiness about them—that is, he/she had developed a false sense of security, a certain kind of independence that led to a belief that he/she had a greater control over his/her life than realistically was true. My response, in such a case, is that the individual did not have that terrific a faith to begin with.

In fact, I John 2:19 confirms this: *"They withdrew from our fellowship. Simply put, they were never really a part of us. If they had been part of our fellowship, they would have remained part of us (remained strong in the faith), but they left our fellowship. This is credible evidence that they really didn't have their heart and soul in the purpose of our fellowship, in the first place."*

People of strong faith respect what their faith does for them and as a result, protect it. A truly strong faith is impervious to the insults, stings, and arrows that are thrown at him/her. Such individuals simply let those hurtful experiences flow, or pass, through them and then run those experiences "to ground". So, those who allow their education to negatively affect their belief in a Living God never really had that terrific a faith to begin with.

Most education, from high school forward, is secular-humanist by nature and is, as a result, an amoral education—that is, it does not teach values and ethics as part of the academic curriculum. However, this does not mean that such an education is all bad when you see the context in which it is attained.

We live in a secular world, not a spiritual one. The world teaches that verifiable knowledge is the only knowledge worth cultivating. In essence, it says that unless an individual can taste, smell, see, hear or touch what is being researched then verifiable knowledge will not be gained. The world is not only disinterested in knowledge that is not ascertained the way I have just described, it also deems such knowledge unprofitable.

The world also believes that knowledge which is not verifiable by scientific standards, does not, and cannot, be proved objectively. Here is the thorny problem with secular education: any knowledge that cannot be proven by scientific standards—that is, be true empirically—is not worth cultivating.

The main purpose of education, when appropriately applied to our lives, is to provide tools to enable us to learn how to process experiences and information, into useful and effective knowledge. This critical thinking also helps us live life at a level of high effectiveness.

However, those of us who are Christians know without a doubt that despite what a secular education can provide us, it cannot give us purpose, meaning, happiness, and fulfillment. Nor can a secular education motivate us to live virtuous lives. These values are found primarily in the spiritual realm not through a secular education.

o **Wisdom Principle:** *No knowledge can give what does not exist at its core/heart. Hence, a knowledge that has no recognition of an Infinite/Personal God at its core cannot provide values, morals, and ethics by which to live.*

5. Experiences

Our experiences are the fifth component of our self-definition. However, a terrific amount of the experiences we have are painful and may not help us as much as they hurt us, especially when we are children. Because of this we often form inappropriate and flawed judgments.

For example, an immature man or woman will usually judge all members of the opposite sex by the worst experience he/she has had with a particular individual of that gender. This is simplistic thinking and categorically unfair and unrealistic. In other words, there are saints and sinners on both sides of the gender equation.

Many simplistic-thinking individuals judge something to be true or false as a result of such an isolated experience. This is not only dangerous but is also a testimony of having a lack of effective and objective intelligence. For example, you and I have bought ball-point pens on scores of occasions. I have on occasion paid for a pen that did not write—not one jot. However, neither you nor I stopped buying ball-point pens, because of this. We simply chalked it up as an unfortunate purchase, and moved forward. Regardless of our experience, we did not believe we would be justified if we stopped purchasing ball-point pens.

How many times have you heard someone say they used to go to church, but because of a bad experience they had in a church or with a particular church member, they quit going. Implied in this decision is the belief that as a result of such an experience, church involvement is/was a waste of time. Again, experience has proved to be a poor teacher. What this kind of experience has served to do is to give a person an excuse to avoid being involved in a church and growing to become more like Christ.

I like what my pastor Dr. William Self said one Sunday morning regarding those who say they do not go to church because of the hypocrites there.

"I would rather be in church with them than in hell with them."

Another example of the profound effect a bad experience can have on our self-definition is when someone lives in a dysfunctional household or associates with sub-par individuals. Such a person can easily believe that the experiences he/she has during that time in his/her life, are normal and healthy, when they could be the opposite.

Truth-enhancing experiences can be of enormous help to us in our development. However, we must have a healthy and objective standard outside of ourselves that helps us judge whether our experiences are constructive or destructive to our well-being. Such a criterion as the Bible will aid in our being able to use our experiences as positive determinates to our self-definition.

6. Passions and Dreams

The sixth component to our self-definition has to do with our passions and dreams. These are usually by-products of what we are interested in as well as to what we give large segments of our time. In his book *The Rhythm of Life,* Matthew Kelly talks about the cultivation of a dream book. This is a terrific exercise and I think that the fulfillment of dreams gives us something to look forward to on a consistent basis. The possible fulfillment of dreams gives birth to hope. What we dream about and the things about which we are passionate profoundly affect our self-definition. The only caution here is, that if your dreams and passions are not part of what it takes to help you become the best you can be, you need to rethink them. Also, all worthy dreams and passions are altruistic in nature.

7. Beliefs

Our beliefs are the seventh and final component of our self-definition. These consist of information we hold to be true about ourselves, others, and about life in general. Beliefs heavily influence our values and convictions. Hundreds of people have related their beliefs to me about certain aspects of life and living. Most of these beliefs are flawed at their core because they have been based on flawed experiences. Again, the safe-guard we have available to us as to whether our beliefs are valid or not is the Bible, not our personal beliefs or opinions.

Think of the Bible as the "center line" on our road of life. We are implored to judge all of our beliefs by it. In fact, Paul, in Galatians 1:8, said: *"But even though we or an angel from heaven should preach to you a gospel (message) contrary to the one which we have preached to you, let him be treated like a plague."*

It is through the use of the Bible that we find virtue—both in thought and deed. Hebrews 4:12 says: *"The Word of God is stronger and more powerful than any two-edged, forged-steel sword. It pierces even to the depths of our soul and spirit, opening both up to scrutiny and conviction. It is a discerner/an examiner of our thoughts, motives, and the deepest intents of our heart."*

o **Wisdom Principle:** *Any solution to a problem, any belief or conviction that one embraces, must have virtue at its core in order for it to be a valid solution, belief or conviction!*

Not only do our beliefs and values determine what we hold is true, but they also reflect how much we like and respect ourselves as individuals. People who truly like themselves do not intentionally put themselves in a position to be easily influenced by destructive experiences and beliefs.

On the other hand, individuals by outside influences are uncertain regarding their values. As a result, they often conform to those individuals whose view of themselves is about the same as theirs. Just as water seeks its own level, so does self-worth and self-respect. This is how important self-acceptance and a healthy self-love are. If our beliefs and values are based on flawed information,

153

how we perceive ourselves will always suffer and we will have a sub-par view of ourselves and of others, too.

Therefore, we must have an objective standard by which to judge our beliefs and values to be either adequate or inadequate. Beliefs and values are rooted in our character, and are key components in defining who and what we become. In turn, our character is reflected in how we behave.

In Chapter One we very briefly discussed the seven components of character. Now I want to talk about a few of those components in a different way from how I did before.

First, our world-view—our attitude—is not inherited, it is learned, or in other words, cultivated, in the environments where we spend most of our time. When you grow up in an "out-to-lunch" household, or a mediocre life-environment, you are at a distinct disadvantage. You do not have a model of faith, hope, and love to emulate. God becomes your only refuge and strength in this context because you have no one to take you by the hand and help nurture within you these three virtues. A lack of guidance puts any person in a difficult position.

This is one critical reason why we have the church—our support group and *divine encourager*. In other words, there must be a "compensatory mechanism" in place, when there are a lack of examples and positive influences in a person's life.

The church is there for us. You need to make a commitment to get into a thriving church and depend on God to lead you to "the warmest incubator", as Rick Warren says. He has promised that He will not leave us alone and that He will be with us always—even to the end of the world.

There are great churches in every city and town in this nation. Trust God by praying for His guidance as you try to find a church family to help you cultivate your soul, character, beliefs, values, and life. We learn the how of faith, hope, and love through the teaching of the Bible. We exhibit how effective faith, hope, and love have worked within us primarily by how we treat others. What we have been taught and how we are treated will determine how we will develop this character trait.

Our world-view—our attitude—is critical to our self-definition. Our self-definition reflects how we have taken life's vicissitudes as well as how deeply our worldview is rooted in the hope that can transcend such life experiences.

o **Wisdom Principle:** *Where there is no hope in the future, there is no power in the present with which to face that future.*

Second, our commitment to being self-disciplined is critical to our self-definition. The first gift we should give ourselves is unconditional acceptance. We should choose to love ourselves because God loves us and He has proved that love through Christ's death on the cross. We cannot love someone else unless we first learn to love ourselves. Proverbs 19:8 says: *"He who embraces wisdom teachings loves his/her own soul."* We should accept ourselves the way we are because God accepts us just the way we are. We cannot have a self-disciplined life without having a healthy self-love. It is simply impossible.

o **Wisdom Principle:** *You cannot give away anything you do not have for yourself.* —Dr. Wayne Dyer

The second gift we give to ourselves is self-discipline, because a healthy self-love helps us to embrace it. Discipline required by others is only as effective as long as those they are there to enforce it. When these "others" are not there, we often choose not to adhere to their discipline.

The only true, long-lasting discipline is an effective self-discipline. Galatians 5:23 lists self-control as one of the segments of the "fruit of the Spirit". If we truly love ourselves, we will be self-disciplined because it is a reflection of our respect and love for the Heavenly Father. It is a signal that we are willing to come under the discipline of the Spirit of God.

To be self-disciplined you must value yourself at the core of your being. When you appropriately value yourself for who and what you are, you will respect yourself and will cultivate self-discipline. A healthy self-love is birthed from a healthy self-respect. Self-respect is birthed by living a virtuous and self-disciplined life. What we respect, we protect. When we have self-respect, we also possess self-trust.

Trust and respect are component virtues. You cannot have one without the other. Those whom I respect, I trust. Those whom I trust, I respect. You cannot trust a person if you do not respect him or her. Conversely, you cannot respect a person you do not trust.

All of the seven components of character are tied to being a self-disciplined individual. If you are going to embrace moral principles that reflect a virtuous life and spirit, and be uncompromising regarding them, then you must be self-disciplined. If you are going to be a truth-seeker of the highest order, you must be self-disciplined. If you are going to be emotionally intelligent, you must be self-disciplined. If you are going to practice a consistent absence of hypocrisy in your life, then you must be self-disciplined. If you want to possess great wisdom and use logistical common-sense in the application of such wisdom, then you are going to have to be self-disciplined.

Finally, as individuals when we can look ourselves in the mirror and say, "I am responsible for my own life," we begin to arrive as a person of character. There is no question that I am responsible for what I think, say, and do. As a consequence, I am also responsible for who and what I become. Mature individuals embrace responsibility! They are no-excuse people. They do not tolerate anything that keeps them from being the best they can be, nor do they settle for mediocrity. Why is being the best he can be the only option? Because insightful and wise individuals know there is an ultimate and final accountability for each of us. Remember, at the core of being the best you can be is a commitment to being completely responsible for who and what you are.

Key to our self-perception is how we have managed and processed the critical components to our self-definition, as well as how we have applied them. If you are like everybody else, you have not monitored the influences in your life very well. You have clearly valued belonging to a clique in contrast to becoming the best you can be. However, if you have decided that being competent is much more important than being cool, you have practiced a terrific amount of self-discipline in the defining moments of your life.

You cannot hide being an outstanding individual if you are a person committed to being the best you can be. Your self-definition cannot help but reflect such a commitment. However, if you settle for being a person who does the minimum to get the most, you will have a nebulous and self-serving self-definition. You will seek to get what you want out of life at other's expense, rather than your own. You will look to others to fulfill the critical components we have just been discussing. The essentials are critical components you must embrace in order to live a fully-functioning life, and the cultivation of such critical components is your responsibility.

Let me close this chapter by sharing a remarkable story told by Dr. Wayne Dyer. He was speaking of Earl Nightingale's cassette tape *The Strangest Secret.* A study was conducted with 100 graduates from one of our most prestigious universities. These graduates were surveyed over the 40 years after their graduation from college. At the end of those 40 years, the following information was discovered:

- ➢ 55 out of the 100 were flat broke.
- ➢ 40 out of the 100 were okay, but would need help from someone else sooner or later just to get by.
- ➢ 5 out of the 100 were financially independent and living fulfilling lives

Dr. Dyer also told of a remarkable occurrence within the organization of a famous east coast department store chain. Corporate advertised that it would soon begin receiving applications for management positions. Applications would be received from outside the company, as well. The union representing the employees maintained that it was not right to hire from outside the company for management positions; that such promotions ought to occur from within.

The management agreed, and, in conjunction with the union, developed a management training program for those who were interested in applying for future management positions. The training would occur on Tuesdays and Thursdays in the evenings from 5:00-7:00. Those participating would receive college credit for taking these classes. Do you know how many employees from "X" Department Stores responded to be part of this management training opportunity? Only five out of a hundred. Incredible, isn't it?

Here were employees all seemingly working for the same goal—to advance—also working in the same environment. All had the same opportunity for advancement but only 5% responded. I am sure the union officials were embarrassed about this response after they had worked so hard to create this opportunity with management.

I believe the two pivotal keys as to why only 5% of the employees responded to this opportunity were attitude and character. It is obvious that 95% of the employees were minimalists in the profoundest sense. They wanted the reward of the opportunity but did not want to embrace the responsibility and commitment it would take to get such a reward.

Somewhere in the lives of the 95% who did not take advantage of these classes, it had been decided that a minimum attitude and a minimum character would suffice. With a commitment to mediocrity, 95% of those who had the opportunity to take the management training for their advancement did not do so.

Perhaps they found it impossible to commit to an endeavor toward excellence, because they had convinced themselves over numerous defining moments, when faced with such decisions, that they were entitled to the best that life had to offer, without working for it. They settled for doing as little as possible, while believing that such a minimum attitude would bring maximum rewards. Tragically, such individuals never become self-honest enough to realize that such an attitude will only bring consistent disappointment and disillusionment into their lives.

Now, fasten your seat belt for this! Only 5% of people in the world will ever reach their full potential and become the best they can be. Also, 40% will get about 60% down the road toward fulfilling their potential, but they will miss out on the opportunities which life will offer. Do you know what this means? It essentially means that 95 out of a hundred people will be just like everybody else.

What do you want for yourself? What group do you want to be a part of? Here is the proverbial "kicker" ... it is mostly up to you.

o   **Wisdom Principle:** *Do more than what you get paid for and you will eventually get paid for more than what you do.*

CHAPTER FOUR
SUBCONSCIOUS COMPLIANCES

o **Proverbs: 14:12:** *There's a path of living that seems right in the eyes and heart of a man, but ultimately, it leads to his death.*

o **Proverbs 16:2:** *All a man's ways seem innocuous to him, but his motives and intents will always be evaluated by the Lord.*

The greatest contribution that Freud made to the field of psychology was his work on the subconscious. The subconscious is sometimes called the super conscious. Whatever you choose to call it, it has a profound influence on who and what we become. In fact, the subconscious knows more than our conscious mind does. There are millions of people in our world who do not realize the power of the subconscious. All of them would be wise to cultivate that awareness, as well as respecting the powerful influence the subconscious has in their lives.

I became aware of the influence of the subconscious when I experienced an incredible tragedy in my youth. This was the realization that my custodial parent was becoming an alcoholic. I also became aware that the physical violence I had witnessed in my home had increased as well.

The culmination of this tragedy is that the addiction and conflict occurred so often that it became part of my expectations of life. After I experienced a brutal confrontation with this parent, I packed my clothes, and everything else that was mine, and asked my best friend—who eventually became my foster brother—if I could come over to his home and stay. I told him what had occurred and he, his older brother, and his parents opened their home and hearts to me. I was a young man with a horribly wounded spirit. Proverbs 18:14 says: *"The spirit of a man can endure physical sickness, but when a man has a broken spirit, how can he bear such a wound?"* I did not realize it at the time, nor could I comprehend the damage that had been done to me as a result of living in such a home.

Over the months I was away from my former home environment, I became aware of things that I would say and do that reminded me of this custodial parent. I was awestruck at how much influence this parent had in my life. I had unwillingly and unwittingly become much like them. I did not like this at all! I wanted to get as far away from being like my family—with the exception of my grandmother—as I possibly could because all I had inherited, as a result of being part of my family, were dysfunctional tendencies and bad memories.

The good memories of my childhood were few. Those I did have had primarily resulted in what I experienced living with my grandmother—being involved in my church, and in scholastic athletic endeavors.

As most young adults, when I started college I lived life on autopilot. My reactions within certain contexts reminded me of the words and ways of the authority figures in my life—specifically my custodial parent. My displeasure of such reminders opened the door for me to dislike myself, and to become self-rejecting. I learned the hard way that simply disliking the self-defeating and self-destructive traits in myself was not enough to bring about positive change.

As much as I tried to quell the influences certain members of my family had on me, I did not know enough about life and relationships—psychologically or otherwise—to take a firm and disciplined hand in changing the self-defeating traits in my life. It wasn't until I was in my late twenties that I began to read about the enormous influence of the subconscious and how I could, with the help of God, reprogram it to have positive and self-disciplined concepts abiding within it.

However, before I could re-condition my subconscious, I had to confront my self-destructive demons. These demons lived in my subconscious. They were my subconscious compliances—the things I did that I did not want to do.

It was at this time that I began to fully understand the words of Paul the Apostle in Romans 7:19-20 when he says: *"For the good things I want and wish to do, I am shocked that I don't do them. What I actually do, and am shocked that I do, is practice the very things I detest and that I find to be abhorrent. These are the very things I do not want to practice."*

I believe that the Apostle Paul was speaking about subconscious compliances—those things that we unconsciously practice, or that were modeled for us, while we were children, by our authority figures whether parents, friends, peers, other relatives, or teachers. These individuals were primarily authority figures to whom we listened, as well as who we emulated. Since we as children have no standard outside of ourselves to determine what is right or wrong in these early formative years, we come to accept dysfunctional behaviors by others as normal. Their dysfunctional influences become part of our dark side. We all have a dark side. Those who disagree with this are not living in the real world. They are being both self-deceiving and downright dishonest. Dr. Carl Jung called this dark side our shadow. Ignorance of this, and the refusal to admit it even exists within us, is precisely the reason most people do not know why they do the destructive things they do.

o   **Wisdom Principle:** *Dysfunctional people often allow the baggage in their lives to <u>run</u> their lives.*

None is immune to subconscious compliances. As a rule, these are primarily the inaccurate assumptions, as well as the unethical and destructive tendencies, in each of our lives. Paul the Apostle wrestled with this dilemma time and again. Romans 7:15-25 speaks to this phenomenon. In these verses Paul says that he had within him the tendency to sin. Like Paul, we have a natural tendency to be drawn toward doing non-virtuous, selfish things. He also says that even when he does not want to do these terrible things, he is helpless to stop using his own strength.

Doing such things is a natural response to what we are deep within—narcissistic and ego-centric. *More often we want to get our own way rather than do the right thing.* Without Christ, we are ego-driven individuals. This is precisely why Christ came to earth and died on a cross. He did this so we could be free from the enormous power of our sin-infected ego, which pushes us in self-serving directions. Christ died to free us from our self-destructive subconscious compliances. Listen to what Paul wrote beginning with verse 24 of Romans, Chapter 7: *"What a wretched man I am! Who shall rescue me from this death-driven body? Thanks be to God, through Jesus Christ our Lord! So then, I myself, in my mind, am a slave to God's law, but in the sinful nature, a slave to the law of sin."*

Hence, if we do not come to terms with the *shadow* in our lives, we will likely repeat the same things we saw our authority figures do.

For instance, if our parents used profanity in their everyday language we will likely do the same. If our parents yelled at members of the family when we or they did something wrong, then we will likely yell at our family members in similar contexts. If our parents were physically abusive to each other and to our brothers and sisters, we will likely be abusive to our spouses and children. If our parents had a tug-of-war for power and control of their marriage, we will likely have the same tug-of-war.

This holds true in conflicts with in-laws; alcoholic abuse; dishonesty; and constant criticism. And, God forbid, if we were sexually abused by our parents, we will likely be sexually abusive if we do not get therapy to help us through this tragedy.

Finally, if we are taught by our authority figures to use fear and anger as a means to a desired end, then we will likely do the same. If our parents were guilt-throwers or guilt-catchers (your dysfunctional self is either one or the other), then we will likely follow their example. On and on it goes. Such is the influence and power of subconscious compliances.

Every dysfunctional act we experience from observing our authority figures when we were children, has seeped deep into our subconscious. Over time, we have been profoundly influenced by such acts and experiences, whether we want to be or not. This is the work and destructive power of subconscious compliances.

I was a product of a dysfunctional home and I did not realize the tremendous influence that environment had in my life and was having in my life. However, once I became aware of it, I was determined not to allow the destructive actions and habits of my family determine who and what I would become.

I made a decision in one critical, defining moment that my subconscious compliances were not going to continue dictating my future. I wanted more out of my life than what I had experienced up to that point—a fully-functioning household; a loving wife, happy children; solid, integrity-based friendships; and personal peace. I asked myself, "What in the world do I need to do to keep subconscious compliances from ruining my life?"

Candidly, the church was not, nor is it today, much help in this situation. It rarely is, because subconscious compliances and their destructive effect on individuals is new knowledge that has not trickled down to the church as a whole. As a result, there is no ministry or strategy in place to counteract the enormous power and influence of subconscious compliances. I came to realize that it was up to me to do something about it.

The first thing I did was acknowledge the kind of person I had become, and the kind of family and economic background I had come from. This was very hard. I was ashamed of the poverty I had experienced as a child and well into my adolescent years. Poverty is stigmatizing. Most middle- and upper-class adolescents as a rule, do not associate with those who are poor. Such individuals are beneath them. Because of my experience and observation of other families experiencing similar poverty, I grew up convicted that poverty was not a matter of being unlucky, but rather a result of being ignorant and un-self-disciplined.

As I mentioned above, I noticed growing up that individuals from similar economic backgrounds associated with each other. Because of this the poverty of my youth affected how I saw myself. Obviously, this in turn affected how others saw me. If something is a big deal to you, others will eventually see this and adjust their attitude toward you accordingly.

Nonetheless, I came to grips with what was real and true about me. I realized that the statute of limitations had officially expired on using my background and the inherited dysfunctions of my family as an excuse not to become the best I could be. I could no longer use such self-defeating influences as an excuse. I had to take positive action to change myself for the better.

I also connected to a truth-seeking exercise about the family into which I was born. My family was, to say the least, uneducated, poor, and unrefined. As a child, I was a victim of their ignorance. However, I eventually realized that there were two things about which I had no control—the family into which I was born, and the physical and personality makeup, genetically speaking, of me and my children.

Once I understood that none of us can choose our parents or our children, I realized that the poverty and the limitations of my life and family were never under my control. I also realized that my family and my subconscious compliances were only one defining part of my life and that only in certain contexts did they define my life. I also realized that my subconscious compliances and family did not have to define what I would choose to become as an individual in the future. If I were treated by others as if these factors would define me forever, I believed that my determination to change was greater than the fatalism which they embraced. Also, I forgave myself and realized that some things are not under my control and are not my fault.

o   **Wisdom Principle:** *There is a statute of limitations on using your family and economic circumstances as an excuse for who and what you have become. Excuses should expire by age 21.*

The third part of what I learned was that I needed to take stock of my life, i.e., look at the assets and liabilities of my background, beliefs, and values. Here is where I began to take inventory of the subconscious compliances that had hindered me from becoming the best I could be.

In this endeavor, I required myself to be objective regarding the influence my parents had on me, for better or for worse. I even compelled myself to look objectively at my grandmother, who, while living, was the most benign individual in my life. She was the one person who truly and unconditionally accepted me and loved me in spite of my flaws, cantankerousness, and immaturity.

I looked at the influence and impact that my childhood friends, extended family, and other authority figures made on my life. I revisited the experiences that were reference points as I cultivated certain beliefs and attitudes about the critical areas of my life. I analyzed, as best I could, why I saw events that occurred within a certain context the way I did and that also reminded me of similar past experiences. I asked myself, "Are my beliefs accurate, appropriate, and fair? Are my reactions to certain events in my life— especially my angry reactions that reminded me of significant past events—mature or immature?" I looked at how I processed all of these experiences and how I applied them to my life in regards to how I lived every day.

When I completed this inventory, I was amazed at how often my actions had run on autopilot, especially my reactions. Reluctantly, I also realized how significant a role emotion had played in determining how I reacted within certain contexts. I came from a family that allowed emotions and feelings, to determine what they did or did not do, and I was following in that same pattern.

I was appalled! I couldn't get over that I viewed as normal the destructive and dysfunctional influences in my life, nor how they had become part of who and what I had become. I wept. My heart was broken—psychologically and spiritually. For the first time in my life, I experienced profound humility. I saw myself as I really was, not the way I chose to perceive myself. My insecurities stood before me and I saw myself as a young adult in need of help and healing.

This experience was not only an enormous help, but it became one of the most illuminating experiences of my life. And this is how life is. Our darkest moments, though scary and discouraging, can become the most illuminating moments of our lives if we let them. I prayed often, while I was processing all of this baggage. As a result, I learned some critical principles in how I, or anyone else, ought to deal with subconscious compliances.

First, one key component on the road to spiritual and psychological health and healing, is acknowledging the dysfunctional and unhealthy ways of relating to others. You can't change what you are unwilling to acknowledge, according to Dr. Phil McGraw. As a result, most people have not, nor will not, work through their own subconscious compliances. Therefore, most individuals who refuse to do the necessary work in this particular endeavor find themselves limited in their ability to rise above the inherent flaws, which they own—whether they admit it to themselves or not—and that also hinder the attainment of healthy and thriving relationships with others. As a result, they will experience more suffering, because of postponing dealing with their subconscious compliances than if they had confronted them earlier.

o **Wisdom Principle:** *Legitimate suffering in one's life increases in direct proportion to the effort being made to avoid it.*

How do you acknowledge such dysfunctional and unhealthy traits? By admitting that certain habits you cultivated as a child are hindering your life now, and are keeping you from becoming the best you can be. It also means coming to terms as to who is primarily responsible for cultivating any and all subconscious compliances in your life during your formative years. If your parents, then you need to say it.

One way to do this is to say: *"My mother is responsible for teaching me that verbally abusing someone while I'm angry is okay and normal. I realize now that it is not. I disown this habit which has been a personality flaw in my life. I refuse to be a slave to my temper, and just because my mother had no problem using anger as a weapon, that does not make it right. My mother was wrong and any parent who does the same thing when they are angry, is equally wrong. Such abuse of anger will not be a part of my life any longer. I disavow and renounce any further nurturing of this horrible, inappropriate, and dysfunctional habit. From now on I will be reasonable in my relationships, as well as in my reactions to the vicissitudes of life."* Say this to yourself until you believe it with all of your heart. Next, do it! This is exactly how you purge yourself from any such subconscious compliance.

Here is a list of the most common subconscious compliances that are part of the lives of most people.

- ➤ Bigotry—the use of racial slang to demean any member of a minority, whether that minority is being demeaned for their culture, behavior or color;
- ➤ Profanity—the use of words that would be considered non-virtuous and vulgar in any environment in which decent people are present or when such language is being used to personally attack someone;
- ➤ Inappropriate anger—the use of anger to viciously attack individuals for self-serving and narcissistic reasons;

➢ Criticism—the consistent and constant criticism of others who do not conduct themselves and their affairs the way the one doing the criticizing thinks they ought;

➢ Kicking others while they are down—receiving pleasure over the suffering of others as a result of their failures, mistakes, or wrong decisions; and expressing such pleasure in an arrogant and condescending manner;

➢ Turning others against someone because you simply do not like them;

➢ The abuse of drugs or alcoholic beverages, being normal in the sense that it is believed that all families deal with such an issue as if it is no big deal;

➢ Gossiping and being a rumormonger with the purpose of hurting others, or simply using such horrible tactics to garner influence and/or control of others;

➢ Manipulation—the use of circumstances or others for selfish ends. Seeking to get others to betray themselves for your own advantage and to fulfill illegitimate wants;

➢ Using physical, emotional, psychological, or verbal abuse for the purpose of maintaining control of others, so that, by your definition, you can be "happy", according to your so-called standards.

I could list many more subconscious compliances, but these are the ten major ones that I believe would be part of anyone's list. Let me say here and now, that if any of these have been part of your life since you were a child, it wasn't your fault. Quit defending those who are guilty of perpetuating these horrible traits in your life. You may convince yourself that they didn't mean it. They may not have. However, how can you love the truck that runs you over? Truthfully, you can't. If the truck that ran over you had appropriately and virtuously loved you, he/she wouldn't have perpetuated these horrible traits on you.

Now, I am not asking you to go to them and seek justice, whatever that may mean to you. I am asking you to disavow these self-defeating traits before they ruin your life and cost you dearly in your professional and personal endeavors, as well as in your relationships. I am also asking you to quit making excuses for the perpetuators of such subconscious compliances. They may have done this out of ignorance, but more often than not it was due to militant ignorance. This ignorance has no excuse.

What I have discovered in observing victims of emotional and psychological abuse by one or both parents, is that in order for the victim to protect themselves, they learn to mirror back what the abusers have been dishing out to them. When a person comes full circle—from victim to victimizer—the cycle of invalidation has become complete. One sign that this is occurring is when the abused defends the abuser. Individuals who have been abused over a period of time often see themselves as the problem and seldom see the abuser as the problem. Next, you hear absolutely glowing descriptions of affection for the abuser from the one abused. Hearing such complimentary descriptions of the abuser is so surreal that you wonder if it were possible to have the abuser canonized, the one abused would recommend such to the Vatican.

Second, you must learn to forgive the perpetuators. I know that most of those guilty of subconscious compliances, don't mean to hurt us and limit our potential. But they did hurt us and they did contribute, to the limiting of our potential. We forgive them not for their benefit, but for ours. Forgiveness frees us to be authentic practitioners of our confessed faith. There is nothing more useless than an unforgiving individual who professes to be religious. Such is an oxymoron—a contradiction.

Third, the Apostle Paul says in Romans 14:7, *"None of us lives to himself alone and none of us dies to himself alone."* The actions we model in front of others affect them for better or worse. We must realize that when we are in a place of authority or influence we can affect the lives of others more than we will ever realize.

It is incumbent on each of us to be aware of our attitude and our actions in the presence of those for whom we are responsible and to whom we are accountable. Use the experiences of how our subconscious compliances have negatively affected our lives as determinates in our commitment, not to perpetuate such either in the lives of those we love or those individuals with whom we have influence.

Finally, monitor the environment where you live as well as the one in which you work. Commit yourself to work to eliminate any destructive habit or trait that will discourage or dissuade others from being the best they can be. Work for justice and fairness in your daily endeavors, and commit yourself to being a person who resolves problems rather than one who creates and perpetuates them.

CHAPTER FIVE

THE FOUR GREATEST HUMAN WEAKNESSES

Most people spend their lives justifying the way they are instead of changing themselves for the better. As a result, it's difficult for most people to realize that inherent and compulsive weaknesses are performance killers. The reason why this is critical to know was mentioned in chapter one—life is a performance business.

Unrecognized or ignored weaknesses prevent most people from maturing, which in turn promotes an attitude of uncaring. Unfortunately, the majority—perhaps as much as 80% of the world's population—does not seem to have a problem staying *small* or *immature*. Perhaps they are just innocently ignorant. However, this immaturity may be due to a person choosing to conform to mediocrity, living life on autopilot, or simply being lazy—unwilling to do the work that is necessary to eliminate such flaws.

Ego is the primary reason people stay small. The ego is a relentless protector and declarer of individual rights and entitlements. There is no question that the overwhelming majority of individuals believe that the world simply cannot do without their presence.

Such people cannot seem to get enough of their "own selves". Of all the people they know, they are impressed with themselves the most. These individuals are narcissistic to the core, therefore, when it comes to life, they believe they are the most important component of it. In this state, they cannot see themselves accurately and do not care to do so. They are ego-driven and getting the results they want is all that matters. *Feeling good about who and what they are is more important than seeing themselves accurately.*

This is the primary reason I don't use the term self-esteem when describing someone who likes himself or herself appropriately. Self-esteem, in a true pragmatic sense, simply means that you like and value yourself. Many self-help gurus teach that positive self-talk, such as saying "I like myself" over and over again, is a key in raising one's self-esteem. My problem with this counsel is that if a person is a jerk or narcissistic, then saying to himself that he likes himself, when in reality he is an impossible person to work, live, or associate with is simply reinforcing that it's okay to be a jerk. This kind of self-talk is just nuts, and the exercise only perpetuates one's weaknesses. In the lives of most people "feeling good" about oneself has taken the place of truly being a good person.

Another reason I do not like using the term self-esteem for describing a person liking himself/herself is due to a profound illustration Dr. Scott Peck used in his book, *People of the Lie*. He describes meeting with an individual whom he considered to be profoundly evil. Dr. Peck asked him what the most important thing in his life was, and he responded, "My self-esteem." When a person uses such a term to describe the most important thing in his/her life and that person is profoundly evil, the term becomes a bad metaphor to use in my opinion. I don't like using terms that evil people are comfortable using to describe who and what they are.

I, too, have been around people, whom I would describe as evil and, from my observation, the common denominator of such people has been a nonexistent self-respect. People who con themselves, are perpetuators of the biggest lies in life. Lies, the poisonous kind that individuals perpetuate on themselves, are the mortar that seals their self-made prisons. Individuals who use the term "self-esteem" in the manner I've described above, and who are also dangerous individuals, are guilty of perpetuating the greatest deceit on themselves.

After almost two decades of working with young people, I believe that there are four major weaknesses of human beings in this world. They are like dominoes neatly lined up. When one falls, they all fall. The same is true when a weakness is confirmed in one's life. When it falls the other weaknesses seem to follow suit. In other words, if an individual has one of the "great four", he or she usually has one or more of the other weaknesses, as well. These other weaknesses are simply not as prominent as the one that has the most visibility in that person's life. What I find astonishing is that in many cases, after such weaknesses have either been self-discovered or pointed out by someone, the individual owning the weaknesses, doesn't seem to be bothered that such flaws exist.

I remember, on one particular occasion, that I was speaking to a group of parents. I laid out the program I believed necessary for their teenagers to become the best they could be, as well as assist them in being prepared to meet the challenges the world would throw at each one of them.

When I began the discussion on character, several parents defended, without any provocation, their role in the development of their children's character. All of the parents who spoke in that meeting, were very defensive and also exhibited signs of insecurity during the discussion of their children's character development. I also found it ironic that those who defended their children's character the most, were those whose children's character was the most deficient. Unbelievable, isn't it?

My grandmother used to say, "When you throw a rock into a pile of dogs, the dog that yelps the loudest is the one you hit."

It was because of this experience, that my eyes began to open to how individuals, whether parents or young people, defended their inadequacies, as well as their ignorance. I have lived long enough to realize that those, who are very good at defending their deficiencies, are the most vulnerable to doubt, insecurity, and frustration. The self-made prisons of mediocrity that such people build for themselves are, in most cases, impregnable to truth and facts.

More often than not, it is impossible for such individuals to identify or recognize any truth that could help them become the best they can possibly be. It is also very difficult for such truth to penetrate their self-made prisons.

o **Wisdom Principle:** *Arrogance is the child of ignorance, insecurity, and confusion!*

o **Wisdom Principle:** *Total self-sufficiency is a myth. It is closely related to its cousin—control.*

The Four Greatest Human Weaknesses

1. Ignorance.

When I learned, as a result of twenty years of working with young people, that most adolescents live their lives on autopilot, I began to realize just how lazy people truly were. They want to live without having to think. You read it right: Most people are too lazy to think. People also want to live life as they wish without having to think about what they are doing. Let's face it, thinking is hard work and most people have never truly learned how. It is clear, based on the world's behavior, that people do not possess the knowledge they need in order to live a fully-functioning life. Other than laziness, other reasons that exist as to why people do not know how to think effectively are: they have never had the opportunity to learn how to think effectively. Perhaps they never had an authority figure who knew such information, nor could share it with them. Or perhaps they simply did not care to research it and cultivate such knowledge for themselves.

o **Wisdom Principle:** *You can't know something unless someone tells you. You can't answer a question unless someone asks it. You can't solve a problem unless someone reveals it.*

Everyone is born ignorant. Only a minority chooses not to stay that way. Consequently, the majority of people in this world do not realize that what think about, matters! What you choose to focus on constantly and consistently, matters. Proverbs 23:7 says: *"For as he thinks within himself, so he is."* What you choose as your focus also makes a huge difference in who and what you become.

What you don't know can kill you—psychologically, spiritually, and possibly even physically.

What I find amazing is how comfortable most people are being ignorant of key knowledge that could make a remarkable difference in the quality of their lives. In fact, statistics abound showing the difference in income between a high school dropout, a high school graduate, a college graduate, an individual with a master's degree, and an individual who holds a doctorate. The gaps between income levels are unbelievable.

One estimate, which I read a few years ago, said that a high school graduate will make between, $100,000-200,000 dollars more in a lifetime than a high school dropout. A college graduate will make between $250,000-450,000 more dollars in a lifetime than a high school graduate. An individual with a Master's Degree will make between $450,000-650,000 more in a lifetime than a college graduate. Finally, an individual with a doctorate—PhD, MD, etc.—can earn at least $750,000-$1,500,000 more in a lifetime than someone with a Master's Degree.

What makes ignorance so deadly is that when most people don't know what they should and need to know, they usually don't know that they don't know. When a person doesn't know what is absolutely critical to their success and happiness, they usually learn the opposite of the saying "ignorance is bliss". Ignorance is not bliss. Ignorance is as poisonous as potassium cyanide. It is a killer of life, of potential, and of character. If you are comfortable living in ignorance then you are on your way to a life of frustration, conflict, lack of fulfillment, disillusionment, embarrassment, and mediocrity.

So, what are the components of the critical knowledge every person must have in order to have a fully-functioning life? That is a question to which I can easily respond. You need to get your hands on every book written by Daniel Goleman, Denis Waitley, M. Scott Peck, Wayne Dyer, Rick Warren, Phil McGraw, Patricia Davis, Laura Schlessinger, Matthew Kelly, Hal Unger, Gordon Livingston, David Richo, and Susan Forward. The knowledge contained in the works of these men and women will propel you toward a level of excellence only experienced by 5% of the world's population.

Another book with which you must become very familiar is the Bible. No, I'm not kidding. No person is considered well-read if he or she has not read the Bible. I know this bestseller is largely ignored by the media. However, it is a marvelous book of history, human relationships, human suffering, human failure, and human ignorance. It is also a book that illuminates the positive possibilities of the pivotal role of faith in human development and accomplishment. When such occurs, you find someone who has chosen to trust in God with all of his or her heart, mind, and soul. The Bible is also the definitive biography of the greatest person who ever lived—Jesus Christ.

I am well aware that the world sees the Bible as a book filled with myths, contradictions, and inaccurate history. I happen to believe that some very smart people in the past 1500 years, who were cynical about the accuracy and claims of the Bible, have tried to discredit it. However, of all the "mud" that has been thrown at the Bible, none of it has stuck permanently. Time and again, the Bible's veracity has been proved. I never cease to be amazed at how unprecedented, the arrogance of disbelieving, secular-humanists can be.

The essential knowledge you ought to have must focus on the five critical areas of life. Please understand that the kinds of knowledge critical to fulfillment and excellence, won't be found while waiting on a bus, watching television, playing video games, or satisfying your sexual curiosity in a car parked "out where the woods get heavy".

Most young adults observe their peers and look at the areas of knowledge these peers pursue (if any), and conform accordingly. Doing so is one of the dumbest things anyone will ever do. Never, never allow someone else—especially if it is someone you don't even know—to determine those areas of life you ought to focus on, and become knowledgeable about. This is too important a decision for your life to leave it to chance because you think a peer, or someone you don't even know is "cool". (Come on; tell me you are not that naïve or ignorant!)

People who influence you must earn the right to do so. This true for me. I have a sifter in my brain, and I refuse to let just anyone influence who and what I become. I made that mistake in my youth and young adult years and I pray to God that I never do that again.

You must have the same discipline in your life. Remember, you are responsible for the influences you choose to embrace. You may not know this, but you will get the blame for listening to someone else's advice which you chose to believe and then blows up in your face. When this happens, you need to face the fact that taking this bad advice blew up in your face and not the face of the person you chose to give you such flawed advice.

Make a commitment from this moment forward not be a victim—one, of not knowing what you ought and need to know, or two, of being guilty of plain stupidity. Don't be like everybody else and operate on minimums all of your life. If you want more out of life, then you must pursue knowledge. Learning, like responsibility and making choices, never takes a vacation! Ignorance is the first and greatest weakness of humanity; and the greatest ignorance is the lack of accurate knowledge of oneself.

If you do not believe me, then you need to read the following:

> *Various news stories state that there are between, 40 to 50 million illiterates in Africa alone. The percentage of illiteracy is skyrocketing in second and third world countries. It is believed that as much as 90% of the African continent is illiterate. It is also not an accident that while the African continent has the greatest natural resources of any other continent on earth, it also has the poorest people in the world. This is not just a continent experiencing a run of bad luck or misfortune. Africa's poverty and absence of a decent standard of living are primarily due to the consequences of ignorance. When I say this, I am very well aware that more despots have ruled in Africa than in any other continent in the modern world. Such individuals have their payback coming and I can assure you, it will be brutal.*

o **Wisdom Principle:** *Poverty, whether physical, educational, or spiritual is primarily the consequence of ignorance!*

If you want to measure yourself by the lowest common denominators in life, knock yourself out. However, if you have even the smallest modicum of self-respect, you will commit yourself to becoming the best you can be. Ignorance is the number one encumbrance individuals will face in this endeavor. It is also believed by many wise individuals, that ignorance is also man's greatest enemy. I have no reason to disagree with such a claim.

2. Lack of Character–In Most Cases, Having No Character at All

Your character is critical to everything that is meaningful and valuable in your life—relationships, happiness, sense of purpose, fulfillment, pursuit of knowledge, and personal peace. Without character, there is no integrity. Without integrity, you have no center line in your life. All you have are feelings and opinions. And, you know what they say about opinions!

What is integrity? It is an individual possessing a sound and unimpaired condition—in other words, being whole. It is living and having a life that reflects truth, a life, which is transparent, prudently flexible, possesses sagacity, is honest, kind, gracious, reasonable, and has a sense of humor. Let's look briefly at these qualities one at a time.

o **Wisdom Principle:** *Never make the mistake of looking for true meaning and fulfillment in the shallow waters of your ego. It is here where your selfish desires reside. Profound and authentic meaning and fulfillment will only be found in the depths of your soul.*

1) **A life of integrity is one that is lived truthfully.** This means two things: 1) Having an absence of hypocrisy in your life; and 2) Being a truth-seeker of the highest order. Truth never takes a day off in the life of a person of integrity and neither does responsibility. Shakespeare wasn't kidding when he said: *"To thine own self be true. Therefore, thou canst be false to any man."* The person of integrity doesn't lie to himself or herself. When a person of integrity makes a mistake or fails, such a person doesn't rationalize what occurred. There is no complexity or confusion in the life of a person of integrity, when it comes to right or wrong. Such decisions are crystal clear—no doubt exists.

   In contrast, a hypocrite is an expert at self-rationalization. Every failure and mistake is explained away. Hypocrites remind me of the Romans. When the Romans wanted to socially accept a "forbidden behavior" and declare it to be "normal," they made a god out of that particular vice. When drunkenness became socially prevalent and desirable, they invented a god for when they wanted to have a drunken feast. They named this god Bacchus. Hypocrites operate much the same way. "After all," they rationalize, "everybody makes mistakes. Everyone messes up." They also say, "So, why do I have to apologize and change? It's just the way I am. I'm programmed to be the way that I am. I can't be but only who I am. It can't be that wrong if I am like everybody else and everybody does what I do." And on and on.

   In the New Testament, the Pharisees also learned their lessons well from the Romans. When they found it too inconvenient to follow a command of Scripture, they simply wrote a tradition to take its place. This is why Christ accused them of such in Matthew 15:6 when He said to the Pharisees: *"You have invalidated the law of God and have rendered it ineffective as the result of your adding on your traditions in place of it."* Christ knew what they were up to. The same can be said of a hypocrite. When a hypocrite can't cut it, as the saying goes, he or she changes the rules.

Many individuals who are not church oriented use the failures of professing Christians as a basis for their not living a Christian life. Hypocrisy is not failing to live up to the standards of Christ. Hypocrisy is professing to live up to the standards of Christ but not caring whether or not those standards are upheld. Hypocrisy is a person being indifferent as well as uncaring toward God and His teachings, while saying the opposite. Again, it is professing that you do live according to Christ's teachings, when in truth, you *know* you *don't*. And, the fact that you don't, doesn't even bother you.

Many Christians fall short of being the best they can be on a daily basis. However, such shortfalls cause great remorse and heartache to committed and consecrated Christians. Christians are also open about their imperfections. However, they are never satisfied with being average. With committed Christians, there is an unwavering determination to be a reflection of the marvelous character of Christ.

I do not give time or consideration to those who expect perfection from Christians while they, in turn, live materialistic, unspiritual, narcissistic, and self-centered lives. Such critics are behaving in an evil manner and are being used by the evil in the world to hurt the church and to discourage Christians. Nonetheless, even though such people are loved by God; He is not present in their lives. God only comes into the lives of those who celebrate His presence in their lives. I am also, deeply convicted that God's presence will not be found in the lives of those who only tolerate God's presence without respecting it.

o **Wisdom Principle:** *Never move in circles where you are tolerated; only move in circles where you are graciously welcomed. Why? Going where you are not celebrated can wound your spirit and demoralize you.*

Am I saying that Christians can't make mistakes and do some very stupid things? No! Trust me, I have been around Christians most of my life. If I lined up all of the individuals who have hurt me and have had a negative influence on me during my lifetime, most would be professing Christians. However, I have come to realize that there are moral Christians and virtuous Christians. Virtuous Christians are in the minority. Most moral Christians are anything but benign when relating to others. In fact, as opposed to virtuous Christians, most moral Christians are lethally judgmental. Even so, I would rather be in church with such people, as my pastor says, than possibly be in hell with those who are not Christian by any stretch of the imagination.

My spiritual development and my "Christian walk" are my own responsibility. My focus is to be on Christ, not on other Christians. I am called to love other Christians, encourage other Christians, and be of service to other Christians. What I am not called to do is judge other Christians by my personal standards and expectations. I am called to cultivate my own garden. A person of integrity lives life truthfully and seeks to consistently do the right thing.

2) **A person of integrity is also comfortable living a transparent life.** I know there are some individuals who don't play their proverbial "cards close to the vest". They play their cards "under their vests". In other words, these persons are very difficult to read. When you see such individuals, they are so self-contained that you can't discern whether they have lost a loved one or won the lottery. When people are that difficult to read, as well as understand, you don't know where they are coming from. In other words, you can't process their intentions.

Transparency is evidence that one is at peace with who and what he or she is and is becoming. Being transparent means that when people see you they actually see you! They sense you without any difficulty. There is an air of competency that transparent individuals exude. If you are self-accepting and you properly nurture a healthy self-love, then you will, as a consequence, be comfortable being transparent.

I love to be around people I can sense and with whom I experience easy silences when I'm in their presence. They are absolutely a joy to be around. A transparent person says to the world: "I'm not perfect and you aren't perfect, but that's okay." When you are at peace with the reality that you are imperfect, you have no problem letting others see you for who and what you are.

In contrast, non-transparent people are not comfortable with their inner person and I believe the reason for this discomfort is that non-transparent people do not speak positively to themselves about themselves. In John 14:27, Christ says: *"My peace I give you, not the kind the world gives, which is superficial, insufficient, and misleading; but my peace, which sets your soul at rest."* People of integrity are transparent, peaceful individuals, and as a result, are visible and easily understood.

3) **A person of integrity is prudently flexible.** To be prudently flexible, one is judiciously and wisely open to new ideas and to better ways of doing things. Flexibility is absolutely necessary in today's ever-changing world. The opposite of flexibility is rigidity. To be rigid is to be inflexible, unyielding, fixed. Rigid individuals, as a rule, are not affected by facts, because their minds are already made up. One of the greatest difficulties that most people have is the inability of knowing when to be flexible and when to be firm in a belief, view, or position. I used to have difficulty with this until I realized that the key to knowing what is correct, is if the idea or "better way" being presented is altruistic,

and has virtue at its core. Once I understood the criteria, knowing when to be flexible was not a problem.

4) **A person of integrity possesses sagacity.** Sagacity is possessing an elegant common sense. It is possessing acute mental and spiritual discernment wrapped in keen pragmatism. I must say that there are few individuals who possess such sagacity—about five out of a hundred. Individuals who possess pragmatic, logistical common-sense, are people who have learned how to process information and make sound decisions. Through all of the challenges life throws at them, such individuals will not panic but rather be thoughtful and contemplative in their decision-making. Make no mistake, such individuals are special. They are cut from a royal cloth.

The key to possessing sagacity is for an individual to be a truth-seeker of the highest order. When he or she is committed to truth and lives in such a fashion, sagacity chases him or her. Persons of great sagacity, who also possess an indomitable spirit, can't help but diffuse themselves.

5) **A person of integrity is honest about himself or herself and about what is factual and true in regards to life.** People who are honest are committed to seeing reality accurately, not the way they wish reality would be. Honesty is upright, trustworthy, and living truthfully. It is being what you say you are and doing what you say you will do. It is also not being what you have said you will not be and not doing what you have said you will not do. Because of honesty, the life of a person of integrity is not complex. Confusion

is the forerunner of complexity. Honest people are rarely confused. As a result, they live lives absent of what I call modern complexity.

All of my life I have heard people say when they have been given a solution to a problem in their lives: "Well, it's more complicated than that." I want to respond: "No, more often than not, it isn't." People-pleasing and politics will make anything in life complicated, if allowed. Honest individuals are not people-pleasers. They are also non-political when it comes to the truth. Why are they able to be so? They have learned how to live without the good opinion of other people. They are immune to the pressure to conform and be just like everybody else.

6) **A person of integrity is kind.** Kindness is being innately considerate and benevolent to others, even to those individuals who can't either help or hurt you. It is, in essence, being benign. A benign person is not acidic, poisonous, or lethal. Kindness means being consistently considerate, with others. To be considerate is the opposite of being rude. Rudeness is a consequence of ignorance and narcissism. A kind individual can consistently be so, because such a person is emotionally self-disciplined. Individuals who are kind don't treat others based on how they feel but rather according to the soundness of their character. Kindness inherently has a warm and pleasing effect on others. A kind person is inherently patient. Kindness and patience are component virtues. You can't have one without the

Proverbial Wisdom: For a fully-functioning life

other. Make no mistake, a person of integrity is truly and consistently kind.

7) **A person of integrity is gracious.** People are gracious, when they are merciful and compassionate to others. Mercy is being compassionate to others when you have the right and ability to be otherwise. When you can be legitimately angry or frustrated with an individual, but choose to still treat them graciously, that is integrity.

A person's decision to act in this manner is ethically driven rather than ego-driven. One is being compassionate, when one is sympathetic to the point of desiring to alleviate suffering. Compassionate people are helpful. A person, who is gracious does what he or she can, when possible, to alleviate another's burdens and suffering. Caring for one another—this is what being a Christian means. In certain contexts, when the need presents itself, an individual who is gracious, is stirred from complacency to do something to help. Anything! It may only be a little, but when one has the ability and power to do something to help someone, he/she does so without expecting anything in return. Gracious people are grateful people, too. Grateful people are joyful. Joy is the fruit of gratefulness!

8) **A person of integrity is reasonable.** What does it mean to be reasonable? It means to be agreeable when it's legitimately possible. Reasonable people are very good listeners. They are willing to listen to another's point-of-view. They reserve judgment until all facts, suggestions, and ideas are known. Reasonable people are consistently and judiciously

cooperative. They do not readily condemn other ideas or suggestions. Rather, they take ideas, as well as plausible solutions, lay them side-by-side, and then consider the worthiness of each one. Once they are satisfied that they have all of the necessary information to make a decision, they choose the best option.

Also, reasonable individuals are not people-pleasers. However, they are champions of cooperation. To be reasonable is to be understanding of others. And, when appropriate, being reasonable means, to be empathetic or sympathetic.

9) **A person of integrity possesses a terrific sense-of-humor.** Better put, such a person has a terrific comic wit. People of integrity find it easy to occasionally laugh at themselves. They are not overly sensitive—they do not wear their feelings on their sleeves. They know laughter can add twelve years to their lives. Laughter, wit, and humor are indicators of individuals who would rather be happy in contrast to having a compulsive need to be right—by right I don't mean being accurate. A sense-of-humor is indicative of one's ability not to take life, as well as themselves, too seriously. People who have a healthy sense-of-humor are warm individuals in contrast to being austere. Individuals who possess a sense-of-humor disarm the insecure, defensive, or cold individual. People gravitate to those who have a sense-of-humor because those who do are benign individuals. They are also an absolute joy to be around.

Failing to know and understand the components of an indomitable character renders you useless in the development of your own character, as well as the development of the character of your children. Remember those parents I spoke of earlier? The second catch to their militant ignorance regarding character occurred when I asked them to suggest what they believed were the traits of a person with an indomitable character.

There were over 25 parents at that meeting and all of them putting their minds together could not come up with more than two legitimate components of an indomitable character. You can't teach what you don't know, right? If parents and leaders of young people don't know the components of an indomitable character, then how in the world can they teach their children about it? Also, how are our youth going to acquire this critical knowledge? The answer is they can't if there is no one to teach them. Just as it takes self-discipline to rid oneself of ignorance, it also takes self-discipline to cultivate an indomitable character and become a person of integrity.

o   **Wisdom Principle:** *Character is more than being moral. It is being whole. A person can be moral without being whole.*

3. Arguing for One's Own, or Another's Limitations and Deficiencies

When an individual argues for his or her limitations, that person is declaring, without realizing it, that there exists in their life a determination and need to be right so he or she can look good in the presence of others. Such a need is not only ego-driven, but it is also rooted in pride—an unaffordable pride. This person needs to justify his or her actions or decisions, declaring them profoundly more important than being whole. This flaw is either a product of one's subconscious compliances, laziness, or it is simply a personality defense mechanism rooted in trying to hide one's insecurity. Parents often argue for their limitations and in turn argue for their children's limitations at the expense of truth, honesty, and personal happiness. Justifying one's ignorance and failures is one certain predictor of a person operating on the minimums in life and eventually ending up with a mediocre outcome in the majority of their endeavors.

o **Wisdom Principle:** *Protecting one's pride at the expense of what is true is a foolish endeavor, which ultimately ends in personal humiliation.*

"He or she would rather be right than be happy," is a phrase I first heard in the mid to late 60s. It describes people who have so much pride in who and what they have become, that they refuse to see their own deficiencies. Consequently, such individuals also believe that their own limitations and deficiencies don't exist. Or, if they are cognitive that such limitations and deficiencies do exist, they rationalize them by saying things like, "Well, I'm not any worse than anyone else." At best, such a ridiculous statement is an assumption, rarely a fact.

Often, these people find it incomprehensible that they could make such a miscalculation, or to believe that they could be that ignorant about themselves, or even be as personally incompetent as they are. However, all of us at one time or another have been. We are imperfect and as a result, we make mistakes ... sometimes embarrassing mistakes. But when we learn from such mistakes, the embarrassment will eventually pass. Life goes on!

Remember, when I spoke earlier about parents who argued for the character of their children when that character was sub-par, at best? What I am describing here is a militant determination of people not to look bad in front of others and to stand firm on the belief that what they have or have not done was correct, when, in an objective sense, was not even close to being so. People, because of this kind of pride, would rather argue for something in their life that will slot them on the path to mediocrity than to look at themselves objectively, and realize that embracing of such habits, ideas, beliefs, or actions, is not within their best interest. Under no circumstances will this belief assist them in becoming the best they can be.

The consequences of arguing for the limitations and deficiencies in ourselves, our friends, or children, are lethal. First, when we argue for our limitations, we literally "shut ourselves down" from the opportunity to learn and grow from our mistakes, miscalculations, and outright erroneous beliefs. When we shut down, we are implicitly saying that we have the proverbial "it" all figured out. Thus, we stay ignorant. People filled with pride, such as I have just described, are determined to be seen as correct, at the expense of their character and at the expense of what is true. And, as you and I know, such pride is obviously unaffordable.

o **Wisdom Principle:** *Pride is a luxury that a person who desires to possess an indomitable character can't afford.*

I can't begin to tell you the number of parents, whose children were irresponsible, childish, immature, and dishonest, who stood up for their children. They blamed their children's actions on anything but their children's selfishness, un-self-discipline and ignorance. Adults who consistently defend their children in situations where no plausible defense exists, are the most irresponsible and ignorant, of parents. The damage they do to their children's future is incalculable. Yet, we have seen this scenario with generation after generation of parents since the early 80s.

Parents need raw courage to see the failures of their children and admit to themselves and to their children that such failures have occurred. When a parent does this, they have taken a step closer to changing what is wrong. Courageous parents will even sit their children down and tell them how they, as parents, failed them. I am convinced that this is what parents who truly love their children will do. It is not surprising that the trust such parents receive from their children grows and becomes much stronger. Such parents are truly worthy of their children's trust, faith, and confidence.

Another aspect of this arguing for our limitations is that when we do, we blind ourselves even more to the truth. In my experience, when individuals embark on a path of consistently arguing for the deficiencies in their own lives, the lives of friends, relatives, and children, the determination and intensity for doing so increases with each defense. After time, such people find themselves in a situation that is beyond reach.

It is rare when truth can penetrate any individual's self-made prison. During such a personal crusade of justifying deficiencies and limitations on behalf of children, family, or friends, truth is not embraced, much less seriously considered. When individuals choose not to be truth-seekers and who argue for such limitations, successfully perpetuate this compulsive yet deadly habit into the next generation—primarily through their children.

A third aspect of this, is that we seriously limit God's influence in our lives, and for all practical purposes, we shut down spiritually. We leave ourselves unaffected by the conviction of the Holy Spirit and remain blind to our own limitations. We also find ourselves on a path of self-rationalization, justification, and outright foolishness that in the end destroys our opportunity to become the best we can be. In the end, what we lose, is respect for ourselves. Besides this, the bitter reality is that we have also lost the respect of others, because they have seen us as unreliable and untrustworthy. Instead of being objective, we are seen as deceitful. Take my word when I say when we are observed in this context, the last thing someone would say of us is that we are truth-seekers of the highest order.

Finally, when a person argues for their deficiencies, those of their children, and of family and friends, he or she is declaring to the world that their predecessors argued for their deficiencies and whether right or wrong they are taking up the mantle and continuing the "tradition," to do the same. Now, I am not saying that those who argue for their deficiencies, are cognitive that they are sending this message. What I am saying is that in the minds of intuitive and intelligent people, the message being given, is that they have no problem perpetuating this weakness.

You are probably asking, "How does one stop arguing for one's deficiencies and limitations?" There is only one way—stop doing it! Is it that easy? No, it isn't that easy to do, but it is that easy to understand. When one is self-disciplined, you can't imagine how easy certain things can become. This is one of those things that's easy for someone to do once one realizes what a horrible weakness arguing for one's deficiencies is. All one has to do is decide to do something about it and then do it.

There are well-meaning people who believe that changing is much more complex. Complexity is often the consequence of confusion. I simply don't buy the thesis that solutions to most of life's problems must have a complexity about them in order for such solutions to have validity. In my opinion, this is not true. Most solutions to life's problems are pragmatic and clear. What most people lack is the courage to face the validity of such solutions and commit themselves to a disciplined plan of action. Complexity is an excuse for doing nothing!

4. Emotionally-Driven Thinking and Decision-Making

The first characteristic of an emotionally-driven personality is allowing feelings to be the decision-maker. I truly believe that at least 80% of the world's population allows feelings to determine what they will or won't do in most defining moments of life. As important as processing your feelings may be, feelings are not intended to be the engine of your decision-making train. However, the majority of the world's people is extremely comfortable allowing their feelings to be the impetus for their decisions.

Even though emotionally-driven decisions rarely turn out well, people seldom seem deterred from continuing to let emotions or feelings determine what they will do. Therefore, it is safe to say that emotionally-driven decisions are totally ego-driven.

Ego-driven decisions are not necessarily made out of a desire to control or just simply out of pride. They may be made as a result of one's spirit being seriously injured. A significant amount of self-injury is due to a wounded or broken spirit. Proverbs 18:14 says: *"A man's spirit can endure sickness, but who can survive a broken spirit?"* My response to the question posed in this verse, is that a person must put their trust in the strength of the Lord.

Going with your "feelings" is like playing the lottery—the chance of winning is extremely slim. In fact, I believe you have a better chance of being hit by a meteor than winning the lottery. Emotionally-driven decisions have about as equal a chance of working out. As I heard a Southern gentleman say once: "Mix your money and heart in your 'how-I-feel' pocket, and you will wind up with both of them broken." Feelings are not facts. Facts are not feelings.

At the beginning of Dr. James Dobson's book *Emotions: Can You Trust Them?*[10] There is a story about a high school football team that was going to play its greatest rival. This rival had beaten them several years in a row. One of the graduates of that "losing" high school who had done very well for himself, was tired of losing to this rival and decided to do something extraordinary to motivate

---

[10] Dobson, James, *Emotions, Can You Trust Them?* (pp, 8-10).

his alma mater's football team. He promised to give every player on the football team a new car, if they beat this rival school.

All through the week, the young men prepared. They were pumped up. The whole student body was whipped into a frenzy. As a result of this unbelievable opportunity, they got behind their team. When game time had arrived, the young men on the team were as emotionally high as anyone could possibly be under the same circumstances. When the team took the field, the players were on an enormous and intense emotional ride. The young men gave it all they had. Every one of them believed that they would win. However, when the game ended, they looked up at the score. They had been trounced. Hopefully, these young men learned that emotion was not a sufficient base upon which to build a strategy for victory. In fact, being primarily emotionally-driven was the team's undoing.

Emotion is not intelligence, nor can it ever take the place of intelligence. An emotionally self-disciplined life is not innate in human beings. A self-disciplined life is intentionally cultivated. Feelings may feel great at the time, but as with every high, reality brings an individual down to earth to deal with what is true. Eventually, one is forced to deal with what is real and not with what he or she wishes to be real.

Emotionally-driven personalities have common vulnerabilities. These flaws are not hard to notice. If one knows what to look for, such flaws will be very evident. One of these vulnerabilities is the inability of emotionally-driven individuals to be consistent in their performance on a daily basis. When people conduct themselves and their affairs based on how they feel, inconsistency becomes evident. There is no question that a by-product of such inconsistency is a lack of predictability. When someone describes one's personality as unpredictable, they are saying that he or she is primarily emotionally-driven.

Emotions are like the ocean tide; they have an ebb and flow about them. Both high tide and low tied will occur on the same day—every day. Emotions are exactly the same. When a person lives his or her life on an emotional treadmill, you don't know which person will show up at any given part of a day—the high person or the low person. You also don't know what such individuals will say, do, or how they will react because of their emotionally-driven temperament.

The television program *60 Minutes* did a news piece a professional golfer with what everyone thought had the best hands in the game. This golfer won was a PGA Tournament Champion and British Open Champion as a young man. However, winning set him on a treadmill of fame and fortune for which few would have been adequately prepared. He couldn't handle the responsibility of his success. He developed a drinking problem and his self-centeredness became his ultimate downfall. During the time of the TV interview, his wife had been arrested and charged with being involved in some kind of drug crime.

When asked by Mike Wallace what accounted for his life being what it was, without hesitation, the golfer said: "I go with how I feel." He could not have said it better than I could have. His life was the result of going with his feelings and allowing his emotional temperament to determine what he decided to do in any given context. At the time of this writing, he has lost significant sponsorships and ranks very low in the golf world rankings. This is where his emotionally-driven life got him. His golf is a reflection of his life—inconsistent. Who wants to be him? This man has such great talent. I hope he can develop the self-discipline to turn his life around. He has a little time but that window of opportunity is closing fast.

o **Wisdom Principle:** *Potential is to performance, what luck is to success—nothing!*

A second characteristic of an emotionally-driven personality is the inability to make solid decisions in defining moments when a decision needs to be made. Emotionally-driven people often have only one voice and one emotion in their mind stating the whys of doing or not doing something. This will either be the voice of defending the right to do what is under consideration (commonly called the voice of the defense attorney), or it will be the voice that protests doing what is under consideration (commonly called the voice of the prosecutor).

The defense attorney, in the mind of the emotionally-driven individual, always defends the desire to do something. The prosecutor in the mind of the emotionally-driven individual always defends the need for doing what is right. Depending on whether the driving emotion is for desire or discipline, neither the defense attorney nor the prosecutor can be objective in the mind of an emotionally-driven individual. Therefore, because there is no judge to decide what is best in the mind of an emotionally-driven personality, whatever decision is made is extremely subjective.

On the other hand, healthy individuals have a defense attorney, a prosecutor, and a judge fulfilling their appropriate roles as they are considering a decision. The defense presents the case for the desires or wishes of the individual, who is considering what to do. Then the prosecution gives the downsides of what can or will occur. Finally, the judge—the person's conscience or standard of virtue—after considering both sides of the issue, hands down the verdict and decides what to do. What makes the decisions of a healthy person more objective and effective than decisions made by emotionally-driven individuals is that healthy individuals will consider the facts and what is true before making any decision.

The emotionally-driven individual who is driven by desire, only has a defense attorney speaking in their mind, and will go with their feelings at least 90% of the time. This is because the defense attorney will argue for going with how a person feels. Since there is no dissenting opinion, it is easy for an emotionally-driven person to decide what to do. Such a person simply goes with his or her feelings. I might also add that when a person consistently goes with their desires at the expense of not using logistical common-sense, such a person is behaving irresponsibly as well as selfishly.

In my opinion, any individual who possesses only a defense attorney in his or her mind when considering what to do is living on autopilot and is therefore emotionally compulsive in how decisions are made in his or her life. Compulsive decision-making is, in actuality, acting without thinking when not stopping to consider the consequences of one's actions. Individuals whose decision-making system in their lives is predominately driven by emotions and are setting themselves up to become self-hating. This is why suicide and cutting are self-centered acts. These individuals are so consumed by emotion that all they can see is life being all about them—their pride, their needs, their hurts, and their pains. Their response to perceived injustices in their lives is to use suicide or cutting as a way to either get back at others or as a way to express their pain or anger. When emotion drives individuals this strongly one must realize that they are in dangerous territory.

o   **Wisdom Principle:** *The points-of-view the narcissistic have about life and living are always one-sided—theirs.*

A person who has in his or her mind only a prosecutor's voice to present the case against doing what is being considered is a person motivated by the emotion of fear. As soon as a desirable thought comes into the mind of such a person, the prosecutor inside immediately and forcefully presents its case. The result of such fear when it comes to one's behavior, is for a person to submit to their fear and do nothing. The status quo is simply maintained.

Such is true in every key moment where a significant decision has to be made and fear seems to completely take over. The voice of the prosecutor in the mind of a fear-driven individual freezes him or her and ultimately, that person simply acquiesces to fear. Again, the presence of an inner judge only occurs in the mind of an emotionally healthy person. A judge is never present in the mind of an emotionally-driven person because desire or fear, depending on the individual, rules.

The third characteristic of an emotionally-driven personality is the inability to defer personal gratification. I am not speaking here of stopping and smelling the roses in one's race toward achievement. I am talking about doing what you need to do in order to protect what is important in your life. To achieve anything meaningful in life you must give up something you want. It is the choice that achievers are consistently confronted with. Individuals who do what they want instead of what is best are emotionally-driven and as a consequence make mediocre choices while living mediocre lives, which in turn produce mediocre results.

Following feelings results in unnecessary failure, because life will always ask for an accounting. You can be led by your emotions and do such things as clown away your life at home, school, or work. Sometimes the company for which you work pays for this misspent time. However, I can guarantee you that life will never pay for such misspent time. Neither will life pay for irresponsible decision-making and behavior. I believe you can trust me on both of these.

Someone might say: "Well, if life is always about the necessity of making decisions, being responsible, and being serious, then I really don't see what there is in life to look forward to." This kind of statement is always an overreaction. What a person is really saying when making a statement like this, is that life should always be fun and entertaining. Those who approach life with this immature perspective and attitude are often ill-equipped to function effectively when the demands of living at a level of excellence are required. Life isn't a party and it isn't a first act for the real thing. Life is the real thing.

When you look at the lives of those who neither respected life nor took life seriously when necessary, you see lives that are in disarray, aimless, and disappointing. Too many people live lives of mediocrity, regret, and heartache as a result of not postponing gratification. The heartbreak, which most experience due to recklessness and selfishness, never seems to end. I and many others are calling the burdened and heavy-laden back to sanity and wholeness. My prayer is that they will listen and respond.

The fourth characteristic of emotionally-driven individuals is their being unable to control their temper or what they say when they have lost it. When individuals lose their tempers, they lose their composure as well. My grandmother once said to me: "You can tell the size of the person by the size of the things that make them angry." Self-disciplined individuals have confessed to me that the two hardest things are controlling the temper, and as a result, controlling what is said. The reason these two areas of our lives are so difficult to discipline is because of the role our ego plays in both of these vulnerabilities. The ego fights for its rights and entitlements. The reason the control of one's temper and tongue are such an important part of life, and relationships in general, is because the loss of one's temper is always accompanied by mis-spoken words. It's hard to take something back once you've said it.

Speaking of the controlling or losing of one's temper, I have heard it said that it is possible to forgive a family member of murder, because it is a crime of passion. However, the same individuals, also say that they would never forgive someone of adultery. I find people with this perspective to be immature, even adolescent in regards to this subject. Also, their concept regarding their idea of the levels of sin is quite skewed. Anyone who would put adultery in a higher category of sin than murder is at least misguided, if not "off the radar screen". Both of these sins are emotionally-driven. One is primarily prompted by the emotion of desire and the other by the emotion of fear. However, there is no question that murder is a tragedy that is caused by the loss of one's temper, as well as misspoken words. Murder is not primarily a crime of passion, but a crime of hate accompanied by a horrific disrespect for life! Adultery is not a crime, on the same plane as murder. If you do not believe that, you need to study your state and federal laws concerning murder. Murder is a capital offense and is punishable by either life imprisonment or death. The same cannot be said of adultery.

Now I can hear someone ask, "Are you saying that you don't believe adultery is that bad a sin?" Of course not! All sin is tragic and brings awful consequences. What I am doing is making an analogy of these two sins. I am also saying that as bad of a relationship-destroying sin adultery is, murder is a much greater sin than adultery. If you have to ask why such is true, I don't think I can explain it well enough for you to understand.

Controlling one's temper is paramount to being an emotionally self-disciplined individual. Over my lifetime, I have been in the presence of individuals who have lost their tempers. In each case, and without exception, these individuals made an embarrassing spectacle of themselves. I have never seen anyone lose his or her temper with class. Class and losing one's temper are on opposite sides of the spectrum.

For an individual to control his or her temper at all times requires emotional discipline and a thorough understanding of what causes him or her to it. There is no question that for individuals to lose their tempers, they must view the context in which they become angry as an insult to their ego. It is amazing how defensive the ego is in such situations. When we allow our ego to determine our reaction in any context where one's temper could become volatile, tempers will flare virtually every time. We must allow our emotions, which are connected to our ego, to flow through us and straight into ground. I can tell you this, for those few who have tamed their egos, controlling their tempers is not a major challenge. Why is this? Because as one tames the ego, one becomes insensitive to the words and opinions of others. Such individuals do not take the inequities and vicissitudes of life personally, but rather, they take them in stride.

Emotionally-driven people are egocentric, i.e., self-absorbed. They are self-centered, selfish, and emotionally un-disciplined. The only thing such people can see is how any context of relating to others, affects their own ego. While such people often behave arrogantly, at the same time they are enormously sensitive to the opinions of others. This kind of neurosis is truly a terrible inferno in which to live day-in and day-out.

The loss of a person's temper and the kind of language he or she uses in expressing anger, are also a reflection of character. When an individual is a person of great character, controlling his/her temper and tongue, is not an issue. Why? Because a person puts the protection of their relationships ahead of their ego. Here is where Essential #9 comes into play. People of character watch their relationships like they do their money—like a hawk! Relationships are precious. Once we understand and respect this essential of life, we will be disciplined in how we speak and keep our temper under wraps. When we are emotionally self-disciplined, defending our ego ceases to be a necessity.

The final characteristic of an emotionally-driven individual is their inability to focus long-term on gathering necessary knowledge that will give them the ability to become self-disciplined and fully-functioning. What do I mean by this? Emotionally-driven people are usually poor listeners as well as poor learners. Their ability to retain knowledge and information pivotal to their effec-tiveness is seriously diminished because of their tendency to listen and learn only when they are emotionally moved. Experiences that truly move us emotionally are rare exceptions. If a person only has the ability to focus and learn when they are emotionally moved, knowledge necessary for living and functioning at a high level of competency will not be recognized nor properly processed into their lives. The critical knowledge needed is based on facts, i.e., truth, not emotion. Emotion has no connection to excellence!

- o **Wisdom Principle:** *It's great to have zeal. However, if one's zeal isn't disciplined with wisdom, it is not only useless, but it is spiritually and intellectually inhibiting.*

CHAPTER SIX

REBELLION IS THE ANTITHESIS OF CONFORMITY

1. Rebellion

o **Wisdom Principle:** *A rebellious spirit is a restless soul in search of a resting place—a purpose. The problem is that the rebel looks without for an answer instead of within.*

A truth, more often than not, is paradoxical. It is rare when it is not. The title of this chapter is a *truism*, which is unquestionably paradoxical. I have always had an interest in what makes a person a rebel and another a nonconformist. For most, there is no difference between rebellion and nonconformity. However, on closer scrutiny, you will find that there is an enormous difference. This brief chapter will give you the necessary information to know the difference.

"**The Parable of the Prodigal Son**" (Luke 15:11-32), is one of Jesus' parable that most people know. However, most may not know that the title was probably given to it centuries ago by a scribe not Jesus Christ. He didn't call the younger son "the prodigal". He simply referred to him as the "younger son".

In my two decades as a youth minister I learned that many big mistakes, if not most, are made when we are young just as this parable illustrates. The story has three principle characters—the father, the younger son, and the older son. I will refer to the older son in the chapter about Difficult People. For now, I want us to focus on the father and the younger son. The core of the interaction between these two will be found in verses 11-24. Let me paraphrase the story for you.

There was a man who had two sons. The younger son came to the father one day and said, "Dad, I want my share of the estate right now. I have reached legal age and I am tired of working on this boring farm. I want to take what is mine and set out on my own. I want to build my life my way while I am young."

The father, sensing that he would not be able to change his son's mind, divided the estate. His oldest son would get his share upon the father's death. The other portion he gave the younger son now. The younger son made his plans, organized his travel, gathered his possessions, and set out to "make his own fortune". Ready to leave, the younger son determined to get as far away from his father's house as he could. The journey was long but he finally got to an exciting place far away. At last, he truly believed, he was now on his own.

He had craved the freedom to be whom and what he wanted to be and now he had it. He gravitated to those who valued the same things he did. He made some friends, shared their lifestyle, and began to "hang out" with them. He lavished food, drink, and gifts on his co-revelers. His lack of discipline and his disrespect for money found him partying virtually all of the time. He spent his money fast—furiously and carelessly. Eventually he ran out of his inheritance and when this happened, his "friends" ran out on him as well. He found himself broke and alone.

With no money and no friends, he suddenly found himself in the middle of a famine. There was little food to be had and most people were suffering from malnutrition and extreme poverty. He, without realizing it, had become one of them—in need and in want.

He, being a Jew, found a job "in the fields" as a farm hand on one of the large farms in that same region. He was assigned the care of the farm owner's pigs. He did what he was assigned to do because he was broke and hungry. The owner of the farm—not a very kind person—paid his farm hands the least he could and fed them as little as possible. This young man never got enough to eat, so he was tempted to eat what the pigs were eating—dirty corn husks!

One day, he took a good look at himself. No longer was he the "hot shot" with money to throw around or the one who had everything all figured out. He had become a slave. He had lived for himself at the expense of his character and lived for "today" at the expense of tomorrow.

He finally realized what he had done. He saw the consequences of his decisions as well as what he had become. He admonished himself. "How many of the servants of your father have plenty to eat, even all they want? I'll tell you what you're going to do.

You're going to get up and go back to your father, apologize to him, and ask for his forgiveness. You're going to tell him that you have sinned against God and have sinned and disrespected him. You're also going to ask him to simply make you just another of his hired servants, because you have forfeited the right to be called his son."

This younger son got to his feet and made his way back toward his father's house. Yet, while he was still a good distance away, his father saw him. He didn't walk toward his son ... he ran to him. With great compassion, tears falling, the father grabbed his son, clutched him to his breast, and with great joy, kissed him over and over.

Without hesitation, the younger son confessed to his father. "Father, I have rebelled against heaven and against you. My sin is before my eyes, as well as before yours. I have embarrassed myself and I have embarrassed you. I am not worthy to be called your son anymore. I forfeited that privilege when I forced you to give me my share of the estate so I could go away and "find myself".

But before his son could finish his confession, the father called out to the servants and said, "Hurry! Bring the best robe I have and put it on him. Put a ring with the family crest on it on his finger as well as shoes on his feet. And ... I tell you what. Let's kill the prized calf and serve it at a celebration dinner this evening. Call our friends and neighbors to join us. And if they ask why, tell them it's because this is my young son who, as far as I knew, was as good as dead, has returned. He was estranged and lost, but now he is home. The joy in my heart is overflowing!"

That evening, with much joy the party began!

Unbelievable, isn't it? What a marvelous story. I can't read it without tearing up. This is a parable that has so many aspects to it that you could do a Bible study on it for six months and not repeat a teaching point.

I have a book in my library by J. Wallace Hamilton that consists of sermons he developed on this one parable. Every chapter focuses on a particular aspect of this story. This is truly a remarkable parable. For our purposes, I want to focus on the younger son and his rebellion.

The younger son made a decision to leave home. He didn't seek anyone's advice. When he made up his mind, he demanded his father give him his share of the estate. Now, we're not told whether his father tried to talk him out of leaving or not. The father may have at least asked him a question like: "Are you sure this is what you want to do?" All we know is that the father complied with his younger son's wish.

I believe I understand why there was an absence of conflict over this decision. The father not only was an intuitive person, but he knew that speaking to his son was of no use. The young man had made up his mind and was not going to be persuaded by logistical common-sense, or the facts, to change it. Most emotionally-driven decisions like this one cannot be changed either by truth or facts, unless the person himself desires to change it.

Parents today are often not as intuitive as this father who focused on preserving the relationship with his son rather than exercising his authority and control over his son's life (which I feel sure he was tempted to do). He saw this situation primarily through "the eyes of love". While today's parents accommodate their children's wishes/desires more than they should, I believe in a like situation they would have immediately deferred to their "position power" and "parental authority", to squash such an unreasonable and outlandish request. There is no doubt that it would have been appropriate for the father in this story not only to question his younger son's request but to deny it as not being with the young man's best interest. This would have been a far better basis for denying his son's request than protecting the family assets. In today's world assets are often more important than relationships ... even family relationships.

- o **Wisdom Principle:** *To the worldly-thinking, money trumps everything!*

The father knew that if he chose to "die on this hill", with his son, he likely risked permanently losing his relationship with him. Again, to him the relationship with his son was more important than his authority and control. He refused to "burn the bridge" between them.[11]

The father knew his son would not listen. Rebels are, consistently, poor listeners. Why? Because they are *know-it-alls* of the highest order. You can tell them, but you can't tell them very much. Rebels won't listen because they are not guided by truth, but rather by selfishly-driven emotions. Notice that the son didn't just quietly leave and go his own way, as well as *make his own way*. He wanted to go his way, but he wanted his father to pay for it.

---

[11] It must be stated that taking into account the tradition within this ancient culture regarding such a request, a son receiving his portion of his father's estate at such a young age was not that unusual. In ancient times, such occurred in families that were quite well-to-do. Of course, our contemporary society has no such tradition.

o **Wisdom Principle:** *All rebellion is primarily ego-driven. Rebels are poor learners because they are arrogant! Arrogance negatively affects one's learning curve.*

Rebels are not only poor listeners and selfish, but they often cannot have lives without others paying a price for them to do so. You need to get this point, because all rebels have entitlement mentalities and their life agendas are self-centered. Rebels truly believe they have a right to ask others to pay the dues for their irresponsibility, as well as for their freedom. Whether a rebel has a superiority complex, or an inferiority complex, an entitlement mentality exists. At the same time, rebels also believe that they do not have to account to anyone. As a rule, rebels can only get what they want at another's expense. The younger son suffered for the choices he had made, but others did, too—specifically, his father and possibly his older brother, as well as the servants of the house.

o **Wisdom Principle:** *Rebels loathe self-discipline and refuse to be held accountable to anyone about anything.*

Rebels also have a belief that their roadmaps of life are *superior* to anyone else's. Again, let's not forget that rebels believe they have life all figured out; if you don't believe it, ask them. They will set you straight ... quickly! They believe they have an insight into life and living that no one else has. They desire to be esteemed by others in a manner that would make them a "legend" in the minds of others. However, the only place rebels are legends are in their own minds.

All of us have a roadmap to life. My questions to you are: "How accurate is yours? Of what does your life map consist? On what is your life map based?" These are all fair questions, but is your life map effective? Your life map is only as effective as the altruistic and purpose-directed results you are getting in how you conduct yourself and your affairs. If your life's roadmap is getting such results as you expected, then terrific. If the results are totally created by your own efforts, and are not at another's expense, then it can be safely said that your life map is an effective one—maybe not the best roadmap, but an effective one, at least.

However, if your endeavor to create your own identity by seeking to find yourself, like this younger son, has caused havoc in the lives of your family and loved ones, then you are guilty of rebellion, and this rebellion is a sin. It is a sin, because rebels disrupt the lives of others—especially those closest to them—in order to get what is selfishly desired, or what is believed to be needed in their lives. I am saddened at what a tremendous burden a rebel's life is to those who love him or her. Why do I say this so strongly?

First, rebellion is a selfish rather than an altruistic endeavor. By altruistic, I mean that rebellion does not serve anyone's purpose except the one who is rebelling. In contrast, altruism involves having an unselfish interest in the well-being of others. Individuals who are altruistic make sure that if they are doing what they desire and they are getting what they want out of life, others share in the positives of what they accomplish as well. When a person has conquered a challenge in life, he/she has also often contributed to the well-being of others. When it comes to rebellion, the only one who wins is the rebel. And that win is only temporary at best!

o **Wisdom Principle: *Rebellion is not a "right-of-passage" for the young; it is a "path of self-destruction".***

Parents worry about children who rebel. Also, I'm sure they're tired of the verbal declarations they constantly hear from their "rebel" children. For instance, "I've got to be me!", which is the code for the mantra of selfishness: "I want to be like my friends." When you hear this declaration, aren't you really impressed with this demonstration of individuality?

I know of children who argue with their parents constantly about being with their friends; about schoolwork, arguing every Sunday about what they want to wear to church. These parents have a constant tug of war with their rebellious children regarding what they will or will not do. The kids' mantra continues to be "I have got to be me." However, at church, school, or anywhere else they go for that matter, 95 out of a 100 children and teens look just like all others their age. Yeah, that's individuality! Or perhaps a new warped definition of it. So, if not individuality, what is it? It's rebellion, pure and simple. Rebellion is someone getting his own way at the expense of doing what is right, ethical, and fair.

One of the things I want you to notice regarding the selfishness of a rebel is that it causes conflict …_always. Conflict is a manifestation of selfishness, and so is anger. Where conflict exists, anger often exists as well.

Anger manifests itself when expectations or perceived entitlements/rights of the rebel are violated. In the mind of a rebel this opens the door to believing that their anger is justified. Such is the case where selfishness is always a visible and significant character flaw.

Parents, you can rationalize giving in to your children all you want in order to avoid conflict or "temper tantrums" by saying, "Well, at least they're not doing drugs." However, what you are doing is letting your children define the life-environment of the home you are supposed to be in charge of. You are also letting your rebels define the identity of your family. Frankly, your children are neither qualified nor intelligent enough to do either. Think about this: if they truly were qualified and intelligent enough to define your family, then their approach would be virtuous and altruistic, rather than demanding, threatening, and filled with conflict.

This is what the prodigal did. He came to his father and as much as said: "Dad, I want to get off of this boring farm and this is what you are going to do. And, I don't care what kind of imposition this creates for you. I have a right to be happy." His approach in leaving home was selfish and self-centered.

Some people may say: "Yeah, sounds just like a teenager." Yes, it does. Unfortunately, ego-driven young people believe they are "bullet proof", i.e., invincible and invisible. It isn't until the vicissitudes of life bring them to their knees that such an "invincibility illusion" explodes before their eyes. Only then is he/she brought down to earth and humbled in a manner that could have been completely avoided, if their ego had not been "running his/her life".

Did you notice something about this young man's demand? He didn't care if it inconvenienced his father or his family. He just wanted to get out on his own terms. Doing the right thing was not part of his concern. I hope you understand that what your children demand you accept as part of their lives is no different than what this younger son did. If you cannot see the truth of this analogy, then God help you.

Second, the basis of rebellion is control. As with difficult people, those who rebel want control of their environment and their lives. In extreme cases, they want complete control of other family members, as well. A rebel with a psychotic bent, in regards to control, actually demands that the family comply with his/her demands. These rebels want to call all the shots in the family, not just some of the shots. They become austere in the sense that they are demanding, strict, and authoritarian in their expectations.

The family watches the television programs their rebel-child demands they watch. The family goes to the restaurants their rebel-child demands they go. In fact, the family goes where and when their rebel-child demands they go.

These rebel children actually turn the tables in their families. In essence, the parents become the children and the rebels the parents. You may ask, "How does this happen?" It happens when a child has no qualms of turning a household upside down—plunging it into horrible conflict—in order to get control. I know what you are thinking: "This is sick." Yes, it is, but it's happening to parents all over the world.

o **Wisdom Principle:** *Behavior permitted is behavior perpetuated.*

Third, rebellion is an attitudinal mindset that says: "I refuse to be disciplined". A common denominator of all rebels is the possession of an un-self-disciplined mind, temperament, ego, and life. Consequently, the life of the rebel is out-of-control. As a consequence, a rebel does not know how to solve problems. Instead, they have an adolescent mentality and temperament.

The opposite of living a self-disciplined life is living an emotionally-driven and ego-driven life. There is no question that emotionally-driven individuals are extraordinarily selfish and lazy. They are also very difficult to work, live, and associate with. They are demanding, believing they are entitled to what they want because of their exaggerated self-importance.

Rebels leave a trail of relational debris as they pursue their selfish and self-centered desires. They don't think about what they do, they just follow their "feelings". Instant gratification is the goal, but in this case, it isn't instant enough.

Fourth, rebels have no respect for the things that truly matter in life. The things that ought to matter—character, virtue, meaningfulness, purpose, and the virtuous meaning of sacrifice—don't. The rebel's respect is primarily for the superficial—tangible things, popularity, prosperity, and power. In essence, rebels respect the wrong things.

Everybody respects something. Respect as defined within this context is a special regard/value for a particular "thing". It is believed that achieving or possessing this "thing" will bring all of the benefits it possesses. This can be something worthy of respect or something that is selfish and which simply fulfills the emotional, physical, or psychological desires of an individual.

For instance, a person can respect—value or esteem—partying and/or going to bars in order to find someone to have a "quick" romantic liaison with. I realize that "respect" is an odd word to use, but, in truth, people can respect the wrong things. It never ceases to amaze me how either the constructive or destructive thing people desire in a very serious, if not intense, fashion, frequently comes to pass. Obviously, what attracts individuals is directly related to their priorities, goals, desires, and perceived needs.

If a person is committed to pursuing character-building experiences, he/she won't take no for an answer when in pursuit of that goal. In fact, this individual will let nothing stand in the way of achieving that goal. The same is true of a destructive desire or perceived "need" in a person's life. On numerous occasions, I have seen individuals accomplish what they set out to do, even though this was definitely not within their best interests.

I am convinced that when a person respects and values something, whether constructive or destructive, and desires it badly enough, he/she will achieve it. Therefore, I'm convinced it isn't the achievement of goals, but the setting of goals in general that is the problem.

The prodigal did not respect what money could and could not do. As a result, he wasted his money. I said in an earlier chapter that what you respect will come into your life and what you disrespect will leave your life. Such is a wisdom principle that will hold true time and time again.

o **Wisdom Principle:** *Be careful what you respect and value. No amount of money will be able to "buy back" the regrets of your past.*

Finally, rebellion always leads to suffering. Suffering may not occur right away, but eventually reality will "bite". The Bible implicitly states in Hebrews 11:25b that there is "pleasure in sin, for a season". You can have your "sinful fun" if you want it ... no question of that. However, you must remember that sin not only has a kick, it also has a "kick-back".

> o **Wisdom Principle:** *Rebellion has as an inherent goal, post-poning all legitimate suffering, but in the end, this costs a rebel more suffering than what would have otherwise occurred.*

Remember Essential #6? *The greatest pains in life are self-inflicted.* The prodigal son did not escape the consequences of his immature choices. Neither did David escape the consequences of his sin with Bathsheba, or the other sins that followed because of that first sin. Isn't it remarkable that one sin begets a "cluster" of other sins? Perhaps it's obvious, but I won't escape the consequences of my sins and neither will you. In this parable in Luke 15, we have an extraordinarily vivid picture of the consequences of the prodigal's actions. It's not an attractive picture. All self-centered behavior eventually leads to suffering. There is no exception to this axiom of life.

My admonition to parents is this: Don't let your pride argue for your children's limitations and deficiencies. If you do, you will see your children experience untold suffering as a result of their self-centeredness. One of your assignments as a parent is to be a protector of your children. In many cases this means you must discipline your children, imparting to them needful wisdom, rather than rationalizing their failures and deficiencies. If your children don't listen to you, you can at least live with yourself knowing you gave all you had to protect them from their ignorance and rebellion.

o **Wisdom Principle***: Often, a rebel never knows the true meaning of peace until just before the "final curtain" is drawn.*

2. Nonconformity

A nonconformist is one who does not conform to a generally accepted pattern of thought or action. Pragmatically speaking, a nonconformist is an individualist—one who pursues a markedly independent course of thought and action. There is no question that a nonconformist is a unique individual.

o **Wisdom Principle:** *Nonconformity is primarily soul-driven rather than ego-driven.*

My observations of nonconformists confirm that their attitudes and behavior are consistently on opposite sides of the spectrum from rebellion. Over the years I've made notes regarding nonconformists I've known or am acquainted. Let's take a look at the characteristics of nonconformity.

o **Wisdom Principle:** *While rebels are "noisy" in their rebellion, nonconformists are <u>quiet</u> in their nonconformity.*

First, let's look at a Biblical example of a nonconformist—David, youngest son of Jesse in the Old Testament. One remarkable story about him which reflects his nonconformity, is told in I Samuel, Chapter 17.

David is obediently attending the family's flocks on the hills outside of Bethlehem when his father calls him in. He wants David to take food to his brothers and some cheese to the commander of the armies of Israel. David's brothers were in the army and engaged in battle with the Philistines in the valley of Elah. David's father also wanted him to return with some assurance that his older brothers were fine. David left the next morning, arriving at the Israelite camp just as the armies were going out to take battle positions.

David left the food supplies with the keeper-of-supplies and ran to the battle lines to greet his brothers. While they talked, a Philistine giant named Goliath stepped out into the valley and dared any one of the Israelites to step forward and engage him in hand-to-hand combat.

There was no question that every soldier in the Israeli army was afraid of this 8'9" giant. Even though King Saul had vowed to give any man in his army enormous wealth if he could kill this giant, as well as his daughter in marriage, no man took the king "up on his offer". (Besides fear, another reason for no one taking up the king's offer is that his daughter could have possibly had the "face of an aardvark".)

While all of the armies of Israel were frightened of this giant, we find in verse 26 of this chapter that this teenager named David took exception to this "monster" insulting the armies of the "Living God". David took his faith very seriously and he respected what his faith represented. This is pivotal to the understanding of this section of Chapter 17.

David took a stand against evil. What happened when he did so? Strategies to discourage him were implemented.

His oldest brother Eliab saw David speaking to the soldiers and the scripture says that he "burned with anger". He attacked David, falsely accusing him of three things:

1) David was derelict of his duty—abandoning the few sheep of which he was in charge. Of course, Eliab ignored the fact that David was obeying his father's wishes.

2) David was conceited—Eliab does not say why.

3) David was a wicked person. Again, Eliab does not say why David was a wicked person—what had he done to deserve this accusation?

David did not take his older brother's accusations at face value. Without arguing he simply asked Eliab what he had done, as well as why he could not even speak. David did a very wise thing by walking away from a confrontation with his brother. He had too much respect for himself, as well as his brother, especially in front of others.[12]

The soldiers who overheard David speaking boldly about the Philistine giant were impressed and reported what the young shepherd had said to King Saul. The King sent for David. Upon entering the presence of the king, David said that no one should

---

[12] David is the only young person in the Old Testament who was used of God as mightily as he was. He learned at a young age that he could trust God—that the Heavenly Father was worthy of his complete trust and obedience. As a result, God used David in a marvelous way. There was nothing David could not accomplish when he lived totally committed to God.

The younger a person is when he/she discovers that God can indeed be believed and trusted, the sooner that individual can "jump start" a personal pilgrimage toward spiritual maturity.

lose heart on account of this giant heathen. He told King Saul that he would go out and fight Goliath.

Surprised, King Saul declared that as David was only a boy, he couldn't send him out to battle this giant who had trained to be a warrior from his youth.

David responded by telling Saul of two times when he faced peril fighting for his life. In each instance, David said, God had delivered him.

"This giant heathen has defied the armies of the Living God. Because he has, the same God who delivered me from the jaws of the lion and the paw of the bear, will also protect and guard me from the hand of this heathen giant—this Philistine."

One of the great sentences in the Old Testament is the last part of verse 37. Saul says to David, "Go David, and may the Lord be with you!"

o **Wisdom Principle***: "Godly confidence is reflected in knowing that when God is all you have, he is all you need."*

Saul offered David his own armor and sword, no doubt thinking that David should conform to the way all of his soldiers were dressed and armed. David walked around in the king's battle uni-form, but he wasn't accustomed to it. It was heavy and cumber-some. He blurted out to King Saul, "I can't use this armor or this weapon. I am not used to it nor am I trained to use them." Then, David took his staff, went down to a stream, picked up five smooth stones and put them in his "shepherd's bag". He took out his sling-shot and he confronted Goliath.

Goliath saw David and walked toward him. When he realized David was only a boy, he despised David and became angry and shouted at the Israelites. "What do you think I am? Am I a dog that you treat me with contempt by sending this boy to fight? Are you daring me to fight this child?" Goliath cursed David by his pagan gods and he shouted to David that he would give his flesh to the birds of the air and the beasts of the field. In today's society, we would call this "trash talking."

David was not intimidated. He responded to Goliath by saying,

> "You come against me with your sword, your spear, and your javelin. But I come to you in the name of the Lord God Almighty of the armies of Israel, whom you have insulted and defied. Let me tell you this … this day the Lord God will hand you over to me and I will strike you down and I will cut your head off. Today I am going to give the carcasses of the Philistine army to the birds of the air and the beasts of the earth. The whole world will know that there is a Living God in Israel. Everyone gathered here will know without a doubt that it is not by the means of a sword or a spear that the Lord protects and saves. For the battle belongs to the LORD and He will give you into my hands."

Goodness; what unbelievable courage and confidence. There is no question that this young man—this teenager—was shrouded in the power and protection of the Living God—and, he knew it!

The Bible states that as the giant moved closer to David, that David ran toward the giant to "face up" to him. David reached into his shepherd's bag and pulled out a stone. Then he slingshot the stone, striking Goliath on the forehead. The stone sank into the forehead of the giant, who fell face down on the ground. With only a stone and a slingshot, David struck down this Philistine giant and killed him. As he promised earlier, David took Goliath's sword and cut off his head.

Upon seeing this, the Philistines fled and the armies of Israel chased them down and killed them all. The bodies of the Philistines were scattered for miles on the left and right of the roads which led back to the "Philistine country". David took the head of the heathen giant to Jerusalem for all of the citizens to see.

What a remarkable story! Here was a boy, a teenager, who took on all odds with only his faith and a slingshot. This story teaches many things. The significant point is this: when god is with you, the world is not strong enough to defeat you!

So, what does this story regarding David have to do with non-conformity? A great deal.

First, while self-centeredness is at the core of rebellion, integrity is at the core of nonconformity. Integrity is related to the word integrate, which means to blend into a functioning whole. A person of integrity is not a divided individual, but rather one who is whole. The word holy has a direct connection, to the word wholeness. The character, of a true nonconformist has continuity. When a nonconformist does not go along with the crowd it has nothing to do with the refusal or lack of desire to be co-operative or friendly. It has to do with what is best for that individual's life.

Second, there is quietness to a nonconformist's actions. For the rebel, nothing occurs in his/her life without a tremendous amount of drama and turmoil. In contrast, there isn't a great deal of pomp and circumstance, or drama, in the life of the nonconformist. There isn't a "notice me" persona. A nonconformist possesses a confident *inner-strength*, which rebels do not possess. Key to a nonconformist's quiet temperament is their immunity to the opinions of others, and the pressure brought to bear by their peers to be like everyone else.

Nonconformists are not noisy people but are thoughtful people who possess a "quiet temperament". They consider what they do and why they do it. There is a steadiness about them—a consistency. Quietness is the result of a person being comfortable with their personhood, their clarity of knowledge regarding life in general, the making of decisions, and knowing what is best in the critical contexts of life.

Third, where a rebel has goals that are primarily narcissistic, a nonconformist has goals that are positive and altruistic. Most of all, nonconformists create a plan to reach their goals. They get what they want out of life the old-fashioned way—they work for it. There is no expectation on the part of others to do for them what they can and should do for themselves. Nonconformists do not embrace an entitlement mentality. They do embrace an "I-am-responsible-for-me" mentality.

Fourth, where a rebel is subconsciously committed to control and, if necessary, engaging in conflict to get control, in contrast, a nonconformist is committed to co-operation. Nonconformists are unifiers rather than dividers. They are bridge-builders in contrast to being bridge-destroyers. They are creators of continuity, rather than havoc. They seek to be problem-solvers in contrast to rebels, who are primarily problem-creators.

While rebels would rather be "right", nonconformists are what they are because they want to be happy. They do what they do because it is best for them as well as for those who are part of their lives. And they are often altruistic in attitude and action. Nonconformists are, rarely a burden to others. This is because they are diligent, in their desire and effort to be kind and gracious to family, friends, neighbors, and acquaintances. Therefore, their achievements in life are never at another's expense.

Fifth, unlike the rebel whose life is lived in fear, a nonconformist lives his/her life courageously. For integrity-based nonconformists, conceding to fear is not an option. They know that the more one fears losing, the more one loses. When the "social tide" says to go one way, the nonconformists often go another. Why? Because integrity never takes a day off and truth is a nonconformist's guide to doing what is best.

Sixth, unlike the rebel, who is usually amoral and unspiritual, a true nonconformist is most often respectful regarding matters of faith. Cynicism does not exist when it comes to the spiritual. God is truly real to the nonconformist and when others disrespect the name of God and His character, the nonconformist does not condone it. Taking a stand for what is right, good, and decent is never an option.

Seventh, people marvel, at what nonconformists have achieved in their lives. People do not marvel at the achievements of the rebel; instead, they marvel at a rebel's lack of pragmatic intelligence and wisdom. The true nonconformist has an enormous faith in the goodness and omnipotence of the Heavenly

232

Father. Very often nonconformists do not know how to live without God in their lives. For them to do so is unfathomable. They know that God walks with those who honor His presence and counsel.

David possessed all of these character qualities. He performed feats that a mere man could never do alone. He achieved what he did because he trusted God with all of his heart and being. Acts Chapter 13, verse 22, tells us that David was a man after God's own heart. This is not said of anyone else in Scripture, only David. At a defining moment in his life David decided that God would be the center of all he became and did. We know David failed God on one particular occasion and that this failure was bitter, embarrassing, and unrelentingly painful for him. However, he got up and asked God to forgive him.

Remember when I mentioned, earlier, that Christians aren't perfect but they have terrible remorse when they fail to live up to God's standards? David failed God but he did not stay down. He did what he had to do to make it right with God. The 51st Psalm is an example of David's remorse and repentance. It is a beautiful section of Scripture detailing the process of repentance and how to restore one's intimacy with God. Paradoxically, David wasn't perfect, but he was Godly.

CHAPTER SEVEN
THE FIVE CRITICAL LINES OF LIFE

There have been times in my life when I believed I was an expert on failure. You may not believe it after reading the first six chapters of this book, but nevertheless, I believed that I was. I have failed at many things in my life and I can testify that the greatest pains in life are truly self-inflicted. What I have come to know by God's grace, is that failure may be an event in your life and in mine, but it need not define our lives. We can learn from failure and use it as a corrective mechanism to realign our lives and move in a more positive and effective direction.

Throughout my life, I have experienced some tough realities, and I have seen others experience tough realities as well. I have lived long enough to realize that there are mistakes of no great consequence, and there are mistakes for which some individuals will spend the rest of their lives paying.

I have charted the mistakes I have made and the mistakes of others that I have observed and have come to the conclusion that some mistakes have altered the lives of those who made them— in many cases, permanently. My goal is to melt down all of these

234

painful experiences and put them in a format that will be easy to process and understand.

Bullies existed when I was a child as they do now. A bully would pick a fight with someone smaller and even anemic looking. In this way as bully could always win a fight he started. Bullies use two methods of starting a fight: verbally abusing his or her target, and drawing a line on the ground daring his target to, cross it to prove he or she wasn't a sissy/coward/chicken—whatever metaphor he chose. The understanding was that once the target crossed the line there was no going back, no matter what the bully did.

As I grew older I found this interesting. This was especially true once I began working with youth. Drawing a line and crossing it came to mean much more than it originally had. I discovered that there are lines all through our lives, which, if crossed, will create circumstances that often prevent us from going back to how things were before crossing a particular line.

From my observation, there are five lines in life that are critical as well as pivotal. We must respect these lines and respect what crossing them will mean. If we cross one or more of these lines of life, we will likely never be the same as we were before. We will change, at least, inwardly. More often than not, our lives will change outwardly, as well.

There is no question in my mind that these five critical areas of life must be managed well, because they are strategic to our personal happiness, fulfillment, and effectiveness. If any person mismanages one of more of these areas, getting his or her life back on track will be extremely challenging. In some cases, it could take years to get back on a positive track.

Much of the subject matter I will mention going forward, I have mentioned already briefly in previous chapters. However, for our purposes here, let's take these "lines of life" one at a time.

However, before we do I want to caution you not to look upon this subject matter simplistically. For example, I have heard that if a person puts God first in his or her life, that all of these things will automatically fall into place. This is not necessarily true. Maturity does not automatically come into a sincere heart, where a whole-hearted commitment to God has been made. For example; if a person is out-to-lunch prior to making a Christian commitment, then after making such a commitment that person will not suddenly become smart, responsible, etc. That person will just be a Christian Idiot. Holiness is a process, as well as a present-moment reality when one commits himself/herself to the Heavenly Father. Please keep this in mind when considering these critical five lines of life.

o **Wisdom Principle:** *"Knowledge is a responsibility for the integrity of what we are; primarily of what we are, as ethical creatures."*—Jacob Borowski, Scientist

o **Wisdom Principle:** *We must know what we ought to be in order to be what we ought to be.*

1. The Line of Attitude

Chapter 1 dealt with attitude, but now think of this: if you do not guard the kind of attitude you cultivate, you could easily develop an "entitlement" attitude—one of those bad attitudes we talked about earlier. Once an entitlement attitude is ingrained in a person's life, it is difficult to then switch to a positive and productive life. Bad attitudes are just almost too difficult to change, although not totally impossible. More often than not, changing a bad attitude is the exception rather than the rule.

Although I have known those who have changed a bad attitude into a terrific attitude, there haven't been enough for me to say comfortably, that this is an easy thing to do. I have come to believe that surviving a heart transplant may be easier than changing one's attitude.

o **Wisdom Principle:** *Your attitude determines how you process your experiences, as well as reality.*

One of my favorite people in this world is Jan E. King, Sr., a retired Florida judge. She wrote a book of poetry a few years ago, entitled *If I Could Say More*. In the book, she has one profound statement on a page. That statement is: "I am not responsible; I am entitled." As a judge, I am sure she saw many a guilty person stand before her because of an attitude that projected the personification of this statement. I believe she would say, without hesitation, that an entitlement attitude was the primary contributor, to a person's deviant behavior.

If you are going to have an absolutely terrific attitude, you are going to have to guard your environment, your relationships and the basis of how you make decisions. The attitude or predisposition you bring to life will make or break your life. I am not kidding about this. As critical as attitude is to a successful and meaningful life, why parents as a whole, do not make it a pivotal part of their teachings to their children is absolutely beyond my comprehension. Could it be that a person cannot teach what he/she does not know?

In Chapter One, I cover how to change a bad attitude into a positive attitude. I believe you must clearly understand that it takes enormous self-discipline to stay on track in the development of a terrific attitude. Reread the points I make in the section regarding attitude. Once you get the points down pat and begin to implement them, you will be on your way.

I need to say here, that many times in many ways, a child's parents are the greatest obstacle to his/her developing a terrific attitude. This is true. Parents can contribute negatively to their children's attitudinal development when they justify their children's inadequacies and deficiencies; wait on their children hand and foot; allow their children to believe they are above the norm simply because they, the children, belong to them. Many parents tend to convey to their children, when they meet their every whim and desire, that it is perfectly normal for children to treat parents as their own private valet, maid, or butler—whichever metaphors are appropriate. When I see this kind of behavior by parents—a behavior I believe is detrimental to their children's upbringing—I'm reminded of the verse in Psalm 106, verse 37 that says: *"They sacrificed their sons and daughters unto the "demon idols" of their blindness."*

Children who are treated this way, grow up believing that the people of the world have been put here to wait on them and to acquiesce to meeting their desires and needs. How I use the word "needs" in the previous sentence can be misinterpreted by the spoiled rotten among us. I would hope not, but then such could be too much to ask. After all, miracles rarely happen when you are looking for them. The expectations of spoiled children who want their needs met, have nothing to do with meeting their legitimate needs, but rather with meeting their illegitimate wants.

Children who are excessively accommodated by parents, grandparents, and other family members, come to believe that they are better than others, opening the door for them to develop an arrogant attitude. Going down this road will kill your children's chances of finding happiness in life, as well as finding meaningful and fulfilling relationships. Arrogance is a sure sign of insecurity, ignorance, and having an unrealistic view of one's self. No one wants to be around, be married to, much less develop a relationship with an individual, who thinks that he/she is better than everyone else.

There is no question that arrogant people usually believe that they are better than everyone with whom they associate. Arrogant people are emotional and psychological "blunt instruments". They have virtually no self-awareness. I truly believe this is because of four things: the unrealistic view parents have about who and what their children are; the excessive attention, as well as accommodation, parents and family give these children; the quality of the lifestyle provided to children by their parents; and issues of insecurity.

Regarding this fourth point, eventually, down deep inside, each arrogant child eventually has to realize that they have not earned the lifestyle with which they have been blessed. They also have to realize that they have what they enjoy because of the sacrifices made by their parents. More often than not, they know that their parents probably gave into their selfish demands as well as fulfilled their request(s) at great sacrifice. Feelings of inadequacy subtly creep into the lives of these arrogant and narcissistic children when they realize they have coerced their parents into giving them things their parents really couldn't afford to buy. However, their parents bought these things out of some kind of misplaced love for them.

Candidly, all of us intuitively know that a terrific life is earned. It is not something that automatically happens. When so much is given to someone who, in truth, has done nothing to earn what has been given, insecurity often surfaces within the hearts and minds of the individuals receiving them.

To compensate for these feelings of insecurity the natural compensatory mechanism used by arrogant children is to conduct their lives in a manner that gives others the opposite impression of what these insecure children believe themselves to be. Hence, they project an "I-am-better-than-you" attitude because they know precisely that they are not. Deep within they have chosen to take the "path of least resistance". This step is nothing more than the path of entitlement they have learned, i.e., a superiority complex. This complex is a compensatory mechanism used by such insecure individuals who possess an entitlement attitude. They, therefore, are refusing to cultivate the self-discipline to change such a bad attitude.

As a parent, you must do all you can to give your children an accurate view of reality. You must also resist conveying to your children two things: One, that you get out of life what you want by simply demanding it; and two, when it comes to your worth as an individual, everyone else is less important than you are and you should never associate with others who are "not as good" as you are.

It's tragic when it's conveyed to children that they are better than those "others" and they are the exception to the rule that states they should be treated the same as everyone else.

- o **Wisdom Principle:** *Thinking you are better than others and knowing you are simply better off than others are on opposite sides of the spectrum.*

As much as we want to believe that our children were born "sinless" and that they were born to be "better" than other children, truthfully, they were not. Our children have flaws; they have sinful tendencies. We can thank ourselves as their parents for having the flaws and tendencies that they have. David wrote in the Psalm 51:5: *"In sin did my mother conceive me."* We sin because we are sinners—not the reverse. Our children will make mistakes. They will fail. They will disappoint us, and they will also disappoint themselves.

I heard about a 10th-grade girl who lives in an upper middle-class home, goes to an upper middle-class public high school and from all reports, comes from an above average home environment. This young lady, illogically, decided to take a nationally known cough syrup and mix it with methadone—a prescription narcotic—and make three "shots" of this mixture for friends at school. She took it to school and gave it to three of her friends. Soon her three friends needed emergency assistance. As they were transported to the hospital, two of the girls "flat-lined" and twice, had to be "brought back." The third didn't flat-line and was released from the hospital that evening, but she was brought back to the hospital later that night. The girl had to know she was having a "slow news day" when the best idea she had was to give three friends a "death cocktail" thinking it would provide a "fun experience."

If it could be investigated, it would, more than likely be found, that the parents gave this teenager everything she wanted and more. It will likely also be found that she was treated as though she was "above the rules" as well as "above the law". This tragedy is the byproduct of raising children to believe that life is all about them.

As you can see, there's no question that parents can be the greatest obstacles to their children's attitudinal development. Parents don't do their children any favors by treating them as though they are above their peers and that they have "God-given privileges" that others do not. Parents also need to stop living their lives vicariously through their children. Parents must be careful not to convey to their children that what negatives they as parents experienced as teenagers can be rectified by and through their children's lives. This is not only unfair to the children, but tragically childish on the part of parents! Yes, the line of attitude is critical. Guard it. Don't cross to the other side without knowing the price you will pay for doing so. That "price paid" will be a life of mediocrity, frustration, disappointment, and disillusionment.

2. The Line of Decision-Making—How You Make Decisions

The second critical line is decision-making. This is the line that reveals true intelligence. There is a correct way of making decisions and a wrong way. The right way is to make decisions based on facts and truth. The wrong way is to make decisions based on emotion—specifically, on how one feels at the time the decision is being made.

We live in a world that essentially has put its brains where its emotions reside instead of relying on facts and truth for help. How we got to such a place is not difficult to understand. Those who struggle with the day-to-day challenges of life are the ones who are the most vulnerable to being led by their egos and "feelings". If one is persistently and consistently led by emotion in decision-making, that person can become vulnerable to depression. Most stay in a place of "emotional turmoil" because they are neither efficiently nor effectively grounded in wisdom.

You would think reasonable people would see the foolishness of being led by "emotional impressions" especially after witnessing what happens in the lives of those who make emotionally-driven decisions. The consequences almost always end up on the opposite side of what was intended and expected. This occurs time and again where emotions and feelings, driven by the ego, are allowed to rule.

- o **Wisdom Principle:** *Emotions are nothing less than signs/signals that communicate to each of us how we have perceived our experiences.*

- o **Wisdom Principle:** *Where the Bible encourages us to use its message as a guideline for decision-making, the ego encourages decision-making based on emotional desire.*

- o **Wisdom Principle:** *Emotion is the vehicle for the ego's expression of its "rights".*

o **Wisdom Principle:** *All decisions which are based on emotion are ego-driven.*

Without foundational principles, we find ourselves in the dark and are confused regarding what to do in any given set of circumstances. Most decide what to do, at any given moment, by how and what they "feel". Cross this line of making decisions based on how you "feel" and you could end up paying the rest of your life for these emotionally-driven decisions. Living your life in the throes of the highs and lows of emotions and feelings, is a sure sign that you are headed for an inconsistent life filled with regret.[13]

I have spoken in this book about the role of emotion in each of our lives. I have stated that perhaps 80% of the world makes decisions based on how it "feels" in most life-contexts. Now I'll add that making decisions based on feelings is often a subconscious compliance. We grow up in homes where the authority figures in our lives made decisions based on feelings and emotions. Such being true, we likely heard statements like:

➢ What does your "heart" (ego) tell you to do?

➢ He (she) makes me feel special?

➢ How do you feel about it?

---

[13] In education, specifically, in the arena in which how people learn is studied, it is understood that there are large numbers of people who are better at learning concepts and knowledge when they are emotionally stirred. I don't doubt such is the case. However, upon observing those who are "emotive" in their learning style, I have found that such individuals are poor at learning and retaining factual information, as well as being able to maintain an unbroken focus when required.

> ➤ Just go with how you feel.
> ➤ What do your feelings tell you?
> ➤ Well, I just feel that this is the best thing to do.
> ➤ I feel like he/she is the one.
> ➤ You have to go with what you feel is right.
> ➤ I just feel that when I meet the right person for me, I will just know it.

All of us have heard these or like phrases used in the context of decision making or simply in counseling a person in what ought to be done. All of these phrases lead one to believe that going with what one is "feeling," is perfectly normal and natural. Such is true when you live in the land of mediocrity and doing what everyone else does. If the majority of the world "thinks" with their feelings and makes decisions based on feelings, this can become a catastrophic problem.

The purpose of feelings is to alert you to areas of life in which your emotions may run strong. Feelings are the reactions of our ego to life experiences. For example, "hot buttons" very often are nothing more than 80% emotion and 20% logic. Hot buttons are areas of life about which we have forceful emotional conviction and to which we react with strongly when pushed.

Areas of our lives that are very sensitive are usually the sources of our hot buttons. However, most people don't recognize that the purpose of emotion is to be a messenger simply telling us how we feel about certain experiences and matters of life. Instead, most people see emotions as message transmitters helping us in the making of decisions. This is absolutely untrue.

o **Wisdom Principle:** *Feelings are transitional. The consequences of acting on them are not.*

You must choose how you are going to decide what is best for you. The making of decisions or choices never takes a day off in our lives. We are constantly evaluating, thinking, pondering, and finally deciding what to do. There are many defining moments, too. One of these is what will be the criteria you will use in deciding what to do in all given circumstances requiring you to make a decision. Consider these points:

The Bible states in I John 4:1 *"Beloved, don't believe everything you hear or embrace every idea presented. However, I encourage you to put what is told or presented to you to the test. Put it through the "truth sifter" in your brain to see whether the information given to you correlates to the principles and teachings of Christ."*

Therefore, the first thing we must do is know the Bible, because it is in this knowledge that we have the necessary weapons to combat evil deception, deception by others, as well as self-deception.

Make no mistake about it. You will consistently encounter people in your life who will have no problem asking you to betray yourself in order to "get along" with them, as well as to be part of their lives. You will be confronted with enormous challenges in your relationships to "go along" in order to "get along". My admonition to you is not to buy into such pressure. If you do, you will end up being disappointed in yourself for doing so. Relationships that consistently or occasionally require you to betray yourself will never give you the payoff you expect in exchange for your self-betrayal. And, as you will come to find out as you become more enlightened, there is no amount of money that can buy back your regrets.

We make decisions every day. In fact, I do not believe I have ever had a day that I did not need to make a decision about something. As much decision-making as an individual consistently does in his/her daily life, you would think some hard criteria would have been given to all of us regarding how good, solid, and wise decisions are made. However, such criteria are rarely, if ever, shared. Why? It is simply because most are not familiar with the criteria that are necessary to make such solid and wise decisions. Therefore, here are some points for your consideration.

One: Be knowledgeable about what the Bible teaches. Sounds uncool to many people, but it is not. There are marvelous stories in the Bible about people, the decisions they made, and how those decisions turned out. We can learn an enormous amount about good decision-making from these stories.

Also, within this wonderful book, there are principles of virtue presented to us that form the foundation of how decisions ought to be made. There is a correlation between the lack of knowledge one may have in how to make good decisions, and one having a lack of effective wisdom, which the Bible provides.

For example, let's look at II Peter 1:5-9:

"There is a reason for applying true diligence and self-discipline in the development of your faith. By developing your faith, you strengthen your life. You do this through the development of moral excellence, which is nothing less than elegant virtue.

Your moral excellence will open the door for you to embrace knowledge that will help you make good solid decisions.

"This virtue-based knowledge will give you the power to develop self-control over your ego and your selfish desires and wants. Self-control gives rise to self-discipline, which in turn develops a godly tenacity and perseverance. Such virtue-based discipline cannot help but produce godliness, which in turn makes you whole. This godliness produces a brotherly loving-kindness, which is nothing less than being kind in a warm and affectionate way.

"These qualities become the personification of who you are and, properly nurtured day-in and day-out through self-discipline, and, in turn, increase the effectiveness and quality of the person you are becoming. As a result, you are neither useless nor unproductive in what you are doing with the true knowledge of Christ our Lord. You have developed praxis. In contrast, those who lack these qualities are blind as well as short-sighted. Obviously, such people have forgotten their purification from their sins committed prior to being redeemed. Such individuals have become mediocre and have become an albatross to the Christian faith. They create doubt in the minds of unbelievers regarding the truthfulness and power of the Christian message."

This scripture personifies what I call the Responsibility Gospel of Christ our Lord. Devotion and holiness are not accidents. They are the result of a person committed to a virtuous and self-disciplined life that is immersed in the giving and sharing of loving-kindness with others. Christianity is worthless unless it translates into being a bridge-builder to others and an encouraging element in the lives of people. Such is difficult to do when individuals are un-self-disciplined, have an absence of scriptural knowledge, and refuse to accept responsibility for their own lives. Contrary to the ethereal among us, the fully-functioning life is not a series of emotional experiences, an accident, or a matter of being lucky. It is the direct result of a person being self-respecting, self-disciplined, possessing a healthy self-love, and living a virtue-based life.

Professing Christians who make decisions based on ethereal visions or primarily emotionally-driven dreams or perceptions, are an <u>affront</u> to the Responsibility-Driven Gospel preached by Jesus Christ, and which is also strongly emphasized in the *Epistle of James*. There is no question in my mind that there has been too much silence in the churches of our country regarding the abuse of the use of impressions, emotions, "feelings", or visions/dreams, and using such experiences as a basis of knowing what God's will is for each of us. This isn't only, scripturally-speaking, unintelligent, it is downright dangerous.

Feelings-driven Christians are an embarrassment to the church as well as to themselves. They project Christianity as primarily based on impressions, feelings, visions and dreams. This kind of Christianity is the laziest kind of religious faith because it is nebulous in how it should consistently function. Such an expression of one's faith becomes an "it-depends-on-the-day-and-how-I-feel" kind of Christianity, instead of what is scriptural, faith-tested, and faith-based. It also lacks integrity and character.

It takes hard work to delve into the Bible and learn the guidelines and principles by which we are to be led as well as by which we are to live. I have stated, on numerous occasions when I am teaching the fully-functioning life, that God will never answer any prayer that He has already answered in Scripture. You may ask why not? Because a person who claims to be a Christian and does not know what the Bible teaches about a particular concern, dilemma, or problem with which they are confronted, has more to do with willful ignorance, rather than whether God is listening to your prayers.

If God has provided us a Bible, which in turn has a wealth of information about life, living, and the answers to the common problems with which we are all confronted, why would He take time to answer a prayer He has already answered in Scripture? He won't. The problem is not God refusing to answer your prayer. It is your refusal to discipline yourself and learn the knowledge and wisdom for life and living provided to all of us in the Scripture.

I am truly convicted that the reason we have so many Christians relying on feelings and impressions to lead them in their spiritual endeavors is because they do not have the spiritual or intellectual discipline to sit down, be quiet, study the Bible, and let God speak to their hearts. As a result, they talk about what they think or hope the Bible says rather than knowing what it says. After a while, such Christians get so used to living on an emotional-treadmill or an ethereal edge, that they actually convince themselves that they are right simply because it feels right. Also, from their perspective, anyone who speaks out against this so-called style as being an invalid or immature way of expressing one's Christian faith, is seen as someone, who is not in touch with the "spirit"—whatever that means—or just isn't as spiritual as they are.

Give me a break, folks! What these so-called Christians are really saying is that they are too lazy to do the work required to be truly and scripturally spiritual, as well as not having a problem being emotionally-driven. Such Christians, without any biblically-based reason, arbitrarily choose to believe that their decisions must feel right in order to be valid. Such "Christians" are way off the pragmatic radar screen. Also, such "Christians" would rather rationalize their laziness by living on an ethereal-edge and, as a result, living an emotionally-driven life.

Solid decision-making is based on Biblical Principles, virtue, and what is truly true. If the way you make decisions does not have, at its core, virtue and truth, then your decision-making is flawed at its core. Making decisions based on how you feel or what your emotionally-driven friends have advised, in contrast to what the Bible teaches, will result in your life being defined by mediocrity. You will live your life on doing the minimum, while expecting the maximum payoff. All I can say is good luck, because you are in for a tough life and a very rough voyage.

Two: Be a lover of truth. I know it's scary to be this way. The reason why is that we may not like what we find when we are truth-seekers of the highest order. However, the more committed you are to being a seeker and lover of truth, the more courageous you will become. Eventually, fear will cease to affect your pursuit of the truth and you will gladly and willingly embrace being a truth-seeker.

In John 14:6, Christ said: *"I am the only way to heaven, the basis of all truth and the personification of what a life ought to be. No one will stand in the presence of the Heavenly Father unless he/she goes through me, that is, has my 'stamp of approval.'"* Our path to being a truth-seeker of the highest order begins at the feet of the One who is the embodiment of truth—Jesus.

Three: Never rationalize your flaws and failures. Never compare yourself to the mediocre among us. If you do, you will always be tempted to feel good about yourself. Your main goal in life should never be to always feel good about yourself. Possessing such a mindset is to live on the proverbial edge of a cliff called Evil. I am convicted that rationalization of one's flaws and failures is to flirt with the possibility of compromising our relationship with Christ. Such is nothing less than spiritual adultery. Always compare yourself to Christ. Are you as good as Jesus? If not, then you and I have some work to do. A shortcut to a dynamic spiritual life does not exist. It takes bold, hard-core commitment. It is a long process to become like Christ but it is worth all we are, as well as all we have.

Four: Analyze why you feel the way you do when you sense a particular emotion seeking to overpower your will, break you down, and get you to capitulate. Feelings are based on something. It could be guilt, anger, fear, bitterness, regret, embarrassment, failure, or most likely, an entitlement attitude. Ask yourself if the particular feeling you are experiencing is trying to get you to do something noble and altruistic. Will it bring you closer in your relationship with Christ? Or is it trying to get you to fulfill an unhealthy, selfish desire? Remember, feelings based on desire are often self-centered. Also, sometimes feelings are neither wrong nor right. They simply are. However, when all is said and done, it is what you do with your feelings that determines if such feelings are moving you toward being better or mediocre.

o **Wisdom Principle:** *Any feeling that, if embraced, will hinder our devotion to God, our integrity with God, our worship of God, and is contradictory to Scripture will never be within our best interests.*

Also, is this feeling, one which affirms biblical principles? Overwhelmingly, feelings do not have a biblical basis. For example, when we read the events surrounding the temptation of Eve in Genesis Chapter 3, we realize that the emotion created by appealing to the ego—what is commonly called pride—was the main reason Eve broke down and fell for the temptation presented by Satan masquerading as a serpent. Eve's feelings were primarily ego-driven, rather than godly-based.

Five: Regarding this point: If you follow the emotional impulse that is trying to get you in its talons, will you truly be a better person as a result of giving in to it? Candidly, asking this question ought to clear up any confusion quickly. Emotionally-driven individuals, when faced with desires that are altruistically questionable, usually become confused as to what to do. A person who is primarily emotionally-driven will experience their desires pulling hard and their nobility pulling only a little when making a decision. Desire very often gets the better of nobility when a decision is postponed and the temptation "flirts". When looking at this objectively, is this what you want—for desire to win at the expense of your integrity? I don't think so. Emotion can confuse and where confusion abounds, complexity is right around the corner. Virtuous choices are easy to make when you decide to do what is right with conviction. The longer you wait to make a decision, the more you are guilty of flirting with temptation. Dr. David Grant, my former and beloved pastor, called this the sin of "spiritual adultery."

I know there are people who will be "egging you on" to go with them and do what they want to do. However, you must realize that going with the group is to be just like everyone else. Your value will always be in your godly difference!

I have heard all of the reasons given for a person not living a virtuous life. It has been said that living a virtuous/Christian life is old-fashioned, boring, unexciting, and lonely, because it ostracizes "normal" people. All of these declarations are clearly deceiving. They are huge misconceptions. The gospel of Christ does not embrace a second-class lifestyle. However, I want to accept the challenge and answer these time-worn declarations one at a time.

When people say that living the Christian life is simply old-fashioned, they mean it is out of style—no longer relevant. But it's not old-fashioned to live virtuously. Such a life is free from guilt and regret.

For those who believe that living virtuously is boring, it should be pointed out that the only way to live, if one does not choose to live virtuously, is to live selfishly. The lack of guilt and regret that one experiences living a virtuous life, results in a peaceful heart, peaceful sleep, and a peaceful life.

When individuals are consistently involved in activities, which they consider exciting but benign, such benign activities would be considered the antithesis of virtuous living by any reasonable person. Those involved in such activities are rationalizing their actions rather than admitting the truth about their true motivation. If I could speak to a large group of individuals who were guilty of such rationalization, I would say without apology that it is the self-disciplined among us who make it possible for all of us to enjoy the freedoms we enjoy in America. When those who are consistently guilty of rationalizing selfish and ego-driven behavior declare that true freedom is being able to do whatever one wants to do, whenever he/she wants to do it, they have no comprehension of the meaning of either self-discipline or responsibility. No! Being virtuous is much more responsible and considerate of others, than the rationalization of such selfishness.

Virtuous living may not have the drama that going with your feelings does, but it does give a virtuous person a complete sense of competence, confidence, and peacefulness. As a result, you never have to fear the consequences of what you have not done when you refuse to go along with the crowd or the clique. Overwhelmingly, going along with the crowd will never be in your best interest when it comes to protecting personal integrity, maintaining your virtue, and preserving your relationships with others and with the Heavenly Father.

o **Wisdom Principle:** *Growth, in godly discipline, competence, and righteous dignity, is the most exciting journey in one's life, because God only abides in the lives of those who love Him and embrace His principles.*

What about the Christian life lacking excitement? It doesn't, but it does lack self-centered drama—what secular-humanists call excitement. The excitement that the world covets is nothing less than narcissism—looking out for number one. Also, excitement is purely emotional. If you take the emotion out of excitement you don't have excitement. One may ask: "Are you saying that it is wrong to get excited about life and certain positive experiences in life?" No, I'm not.

What I am saying is that excitement, or drama, in one's life can be addictive, as well as deceiving. God doesn't work with us primarily through emotion, but by what is true. Doing the right thing at the right time is worth getting excited about. Ninety-five percent of the time people get excited about doing the selfish thing, which is wrong. Today we see people get excited about fulfilling selfish desires and illegitimate wants. It is rare that I see individuals getting excited about doing the right thing. Why don't people get excited about doing the right thing? Because more often than not, this goes against what their ego desires. The ego cares about one thing ... getting what it wants, when it wants it.

o **Wisdom Principle:** *Godly excitement always comes at the conclusion of doing what is right. Ungodly excitement always comes at the beginning of a temptation that is seeking to have one do what is selfish.*

What about the Christian life being lonely? As a Christian, you may find yourself alone on occasions, but when you are in fellowship/in touch with God you are never lonely. Do you remember when I mentioned that loneliness is not a lack of companionship or the sharing of affection, but rather not having a passionate purpose? Once you understand this, you come to realize just how insecure a person is when a sense of purpose is absent from life.

Just remember, God is with us when we are alone. In Revelation 3:20, Jesus says: *"Pay attention, I am standing at your door and I am knocking. If you hear my voice and open the door to your heart, I will come to your side and be there to listen and to fellowship."* Christ nurtures our hearts and souls in positive and wholesome ways. The world nurtures a person's un-self-disciplined and selfish ways. The four key questions you should ask yourself, before you make a decision, are clear and simple:

1) Does it make sense? In other words, is it spiritually logical?
2) Is the decision virtuous at its core? Is the character of Christ reflected in the decision under consideration?
3) Does it contribute to helping you become the best you can be?
4) Does someone besides you benefit from the decision, which is under consideration?

When and if, you consider these questions, I think you will find your path to making decisions much clearer. Doubting about doing what is best for you will vanish. Emotion has a role in how we relate to others, but virtue and godly purpose will always trump the importance of emotion/how one feels, in any given context.

o **Wisdom Principle:** *Each time you give in to your narcissistic desires, you will ultimately experience disillusionment. Eventually, narcissism will leave you with self-loathing.*

3. The Line of Professional Endeavors

There are too many people in this world getting up every single day to go to work at a job they positively hate. I don't know how many times I've heard, over the course of my life, people complaining about their work—what they do for a living—as well as about the challenges they must wrestle with while doing so. Doing work, which you don't like ultimately has a cumulative negative impact on your life.

If we listen to the media, we will definitely get the impression that if we are not on radio or television, being in front of a camera and talking to people about the critical whatever(s) of life, then we are just not part of the cool crowd and we are not doing what we ought to be doing. Implicit in these messages is that we can't possibly be happy unless we are a part what is happening—reporting, being one of those special people who are being interviewed/talked about or simply obsessed with what those in the media say about such individuals. The reality is that those who are involved in such highly visible endeavors have just as many problems as those who are not part of such professions. Such a simple truth seems to just simply go right over the heads of those in the media as well as those who avidly covet being part of this whole "media thing".

Some of you may be shocked at what I am going to share now from Rick Warren's book. He said that God is not nearly as interested in what we do for a living as He is in our fulfilling the purpose for which He created us, the development of our character, and the development of our soul. I mostly agree with this and at the same time find this statement somewhat incomplete.

My reason is that I strongly believe our professional endeavors can positively contribute to the development of our character and our soul. We can serve others through the financial rewards of what we do professionally. Anyone who does not believe this has never been part of a church budget campaign. I also believe that our professional efforts can contribute positively to the lives of family, friends, and acquaintances for the same reason. They can provide meaning and temporal fulfillment in our lives by our doing them extremely well, while contributing to the well-being of others. I refuse to make light of the choices we make concerning our professional goals. I see too much misery in the lives of people when it comes to the choices made regarding their professional achievements to believe that this line of life does not or cannot contribute to our happiness and fulfillment. I believe it is critical that it does.

In the Epistle of I Timothy 5:8 says: *"All authority figures in the home have a responsibility to provide as best they can for their loved ones and families. The failure to do so is to become a living* denier of the faith *and to be guilty of having an unbeliever's attitude."*

This verse states that there is an inherent responsibility, which adults in a family, whether immediate or extended, have toward those who are vulnerable, sick, or in need. We have the responsibility to specifically be providers and protectors of these precious people. The ability to provide for and protect these individuals is only possible by having a strong economic base that is made possible by one's professional efforts.

First: I believe that everyone has a song in their hearts, regarding what they want to spend their life doing. This song, as Dr. Wayne Dyer has justifiably called it, is also part of our pilgrimage in finding our mission in life. I am convicted that this song begins to whisper its melody in our hearts by the time we turn 17. I have known of individuals who began to listen to this song when they were much younger. It depends strictly on the individual and how cognizant he/she is in recognizing what their heart/soul is communicating.

Second: I believe this song works in concert with the passion each of us has in our life. As we mature, we learn that the passions of our youth, which specifically contributed to a sense of fulfillment during our adolescent years, begin to fade in importance. Such adolescent passions or interests often fade in direct proportion to the gradual disappearance of those peer influences, which contributed to our decisions to become involved in the activities that we were a part of as teenagers. However, the more intense heart-felt passions in our lives will remain strong. Often it is these passions that are key in leading us to what we decide to do professionally.

o **Wisdom Principle:** *Those who love what they do professionally are better at what they do than those who don't.*

o **Wisdom Principle:** *Your "mission in life" is closely related to what unlocks your passion and compassion.*

Third: I believe the role of parents regarding this particular aim, is to help their children cultivate those areas about which they are passionate, and assist them in determining how they can earn a living doing what gives them a sense of fulfillment

and meaning. It is appropriate for parents to let their children know that the cost of what it takes to succeed in what they are passionate about, ought not be their primary concern once they know what it is they truly want to do with their lives professionally.

Fourth: Remember that it is not unusual for someone to wind up doing professionally what he/she did not study for in college. For example, many people have studied to be college teachers only to discover themselves working in corporate America. I have known a few people in my life who graduated from law school but did not stay in the law profession. I personally know of a building contractor who graduated from University of Houston Law School. He did not enjoy being an attorney and decided to leave that profession. There are probably many others who studied law only to end up doing something else. However, their background in law became strategically important in what they did. Their law background gave them a greater dimension of contribution to the professional venture in which they became involved. Such can be said of any kind of education. Higher education can at least indirectly help us in professional careers, which are not closely tied to what was studied.

When all is said and done, a person ought to be settled in what he/she wants to do professionally in life by age 35. To be over 40 and still undecided about what to do with your life has to be frustrating and disappointing. It is also a sign that a person has either not disciplined himself/herself to make a decision about this important area of life, or he/she simply did not have the knowledge to be able to make such a decision.

Either way, people's professional endeavors are a critical line of life that must not lend itself to confusion and frustration over the long term. There will not only be confusion, frustration, and disappointment to those who are still undecided about their professional lives past age 35, but economic turmoil will be part of their lives as well, if this line of life remains nebulous and confusing.

Let's face it, what most people do is odd-jobs while in high school and then, very often while in college, become involved in part-time work to help pay their bills. The majority of college students have to contribute to their expenses in order to go to college. Young adults who go to college on Mom and Dad's tab are by far the exception.

Just before a college student graduates, if his/her major is not *task-specific*—like marketing or business—it is going to be easy for him/her to fall into the trap of staying with the company where he/she worked part-time while getting an education. Right about the time the student graduates, the boss asks, "Why don't you consider staying with us after graduation? We can give you management training and slot you into our management program." Very often, such a temptation is hard to resist, especially if you are well-liked, there.

Another scenario is the possibility of a family member or friend recommending a company with which they are currently employed. They may open a conversation by telling the college-graduate-to-be that the company is currently hiring. Such a family member or close friend will encourage the student to apply for a position and tout the great health benefits, retirement program, continuing education program, and the opportunity for advancement. Again, such a temptation may be too good to pass up.

As suggested, the college-graduate-to-be goes down and applies for a position and unsurprisingly is hired. The student is single, often moves back home after graduation and enjoys free room and board, while working at what was considered a terrific position to begin a professional career.

In the beginning, the money is okay, primarily because the traditional expenses that most people have to maintain—a home, insurance, utility bills and other life-expenses—are taken care of by proud parents. The full impact of not having to pay such expenses, more often than not, goes "right over the head" of the graduate. Very often, reality will not hit the young adult until he/she decides to permanently and intentionally alter his/her life.

This occurs when love and marriage enter the picture. All of a sudden, the new couple is confronted with the purchase of a home, as well as paying other bills associated with "couple hood". Such new expenses start to eat into salary and savings and all of a sudden, the job that was terrific in the beginning no longer pays the bills. Sacrifices must be made such as cutting into pleasures and activities that are enjoyed by both and are also perceived as a must-have for life.

All of a sudden, the enjoyment of the job is not there and the focus is more on the dissatisfaction of their monetary compensation, instead of the focus being on how he/she can increase their service and contribution to the company as well as to the customers of the company for which he/she works.

This scenario is replicated, more often than not, in the lives of millions of young adults across our land. It is nothing less than a terrible tragedy. Therefore, I must say to each of you, "Please don't do this to yourselves." When it comes to your professional achievements, don't be careless in deciding what you choose to do. Don't reach 50 before you find your true calling. Robbing yourself of professional joy is tantamount to robbing yourself of years of enjoying life, while having to give large segments of time, to an unpleasant job. Over your life, you will give more time to your professional endeavors than you will to any other single under-taking. Making a mistake with this line is a regret you won't easily be able to overcome.

I recommend you listen to your heart. Specifically, listen to the Spirit of God, in regards to what you will do professionally in your life. Focus on your passions and what also unlocks your compassion.

First, in your professional career, be aware that excellence in how you perform will be a reflection of your relationship to God. I am convicted that you will have God's guidance in your life when it comes to this critical line of life. I don't believe God wants you to leave this choice to chance. He wants to help you with this important decision. You should allow Him to do so.

Second, ask yourself if the profession under consideration will help you become the best person you can possibly be, both for yourself and for others. To be truly successful in life, your focus ought to be to excel at becoming the best you can be rather than focusing on just how great your financial compensation is. For most, making a great deal of money at what they do profession-ally is all that matters. However, such individuals often lose when it comes to the cultivation of a terrific character and learning to live a life of virtue.

I asked above if you, as well as others, be better off as a result of the choice you make for a professional career. Will it provide opportunities down the road for you to increase giving to needed ministries in the world and especially to the community in which you live? Will it help bring you and your family closer, rather than propel you farther apart? Putting it more succinctly, will your professional life cause you to be away from your family for extremely large segments of time, to the point that the closeness of your family, one to another, is negatively affected?

Professional achievements can be used by God to help you in the completion of your Godly assignment, as well as in fulfilling the purpose for which God created you. Make this line of life a serious matter. Your professional endeavor can be a terrific servant in the fulfillment of God's purpose for your life. However, it can also be a horrible master if you make the wrong choice.

4. Money—Your Attitude Toward It & the Role It Has in Your Life

A person's management and use of money is an absolutely critical line of life. There is no question that money has been a subject of controversy throughout the history of the protestant church in America. I Timothy 6:9-10 says:

> *"There exist people who want to get rich so badly, that the end of getting rich justifies the means used to do so. Such a lust for wealth becomes an irresistible temptation to such people, and this temptation traps them into considering many foolish and harmful strategies that appeal to their egocentric desires. In the end, succumbing to such desires brings life-destructive forces upon their lives, which*

inevitably lead to personal ruin. The reason, for their destruction is their lust and love for money.

"Loving wealth for wealth's sake is the root of all kinds of evil. Many people have longed for wealth, thinking that having it solves all problems. It doesn't. Such a lust for wealth will lead to a person's wandering away from the faith, which they have always known to be tried and true. Ultimately, the tragedies that befall those whose lust for wealth has compromised their faith and character, are tragedies that have all been self-inflicted and have become ultimately regretful for the rest of their lives."

And from Ecclesiastes 5:1: *"The individual, who obsessively desires money, shall never be satisfied with money in and of itself, because money cannot bring happiness and fulfillment. Also, the person who passionately desires the abundance of things and any tangible wealth that such things bring, will realize the very same thing. Loving money because of choosing to believe the fallacy that it can bring happiness, meaning, and fulfillment to one's life, is self-centered and foolish."*

Again, in Ecclesiastes 10:19: *"There are individuals who live for three things: enjoying an extravagant meal; drinking wine till all inhibitions are gone and lascivious merriment is experienced, as well as enjoyed; living and working for money because it is believed that money is the answer to everything."*

Amos 2:6 describes Israel being punished by God because the inhabitants sold the righteous among them for money. There is no question that the times when money is mentioned in the Bible have not been complementary of its effect on people. People seem to have an inherent weakness for money. And, in most cases, will unfortunately do just about anything to have it. There is no doubt that Christians have picked up on this negative view of money from the Scripture, and as a result, have, in turn, taught in churches throughout the world that money is unimportant, as well as bad.

Obviously, at this point, what is needed is a more thorough analysis of the subject of money. On one particular occasion, Jesus instructed one of His disciples to go and catch a fish (Matthew 17:27). He further instructed the disciple that the fish would have a gold nugget in its mouth. The disciple was to extract this gold nugget and take it to the tax collector so that the taxes for Jesus and the disciples could be paid. I am fascinated that Jesus gave this disciple some very pragmatic, as well as specific, instructions for the resolution of this dilemma. Christ took specific action to resolve an issue in a specific area in which money was the only thing that would work. But this illustration is either ignored or glossed over by many Christians.

The last scriptural illustration I want to use is the story of the *"Widow's Mite,"* in Luke 21:3 & 4. Christ was in the synagogue observing well-to-do people walking by and putting offerings in the treasury. He also noticed a poor widow putting in two small copper coins. His response to this dramatic contrast of giving is in the fourth verse:

> *"The rich have put into the treasury what they could easily afford to give. However, this poor widow did not give from her wealth but rather from her poverty. She gave all she had. I want you to listen; this widow gave more than any of those who were rich because she gave from her lack and the rich gave from their abundance."*

Here is what we find in the Bible. We find that money is not only important but that money can be used for many purposes— many of them good and decent purposes. Therefore, money is not inherently evil, or bad, but also, it is not unimportant. Quite frankly, money is vitally important! Read closely what I have learned about money: "Nothing can take the place of money in the arena in which money works and where it is the only thing that will work."

If you recall, it was a rich man who provided the tomb in which Jesus could be buried after He died on the cross. That man was named Joseph of Arimathea, also a disciple of Christ—specifically, a *secret* disciple of Christ (Luke 23:50-55). Also, in all of the transactions described in the Bible that involved the selling or purchasing of land; it was money or something else of equal intrinsic value, which was used in order for the sale or purchase to be completed.

In Matthew 6:24, Jesus stated: *"No individual can have two equal allegiances. That person will either love one or loathe the other. He will hold fast to one and completely despise the other. A person cannot put God and money on the same throne. Eventually one must take precedence over the other."* Christ is stating a psycho-spiritual truth. You cannot serve, as it says in the Bible, "two masters". One must eventually take preeminence, over our lives.

Traditionally, there have been three things that have, in place of God, vied for first place in the lives of people. These are selfishness, materialism (which includes money), and the fulfillment of sensual desires. All three vulnerabilities fall under the umbrella of ego. Humans have a natural tendency to covet these things in their lives because it gives them a sense of self-importance, which, in turn, feeds the ego. Also, such things foster a belief that the pursuit of these obsessions, are equally significant in the eyes of others. While such beliefs may be true to the majority of the people in the world, truthfully, they are shallow and obviously flawed.

There is no question that you can have a healthy respect for what money can and cannot do, as well as possess the discipline to handle money and use it for God's glory. However, we won't be able to accumulate money and use it for altruistic and godly purposes if we don't respect it … especially in what it can and can't do. Notice I did not say love it; I said respect it. Money, like anything else in life that is temporal in nature, makes a terrific servant. However, it also makes a lousy master.

Money is like our health. We are concerned about it, until we do not have it. The only people, as a rule, who do not worry about having enough money, are those who have enough. Money is important to any reasonable person living in a civilized society. So, let's talk about money.

The best place to start is the proverbial question: "What is money?" Simply answered, money is the reward we receive for the effort each of us gives. If you were a farmer, you could understand this when I say that money is the harvest of our production. Many people miss this point.

o   **Wisdom Principle:** *Money is an effect, not a cause.*

Think about this: there are only five things you can do with money. You can spend it; pay taxes; invest it; save it; and finally, you can give it away. Let's look at each of these.

Most people do not have a problem spending money. Spending money is an American pastime based on the amount of credit-card debt we are told we have in our nation. Paying taxes is not really that big of a problem since 98% of working Americans have their taxes taken out of their paychecks before they get what is left. Investing money is a long-term project. Putting money into a diversified portfolio is a life-long project.

It is recommended that 5% of what we make should be placed in long-term investments. Emergencies are a key reason we should put money in an easily accessed account. One of the areas of which the Bible speaks regarding benevolence is the caring for orphans and widows. In more modern terms, this means taking care of the basic needs of those who aren't able or don't have the means to do so themselves. In this context, money is, metaphorically speaking, God in circulation.

Also, when it comes to money, I am surprised that so many people complain about what they make and refuse to knock themselves out for the pay they currently make. However, what every single person who embraces this attitude fails to realize is that unless he/she is willing to extend himself/herself, and provide a greater service than for which he/she is getting paid, the opportunity to make more money will likely never occur. It is simply the law of cause and effect. What I don't want you to miss here is that *the cause*, occurs, *before the effect*. You must give greater service to the company for which you work (cause), before you will get paid more for your service (effect). Remember, you always pay the price for success in advance.

Money is also a tool which keeps our economy going. Once we earn money, we can, in turn, use it to purchase the products and services we need from others. More often than not, the quality of what we do can be measured by the amount of money we get, for what we do.

I have heard Christians say that money doesn't bring happiness. Yes, that is true. However, money has aided in bringing more happiness into the lives of people than poverty ever will, even though such happiness, at times, may be temporal. Realistically, money pays for a warm house in the cold of winter. It pays for the food we eat, the clothes we wear, birthday and Christmas presents, vacations, a college education and a means to help those in need. As Earl Nightingale has said, in his speaking engagements, *"Money is important, because it is the only reward for the effort we make, which is completely negotiable and can also be used by anyone and everyone."*

I have always been fascinated in what others are paid in correlation to what they do. I am amazed at how a doctor can sometimes make more in a day than a janitor can make in a year. On the surface, this seems unfair. Objectively speaking, a janitor is not any less important than a doctor. A doctor could not do his/her job without pristine-clean facilities. However, there is a universal law in monetary economics that says that one will be compensated in direct proportion to the demand for what they do, their ability to do it, and the difficulty that will be experienced in replacing that person, should they leave for a greater opportunity.

Realistically, you can teach a person how to clean a building in a week or two. However, it takes years for an individual to become a doctor and usually at a tremendous personal sacrifice. I have never heard it costing a janitor $60,000 a year, to learn how to become a janitor.

We know that only 5% of the world population is financially solvent. What I mean by that is that this 5% is able to meet the financial needs in their own lives on a consistent basis without outside help of any kind. In contrast, 95% of the world's population will live, as it is said, from hand-to-mouth.

Obviously, we all want to be in the top 5%. This being so, what must we do to insure that we are? That is a fair question and is worthy of a clear and uncomplicated response. Let's look at five primary things.

First, we must understand that people do not become rich as a result of being lucky. Luck has nothing, to do with becoming rich. Once all of us come to terms with this, we will approach the dynamics of money with a different attitude. Most people who possess wealth have certain markers about how they conduct themselves and their affairs. One marker is that most are well-educated. The second marker is that most possess an excellent work ethic. They can be depended upon to be on time, and do their job as effectively as possible. The third marker is that wealthy people are goal-setters. The fourth marker is that wealthy people respect what money can and cannot do. Finally, wealthy people pay more taxes than anyone else in America. Also, the top 5% invest the bulk of the wealth in this country in order to build strong and viable companies, and, as a byproduct of such investments, are the primary creators of jobs. [14]

o **Wisdom Principle**: *Government does not CREATE income; it takes it from those who do.*

It is important that we understand the contribution that wealthy people make to our economy and how vital their investment capital is in creating jobs. Individuals such as Brian Tracy, Earl Nightingale, and Wayne Dyer have taught and shown, time and again, that those who are wealthy have developed a plan to achieve their wealth, and then executed the plan. Creating wealth in one's life can be planned and if the plan is implemented, wealth can be expected to be the "effect"—the "payoff."

Second, understand that the accumulation of wealth requires setting income goals. Again, only 5% of the world's population sets income goals. To go through life believing that making "big

---

[14] Many people erroneously believe that the federal government creates jobs. This is so far from the truth that once you see the fallacy of it, you will realize that it is nothing less than laughable. Such a belief has been circulated so much that even the politicians, who are the primary source of such "bunk", believe it.

However, in no way has it ever been proven, nor can it be, that government has ever created jobs on its own. The government cannot provide jobs without taking money from those who pay the taxes to do so. As a rule, government is bureaucratic; often financially irresponsible; possesses an entitlement mentality when it comes to its citizen's pocketbook; operates on minimums; says more than it actually does; and is incompetent. The only truly functional part of government, which has proved itself to be worthy of our confidence and investment, is the military. This confidence is merited because of our military's past demonstrations of its competency.

money" is a matter of being in the right place at the right time is again naïve. Those who accumulate wealth work at it. They study and learn what it is going to take to earn what they want, and then they pay the price to earn that income. Your income goals ought to include four critical components:

1) **Yearly Income:** This involves the amount of money you want to earn in order to reach your goal. You also need to understand that points 2-4 are contingent on this number.

2) **Yearly Amount Committed for An Investment Account:** It is wise to invest in low-risk mutual funds, S & P stocks, or precious metals.

3) **Yearly Amount Committed to Savings Account:** This account allows you to get your hands-on emergency funds without disturbing either your investment account or your retirement account.

4) **Yearly Amount Committed for a Retirement Account**: It is important to start conservative on this account and maintain the percentage you have chosen to invest through age 35. After this age, I would increase the contribution 1% every five years.

Those who are determined to do well financially do two more things. He/she becomes the person necessary to qualify for the income desired. In other words, a person becomes highly skilled at what they do professionally. The job at which they become highly skilled is something they also enjoy doing. Secondly, they then work the plan to achieve that goal. I said this earlier and it begs repeating: if you want to make a million dollars a year, you had better have a million-dollar self-respect and self-worth.

A word of advice regarding your income, investment, and savings goals. Once you set these goals, forget about them. Next, you should do three things.

1) Focus on performing your skill better and better, i.e., learn to do what you do professionally better than anyone else.

2) Focus on serving the company for which you work, as well as the customers, of that company. Never put a limit on the service you give. People who refuse to do more than what they are being paid to do will seldom get paid more for just doing the basic job.

o **Wisdom Principle:** *People internally become the goal before they can reach the goal.*

3) Always be mindful of making and the accumulation of money. Financial success is directly related to how skilled a person is in their professional endeavor, the demand for what they do, and how difficult it would be for a corporation or organization to replace that person. If what a person does can easily and quickly be taught to them, then it can be confidently believed that the demand for what he/she does will not be that great, because finding someone to do that work will obviously be relatively easy.

My advice is to pick a field in which a tremendous amount of skill is required, and as a result, those who possess such skill will not be plentiful. By doing this you will always be in demand for your highly-sought-after skills. As in any profession, there are highly skilled individuals who are also well-trained. However, there are also those who are well-trained but whose skills are mediocre at best. You must have the determination to be in the category of the highly skilled. If you are, you will never lack for opportunity and you will most certainly be able to name your price when it comes to your professional excellence.

4) Be clear in your understanding that there are two paths to wealth.

    a. The first is the path of being of service to others. Whatever you seek in the form of monetary reward, you must first seek through your service to others. These are your friends, neighbors, acquaintances, colleagues, or anyone with whom you come into contact. The more effectively you are able to serve others, the greater your monetary reward.

    b. The second is the path of creative ideas. Over the years I have realized that money gravitates to the right ideas. Everyone who has become wealthy in the past fifty years did it with terrific ideas—ideas that filled a gap in the economy of their country whether that gap was local, regional, or national. Such ideas provided a service to others that, until that time, had not been provided before, and in a manner and style in which it currently exists. It is also possible that the idea could not have been in existence or even possible until the time it came into being.

      People, who understand this principle of wealth— the principle of ideas to which money will gravitate—often spend thirty minutes a day writing down ideas. Most of the ideas they write down are useless. However, over a year a person can come up with fifty ideas that if implemented could create wealth. All individuals who have become wealthy in the past twenty years did so by coming up with an idea that, when implemented, was timely and needed by a significant number of people.

o **Wisdom Principle:** *The greatest ideas are discovered by those who love what they do, i.e., Thomas Edison.*

5) You must remember that making money is an effect not a cause. The cause in making money is your service to others. I truly believe that the distance between one's discontent in what they are making and their income goal is the amount of service they must provide in order to achieve that income goal. Don't be deceived. The world will pay you exactly what you settle for, no more and no less. You will receive that which you have justly earned, not that for which you idly wish. Wealth will always be the result/effect of your effort and service.

Remember, you will never be successful because you make a great deal of money. You make a great deal of money because you are successful. Your achievements are always a reflection, of who and what you are.

5. The Line of Love

Although I am going to cover the subject of love much more thoroughly in Volume II of *Proverbial Wisdom for a Fully-Functioning Life*, I choose to introduce the subject in this final Line of Life. When I was a young man my view of love was exactly as Robert Frost wrote below. Experientially, for most people around the world, their view of love is extraordinarily similar. If this area of a person's life is mismanaged, a bad decision will bring tremendous suffering and pain. Let's give this subject a closer look.

➢ *"Love is an irresistible desire to be irresistibly desired."* — Robert Frost

➢ *"Love in its essence is spiritual fire."* — Emmanuel Swedenborg

➢ *"A loving heart is the truest wisdom."* – Charles Dickens

➢ *"Love is the only gold!"* – Alfred Lord Tennyson

➢ *"Love is the only sane and satisfactory answer to the problem of human existence."* – Erich Fromm

➢ *"People think that love is an emotion. Love is good sense."* – Ken Vesey

➢ *"The first duty of love is to listen."* – Paul Tillich

➢ *"Who, being loved, is poor?"* – Oscar Wilde

o **Wisdom Principle:** *Pragmatically speaking, tens associate with tens, sevens associate with sevens, fives associate with fives, and zeroes associate with zeros.*

There is no question that this is a pivotal line. Your choice of the person you marry will bring you 90% of the joy in your life or

90% of your misery. If you think I'm kidding, you have not paid attention to what I've already written. This one decision is the one 95% of us are least qualified to make when we make it for the first time. Like knowing and understanding the dynamics of parenting, our knowing and understanding the dynamics of authentic love is another area of which we Americans are very ignorant. Why was I so ignorant about this subject? Primarily because my parents and other adult authority figures in my life were ignorant about the subject of love as well! My peers were even more so. As I have repeatedly stated throughout this book, you can't teach what you don't know. This equally applies to your parents or mine! If your or my knowledge of love only consists of what we have learned from our parents, other authority figures, and our peers, such knowledge will always be an insufficient base upon which to build a marriage. I want to clarify a few points.

First, do not allow your feelings to determine primarily whether or not you think you are in love. Candidly, feelings have very little to do with authentic love. We have the power and choice to love whomever we choose. Love is not something that overwhelms us and takes over our hearts. When feelings are overwhelming you in regards to a particular individual, and these feelings are in control of what you are thinking and feeling, such isn't love, but infatuation. True, authentic love is not an emotional tidal wave. One may not be able to make his/her heart romantically attracted to someone when the desire is not there, one can choose to love anyone he/she desires. Feelings, strong romantic feelings, feel like love, but are not love at all. Such feelings are nothing more than infatuation. Infatuation is a totally physical and emotional experience. Infatuation has an indirect relationship with love. However, calling infatuation love or confusing infatuation with love—which most people do—in reality makes no logistical common-sense.

Individuals, who believe that love and infatuation are synonymous, are deceiving themselves. And, as I've learned from Dr. Gordon Livingston, the worst deceptions are those we perpetrate on ourselves. Love, unlike infatuation, is being committed to another person's positive social, personal, and spiritual development and well-being. Any definition of love, other than the one I have just given, will be woefully insufficient and shallow. Infatuation has little to do with love. Infatuation is unpredictable in the sense that you cannot control it when it occurs. It is all about what is happening to you and what that relationship does to you and for you. Infatuation is also serendipitous, i.e., you cannot plan to be infatuated with someone. Infatuation is similar to lightening striking. Infatuation, like lightening, is unpredictable and also dangerous. You are most vulnerable to making a mistake when you are in the throes of infatuation. That mistake is thinking that the infatuation you have for someone is love. If you choose to believe that infatuation is love you have just become a member of the "Morons Love Club".

In fact, married people have confessed in surveys and polls that they have been infatuated with other individuals on more than one occasion. This is strong evidence that when it comes to relationships with the opposite sex, being affected by someone's looks, style, and personality is primarily emotionally-driven. Emotions, as I have said, do not have brains even though most people in the world treat them as if such is true. This misplaced faith in romantic feelings is nothing less than crazy.

o **Wisdom Principle:** *True love is logical and altruistic ... infatuation is neither!*

Second, focus on how that person affects your character, your temperament, and your decision-making when he/she is around you. It is important that you realize that relationships, whether they are love relationships or otherwise, are best for you when they help you and inspire you to become a better person. Relationships create a significant amount of warmth, laughter, and camaraderie when this is true.

Also, I do not care how physically gorgeous you may think a person is, if being in their presence is not consistently "easy and comfortable", you must have the intelligence and courage to realize that this person is not "rubbing off" on you well. Be observant regarding what kind of effect this person is having on your temperament when you are with him/her. If you often sense yourself emotionally flinching when this person does or says something to which you take exception, you are getting a huge red light. You need to observe and heed such lights and respect them. What is happening, in this context, is that your "temperament radar" is putting you on high alert that something isn't quite right. My advice is to find someone else before you make a horrible mistake. The idea that good-looking people are also automatically easy to work with, associate with, and live with, just because they are good-looking, is just dangerous!

I knew a young man in college who was a terrific, common-sense kind of fellow. He looked at life the way he looked at math. Two plus two was four then, just like it is still four today. If something in life added up, terrific. If it didn't, it wasn't worth his time and attention. He was not the snappiest dresser on campus and he didn't pay much attention to his hair—specifically how or whether it was combed or brushed. He was just a quality-stuff guy, who possessed very little self-perception.

On one occasion, some of us noticed that something was happening to him. Those of us who knew him didn't see it coming. He started sitting with a girl during mealtimes instead of with us. Over the next few weeks I saw his life change for the better. He started to send out his shirts and pants to be laundered. He was shaving consistently, and he began paying attention to his hair and how he generally presented himself in public. His etiquette also dramatically improved—not just when he was with her but around us as well. He was changing for the better—improving. This girl was having an enormous positive effect on him.

He got engaged to her in the spring of his junior year and they married when they both graduated college. They are still very happily married today. They rubbed well together. Consequently, they enjoyed being in each other's presence for extended periods of time. This is one of the good stories regarding relationships.

There are men and women all over this world who are physically attracted to each other, but as they begin spending long periods of time together, they match in other areas of the relationship. When there is an intense physical attraction, most are not cognizant that they don't match where and when it counts. Nonetheless, certain insecure individuals have a compulsive tendency to press too hard in a romantic relationship once they find themselves intensely and emotionally tied to someone, in spite of the reality that they don't really get along in the real world.

Dependent individuals want to constantly be with someone they can couple up with once a strong attachment has developed. It is as if they won't be able to breathe unless they are constantly with the other person. Again, such people call this kind of emotionally intensive relationship love, but it isn't. In fact, it's nothing less than the old "I-don't-want-to-lose-this-person-because-I'm-too-insecure-and-don't-have-a-life-without-them" syndrome. Very often, the goal of such individuals is to isolate the person to whom they are intensely attracted from everyone else so that he/she can have that person completely to themselves. Needless to say, this is warped, as well as dangerous. Individuals who are this possessive are often suicidal and homicidal. Obviously, not good!

o **Wisdom Principle:** *Oppressive individuals suffer from a belief that they are unworthy of love and attention. Such a belief is rooted in gross self-rejection and insecurity.*

o **Wisdom Principle:** *A marriage partner ought to be the most important person in your life, but not everything in your life.*

Such people as I have just described possess an oppressive spirit. Oppressive personalities are constantly anxious and prone to depression. Being possessive when it comes to their relationships brings out jealousy, and they see their difficulty in finding someone to love them as a matter of life "not being fair". For such individuals, finding themselves in such a predicament is not only harsh but unacceptable. A person who has an oppressive spirit is one who becomes burdensome to others when spending long periods of time with them. A person with an oppressive spirit can also become tyrannical when the fear of losing someone from their life becomes possible.

When you are around someone with an oppressive spirit you can't wait to get away from him or her. You sense that you are a prisoner when you are in their presence. Such a person is constantly asking you questions—what are you thinking, where are you going, or with whom did you spend time that day. It is as if that person is a policeman interrogating you. The reason you sense that you are in some form of a prison is because this person is constantly probing, trying to keep track of you.

Such a person is, in reality, a major loser when it comes to maturely managing relationships. He/she has not come to terms with who and what he/she is and is doing everything in his/her power to avoid doing so. Walk away! On second thought, don't walk away, run away … quickly! Don't look back. He/she may be gaining on you!

Another thing about this kind of person is that he/she is completely oblivious to the obvious, which is that he/she affects others this way. Such people do not believe they are doing anything wrong. To them, they are just spending time and giving attention to someone special—someone they are very fond of. They don't realize that the way they are showing their fondness is extremely intrusive and oppressive. Also, they do not realize that there are three things driving them to attach themselves to the one they think they love in such a fashion: insecurity, loneliness, and the fear of the loss of something significant; which in this case, is love. If you marry someone like this, the obsession of trying to hold on to you—refusing to give you space to be yourself—will get ten times worse after marriage. The only way you will likely be able to escape such a person, is to perhaps plead with the U. S. Marshall's Office to accept you into the Witness Protection Program.

I have an acquaintance who married a young woman such as I have just described. It was his first marriage. This girl possessed an oppressive spirit. The first guy who gave her a great deal of attention—my buddy—found himself with a girl who refused to separate herself from him for any amount of time. She attached herself to him like white-on-rice. He couldn't get rid of her, so he married her.

Now, even in his youth he was a terrific golfer. He continued his interest in golf but after he married her his wife literally cried each time he left her to play. Her attachment became a character disorder and she escalated her displeasure for his playing golf by resorting to grabbing one of his legs as he tried to walk out the door. She was resorting to desperate means to keep him from leaving her for a four-hour game of golf.

While I was listening to this story, I was saying to myself, "You've got to be kidding me!" But he wasn't kidding. Tragically, there are people who believe that such behavior is an expression of genuine love. But anyone who believes this behavior is some form of love, has literally lost it. Love has no place in such behavior. This is nothing less than an obsession gone crazy!

Third, ask yourself if you admire and respect the person who has captured your undivided attention. How do you know if you admire and respect someone? Simple! Ask yourself these questions.

1. Does this person possess character qualities that you want and are you willing to allow them to "mentor" you while you incorporate such admirable traits into your life?
2. Would you be proud for this person to be the mother or father of your children?

If your response is something like, "I admire their physical attractiveness," you are infatuated, rather than being in love. When you love someone, you want to be like them in more ways than one.

Fourth, get to know the family and see how it responds to you. For me, this is a deal-breaker. I know that 90% of individuals will not give the character and temperament of the family into which they are going to marry any serious consideration. This is tragic. The usual attitude regarding this is that most individuals say to themselves, as well as to others, "I'm not marrying his/her family. I am marrying him/her." My response is, "Yes, you are marrying his/her family." If the person you believe is "the one" is close to his/her family, what they think about you, as well as, what this family believes about you is critically important.

Finding out after you marry someone that you cannot stand his/her family is "major bad news". Before you know it, you will be coming up with excuses as to why you can't visit your spouse's family. The next domino to fall, in this kind of context, is that your spouse is now going over to his/her family's home—for Thanksgiving, Christmas, birthdays and other special occasions— all alone. I don't think you have any idea how much tension you are creating within your marriage when your dislike of your spouse's family has escalated to this.

One of the proofs of loving someone is that you don't trample on the things they deem important to their happiness and well-being. You respect what is important to your spouse. I think one of the greatest things I can do for my wife is to love, live, and work with her family the very best I know how. I try to make sure that I don't interfere or hinder the cultivation and involvement she has and wants with her family. I would strongly advise you not to scoff at the importance of this point. If you do, I believe you will regret it.

In the end, there will not likely be many, if any, good memories of being with your spouse's family for special occasions. You need to pay attention when I say to you that you will need all of the good memories which you can be a part of in order to keep your marriage thriving. If you don't make getting along with your spouse's family a priority, eventually, when your spouse thinks of being married to you the bad memories will outnumber the good ones. When this happens, the relationship is in huge trouble. In other words, there are "problems in Mayberry".

o   **Wisdom Principle:** *The quickest way to lose your enthusiasm for life and living is to marry the wrong person—especially a self-centered person.*

Fifth, beware of the "bait-and-switch" strategy, which, more often than not, is quite common in relationships. What do I mean by this? Most individuals do not have any problem putting their best foot forward in relationships as well as project to another person a persona of how they want to be perceived rather than projecting the persona that is truly who he/she truly is. This "bait-and-switch" is so common in dating that many marriage counselors don't think it's all that abnormal. It is abnormal! It is also very dishonest!

Presenting yourself to be someone who is substantially different from the person you will reveal yourself to be once you are married, is about as dishonest as you can get. If you are hesitant to reveal the real you in the initial stages of a relationship you need to back off and not get into a relationship. You are going to hurt someone doing this and that's simply unacceptable, as well as unethical. The reason I say this is because you are not qualified to be in any kind of relationship if the person you reveal yourself to be, once you get comfortable in a relationship, is different from the person you sold yourself to be in the beginning. When you sell yourself to be someone you are not to anyone, you are not integrity-based enough to qualify for any relationship. The end does not justify the means. Love isn't about getting; it is about giving.

Selling yourself to be someone you truly are not, to someone you purport to love, is a combustible scenario, which ultimately leads to heartbreak for the one being deceived. It shows you as being a person who can't be trusted. Authenticity is pivotal to any successful relationship. I can tell you this. If you are not comfortable exposing your failures, frustrations (hot buttons), fears, and flaws to the one you say that you love then you are not ready for love ... or even friendship, for that matter.

I am so convicted in regards to the importance of your being authentic when it comes to love, that I believe in my heart of hearts that annulments ought to be granted in relationships where such dishonesty has occurred. Our legal system has not arrived at this conviction as yet, but I am praying to this end.

In the church, especially among conservative denominations, it traditionally has been the position that if someone is a victim of such dishonesty, he/she must stay in that marriage and work to make it a success, no matter what. "After all," such denominations say, "the New Testament condemns divorce except for the sin of adultery, doesn't it?" My response: "Yes, it does."

However, think about these two things regarding this perspective.

1) When a denomination teaches through doctrine and also enforces that same doctrine with the threat of some form of stigmatism toward any individual considering leaving a relationship where gross dishonesty has occurred, that denomination is implying a 100% guarantee exists that all will eventually be well, and the wounds from such dishonesty will heal if a couple stays together. Whether the couple truly works things out is irrelevant to these religious groups.

   The denomination is also saying that time heals all wounds. But, if such is true then God is not necessary. Such a position on the part of any denomination is as deceitful and equally as lethal as the dishonesty the innocent party is being forced to accept. There is no denomination that can give any such guarantee. If a denomination is comfortable enforcing such a doctrine and giving this guarantee, then it ought to be committed to doing all it possibly can to make sure that couples being advised to stay together, in the midst of such deceit, actually stay together.

   If the truth were told, most denominations that teach no divorce under any circumstances except for physical adultery, are not that committed to making sure these couples stay together. Most authoritarian denominations are very good at making these kinds of edicts, but are very poor at truly ministering to couples trapped in situations by those edicts.

2) Physical adultery is not the only kind of adultery. There are other forms of adultery that equally breach the trust in a marriage as destructively as physical adultery does. In fact, there are seven kinds of adultery, among them spiritual adultery, psychological adultery, and emotional adultery. I know this comes as quite a shock to those who think simplistically regarding this subject. To those who have taken the conservative position regarding adultery, I have the following response:

If you have committed yourself to complete authenticity in your relationships, then you are truly arriving in your maturity. When you can emotionally undress yourself, and show your true self to those about whom you truly care a great deal, then you are becoming mature enough to be in a relationship. If you are not comfortable enough to do so, you are not ready for any kind of significant relationship in your life. A mature individual is an authentic individual. Mature people do not need to apologize for what they are and have become. All of us are a work in progress. If you are rejected by someone because you have shown your true self then it is good to know this before making a big mistake. Most people are not ready for authenticity. They are intimidated by it because there is so little of it in the world. There are billions of people in this world who make the mistake of undervaluing what they are, and overvaluing what they are not.

- o **Wisdom Principle:** *Never apologize for being you! God doesn't, so you shouldn't either.*

The Line of Love is a line you must handle with great care and respect in order not to make a critical mistake for which you will pay the rest of your life.

CHAPTER EIGHT

INSECURITY: LIFE'S ULTIMATE NEMESIS

o **Wisdom Principle:** Make no mistake, insecurity is an emotional and psychological dysfunction, which consequently is drawn to social groups, which feed this dysfunction.

o **Wisdom Principle:** *Your comfort in "the growth zone" is directly dependent on your hunger to excel.*

Chapter Introduction:

This chapter will describe and explain the debilitating effects that insecurities have in our day-to-day interaction with those who are terribly afflicted by them. I will, in my second volume, discuss in more detail about the difficulties of living in a family with, as well as being married to, someone who has "masked" insecurities during the gestation period of a relationship, and who, after he/she has become comfortable in the relationship, begins to reveal those insecurities. Other than being married to a truly difficult person, being married to an enormously insecure individual will bring a person the second greatest amount of misery possible. For our purposes in this chapter, we will discuss how insecurity affects each of us as we associate with and work with insecure individuals.

Everyone has experienced insecurity. Insecurity is inflicted upon each of us in three different ways—self-inflicted, other-inflicted (inflicted by other individuals), or socially inflicted. Most people experience life-long insecurity in one form or another. However, it doesn't have to be nor should it be this way. Insecurity is so prevalent that it has become accepted as a permanent part of the lives of most people in this world. For this reason, I call insecurity life's ultimate nemesis. It will keep individuals from becoming the best they can be. Insecure people are consistently afflicted with self-doubt and the fears of rejection and failure. If you want to be the best you that you can possibly be, then you must confront your insecurities and do something about them. Unless you do you will always be haunted by them and, as a consequence, you will always face needless self-doubt and the limiting of your effectiveness in your career.

Only 5% of the world's population knows what it is like to pursue life and all of its challenges, with a sense of peace and assurance that all will be well, regardless of the paths that must be taken to arrive at the desired place. For this small but significant group, success is an intuitive expectation. These group achievers expect to arrive at the place to which their goals lead them. You may be thinking that this percentage is very small, but I assure you, based on performance statistics, it is not.

While I was growing up no one ever spoke to me about insecurity and how such thoughts, feelings, and beliefs could be abated. Because I experienced insecurity for much of my childhood and adolescent years, I know what being insecure is like. My parents had so many insecurities they spent too much time and energy dealing with their own issues to have time to help me with mine.

And, if you have parents who are battling their own insecurities, then your parents, realistically, have nothing to offer you that can assist you in your battles with your insecurities. I believe that what I have learned over the decades about insecurity can help you. Make no mistake. You can do something about your insecurities so that you will rarely, if ever, be bothered with them again.

o **Wisdom Principle:** *The longer any insecurity stays in your life, the greater a foothold it gets and the harder it is to eliminate.*

There are several causes of insecurity. Here is a list with details about the most significant. Keep in mind that we are entering the discussion of a very sensitive subject. Fasten your seat belts and realize that eliminating insecurities from your life will be painful, but the healing will often be fast and liberating.

The first cause of insecurity is poverty. I grew up poor and know how stigmatizing poverty can be. The majority of those who are not poor and did not grow up poor, as a rule, see themselves as better than those who are. This daily intensifies the negative aspects of poverty. There is little that is more dehumanizing than being treated as less than those around you who are not only more economically advantaged but also believe that they possess a significance you do not possess.

I mentioned in an earlier chapter that the greatest cause of poverty is ignorance, not bad luck. Here's an example as to why I not only said this but believe it as well.

Parents who have not adequately prepared themselves for life with at least the cultivation of a skill set that those who employ others would find valuable and important, are at a distinct disadvantage. When such occurs, these individuals have no one to blame but themselves for the poverty in their lives. People are not owed a skill, but instead are responsible for cultivating one and looking for the opportunities to do so. Once a man and a woman marry and have children, for whom they have not adequately prepared, poverty and all of the baggage that comes with it falls upon all of the members of that family like an avalanche. This is a preventable tragedy. However, in order to prevent it you must want to prevent it. Those, who believe they will get a break and overcome poverty with "lotto luck", are in for great disappointment and disillusionment.

- o **Wisdom Principle:** *You are never able to change what you are willing to tolerate!*

- o **Wisdom Principle:** *You cannot change what you don't acknowledge.*

A second cause of insecurity is the media-created social standard that makes an individual a victim. This social standard defines what makes a person physically attractive, and as a consequence, more valuable, accepted, and liked, over those who are not as attractive. This cause of insecurity does an enormous amount of damage in people's lives and this damage is absolutely needless. It could be avoided but the selling of sex in this world is so pervasive and addictive that it has the majority of the world in its talons. The greatest reason for this cause of insecurity is the shallowness of its adherents.

Thanks to *People Magazine,* and other publications like it, a person possessing physical attractiveness, musical talent, theatrical talent, athletic talent or, in some cases, extreme academic intelligence is much more apt to be accepted by others than those who do not fit the bill, as they say. Such standards are hailed by the shallow among us, as being the ultimate determinates as to whether a person is valuable and worthy of our attention and time. Such a so-called standard is not only "puddle deep" but cruel and insensitive.

Insecurity is a constant nemesis to most American teens since most of them struggle with the perception that they are very unattractive as the result of either having acne, being overweight ... or thinking they are, or simply being unable to meet the arbitrary and unreasonable media standards regarding what makes a person attractive. The overwhelming majority of young people who do not meet this shallow and arbitrary media-created standard are seen as second class by the so-called "elite minority". This perception by the young has not been much different from generation to generation until the last several decades.

There is no question that the difference from earlier generations to today's generation has been the intense visibility of this arbitrary standard, as to what makes a person attractive and valuable to society. The pressure, the stigmatism, and the labeling of those who have not met this arbitrary standard, have all intensified to a level never known before. Once a child enters school, he or she begins to experience this horrible labeling regarding just who or what is considered physically attractive, and who or what is not. This is especially true at the well-known "social event", we call high school. It's time for a change. It seems that *People Magazine* and its media cohorts are not going to do it, therefore we are going to have to. My contribution is to write about it and give you a strategy on how to eliminate insecurity from your life—permanently!

What I think the pop culture magazines fail to understand is that personality, a sense-of-humor, and character are, objectively speaking, very attractive in others. However, you will hardly ever see such traits commended, much less applauded, by the members of the media. Why not? The media do not respect nor value such traits enough to give them the visibility that, in contrast, is given to physical attractiveness, talent, or extreme intelligence. Also, such publications perceive this nobility of life and living, boring. The people publications that embrace the shallow standard can deny all they want that they do not embrace a standard for physical attractiveness but their actions belie their more so-called noble intentions.

One of our leading publications has an annual "swimsuit edition" that not surprisingly outsells all of its other monthly issues by hundreds of thousands of copies. Another one has an annual issue lauding the "100 Most Beautiful People in America". If just these two illustrations don't magnify my point then I don't know what will!

Let's talk about horses for a moment. When you put a bit in the mouth of a horse, you do it to control the movements of the horse's body.

Ships that sail on the open seas, are another example. Many such ships are huge and can only be propelled forward by strong winds. Did you know that these ships are also steered by a very small mechanism known as a rudder? Wherever the pilot of a ship wants to turn a ship, all he has to do is control this small rudder to get the ship to turn in the direction he wants it to go.

It's the same with the tongue. It is a very small part of the body, but it is so pervasively powerful. With it we boast greatly. Have you ever considered that every forest fire is started by a spark? It is! The tongue can be like a forest fire. The tongue can rage with evil and it can arouse various parts of the body to consider doing things that are blatantly wrong. In fact, an undisciplined tongue can contaminate and corrupt the whole person. It can set the entire course of a person's life on fire and that fire can be so destructive that it can even be said that it comes from hell itself.

All kinds of earthly creatures, whether on land or in sky or sea, have been tamed by man. However, no man has ever been able, to permanently tame the tongue. It can express, as well as be guilty, of all kinds of evil. It is the only part of our physical body that can drip with deadly poison with every word it speaks.

Isn't it ironic that with our tongues we can praise our Heavenly Father and also be capable of profaning men, who, by the way, have been made in God's likeness? Imagine, for a moment that out of the same orifice comes praise and cursing. This doesn't make sense, does it? This should not be. Can pure, cool, fresh water and brackish water flow from the same spring? Can a fig tree bear other fruit such as olives? Can a grapevine bear figs? The answer is so obvious that these questions are not worthy of a response! Neither can a brackish spring produce pure, cool, fresh water, because it is contrary to what makes it what it is.

If you cannot comprehend the terrible damage an undisciplined tongue can cause, after reading this section of the New Testament, all I can say is, God help you. Just as a person's education, or lack thereof, can be determined by their knowledge and use of their native language, so can the self-discipline of a person be determined by the use of their tongue. Possessing a disciplined tongue can move a person toward excellence and authentic confidence as quickly and as much as anything I know.

A third cause of insecurity is an individual being rejected because the "in crowd" doesn't believe that he/she fits in. I have an idea what this fitting in really means. However, I am equally confident that the ones doing the rejecting cannot articulate what *it* means to them. I know that it is some arbitrary standard used by unthinking individuals whose "standard" of what it means to be cool varies with the social temperature.

I spoke in the first chapter about cliques. What I want to mention here is that "fitting in" actually means fitting the idea the leaders of a clique have regarding what it means to be *cool.* Being cool to these leaders means "kissing up" to them and making them look good because it is obvious they can't be "cool" on their own. If they could they would not need your help to do so. Get my "drift"?

Rejection is a big deal to children and teens who do not have a terrific and empathetic support system at home. These teens don't have an authority figure who can help them stand up to those who have become self-appointed kings and queens of their world. Hopefully, this chapter will give them fodder for their battle. Also, reading about what seemed to be insurmountable odds in the life of David should inspire each of us to trust our Heavenly Father and cast our cares upon Him for the simple reason that He truly cares for each of us.

If a child or teen has loving and nurturing parents who are there for them in such times as those described, these children and teens can overcome the pressure from cliques, as well as "clique-hounds". These children can also overcome as well the pain of the put-downs they have had to endure. However, even children and teenagers as fortunate as these need to trust the Heavenly Father and garner strength from their relationship with Him.

o **Wisdom Principle:** *Cliques are the refuge for the insecure and the narcissistic among us.*

o **Wisdom Principle:** *The less self-defined an individual is, the more conforming to external standards he/she will be.*

A fourth cause of insecurities is someone growing up in a family made up of members whose personal and social behavior are embarrassing, whose actions deem them incompetent, and whose expressions and mannerisms communicate a lack of intelligence and good judgment. Such family members are misfits. Members in my immediate family had behavior and intelligence that were sub-par, to say the least. I cringed when I was with them in public, because I had unfortunately become accustomed to their doing or saying something embarrassing ... even outrageous.

Also, as a teenager I had friends who worried about the behavior of a parent or a sibling when they were with them in public and especially at a school function. The behavior of their families caused great concern to them because they were apprehensive that something embarrassing might occur. Any individual in a like situation fears being lumped in with the family members who are socially inept or who are simply uncouth. The innocent family member fears being ostracized by those who happen to be present when these family misfits are making fools of themselves. Those of us who have been in these situations fear being talked about as well as being perceived as just like these misfits in their families.

The only way, to avoid this scenario is either to make sure your uncouth family members are not around you and your friends at all or better yet, that you conduct yourself in such a manner that when your friends see the antics of your family, they are sympathetic toward you and respect and admire how far you have come in spite of your family.

Through the various stages of my growing years, I knew friends who lived with such an apprehension … too many to count. As a middle adolescent, when I was playing summer baseball, I recall seeing the dad of one of my teammates come to watch us in a game. That wouldn't have been such a big deal except that father came to the game drunk. He staggered around the perimeter of the fenced field and yelled obscenities at the umpires when he didn't like a particular call. When my teammate came up to bat, his intoxicated father became more obnoxious and embarrassing. All of us hurt for our teammate. We knew that he couldn't control his father. When I looked into my teammate's eyes, I knew that the pain he experienced every time his father behaved like this was too horrific to comprehend or talk about. Parents like this are such a burden to their children. What is even worse, they are so unconscious when it comes to their irresponsible behavior that they are not even aware there is a problem. This is tragic!

A fifth cause of insecurities is having a lifestyle that is just too easy ... a lifestyle that doesn't challenge a person to grow and mature daily. Individuals who are given so much while so little is demanded of them, as a rule, will not be able to meet any significant challenge with confidence due to their lack of growth—their immaturity. They have never had to face these kinds of challenges on their own. Mom and Dad have always been there to buy or otherwise help get their child out of trouble or defend their child's deficiencies.

No child or teen can be tough enough to meet a significant challenge if he/she has never developed the discipline to be able to do so or has never seen the need to cultivate such a necessary self-discipline. Parents are the primary cause of this inferiority. Protecting children from the world is not as effective as preparing them to protect themselves. Parents need to realize that they will not always be there to protect their children from the world when things get confusing, difficult, or tough.

Also, when everything is provided for a child, especially in an environment fixed by the parents in so far as to insulate a child from any possibility of failure, no accurate view of reality is possible on the part of the child. When this happens a strong sense of unworthiness usually comes over children, who intuitively know that they have not earned anything. In other words, they have simply had it too easy and are unprepared for life's challenges.

Anything unearned in one's life does not result in one being filled with self-confidence. Self-confidence is earned—it is not a gift. Self-confidence doesn't just happen. It is a byproduct of discipline, commitment, and hard work. Without self-confidence, competence in any endeavor is only a wish—never a reality.

o   **Wisdom Principle:** *Parents, there is a difference in encouraging your children in their performance and in deceiving your children about their performance.*

A sixth cause of insecurity is possessing a low social IQ. I have two brothers—specifically they are my foster brothers. Both of them have a very good social IQ. In fact, our Mom had a wonderful social IQ and she passed her very competent skills in this area of life to the both of them. I knew my brothers in high school, prior to my becoming part of the family. I quietly admired both of them as they navigated the "social waters" with ease ... even as teens. I did not have that skill, because at the time I had no one to teach me.

When individuals do not have the knowledge and skill to navigate the social waters, it is clear they have not had anyone teach them these skills, have not had the opportunity to mix socially with others regularly, or have been reluctant to do so when the opportunities arose.

The cure for a low social IQ is learning what makes one likeable and having the discipline to implement these traits in your own life. Likeability is not luck, charisma, or being genetically blessed with an engaging personality. Likeability is character-centered. I will speak on this in a later chapter. Nevertheless, being likeable is a quality that can be cultivated. To those who believe that likeability is genetic, please don't say that out loud to anyone. You will come across looking foolish, if you voice such an opinion.

Another reason for a low social IQ is simply when someone is very difficult to get to know or get along with consistently. In the last chapter, I spoke about individuals not rubbing well in a romantic relationship. How well someone rubs gets along with another person can be determined when he/she is around a particular individual over a long period of time. People who consistently don't get along well with others simply are not likeable. They don't have the key likable temperament components. A person who is unlikable as well as non- transparent, is one who is not qualified to be in any kind of social relationship. This person is not going to have the necessary relational skills to have successful social encounters. The primary reason such individuals are not likable is arrogance, which is a compensatory maneuver used by most insecure individuals to hide deep inferiorities and ignorance of the smoother aspects of social etiquette.

The seventh cause of insecurity is the lack of certain skills in a particular context that would help someone perform well in his/her career. I must tell you that this insecurity can be caused from the lack of skill in playing a card game well like Bridge, or not playing a particular sport well. Whatever the cause, not having a skill that is needed at a particular time and context can bring about a sense of insecurity as well as the fear of failure.

To be clear, I am speaking about experiencing this specific insecurity consistently. Within such contexts, individuals who experience this kind of insecurity have usually lived a very isolated life. Most of the time they live their lives within a tight social circle, made so either specifically by them or for them by an authority figure when they were younger. Because of this they have had a very limited exposure to the world most of us know. Instead, they have developed an insufficient social base and will find it difficult to be comfortable and effective in contexts like those described above with any sense of competence or confidence.

These individuals also live with what I call the "angst of inadequacy". It is a sensation right behind the proverbial "belly-button" that springs up at a time when one feels inadequate or incompetent to accomplish something or participate effectively within a group. Those who possess such angst are unskilled in certain abilities. Make no mistake, self-discipline leads to competence and competence leads to confidence.

The eighth cause of insecurity is a lack of self-identity. Those who have a clear self-identity are more competent and confident in facing the challenges of life. These individuals know that the most important words ever said to anyone are the words said by that person about himself or herself. However, when individuals don't have the knowledge necessary to cultivate a solid and stable self-identity, they find themselves with a vague or nebulous self-identity, which in turn is compounded by having enormous insecurities.

A strong self-identity is like an anchor. The winds of life blow, the waves on the sea of life rage, but the stability of who and what a person is remains unmoved. When such a strong self-identity does not exist in one's life, instability becomes a key component of that person's life. The reason is due to how easily one is influenced to think and do things that are not within their best interests by the mediocre individuals around them. Those who are easily influenced in what they say and do are overwhelmingly outer-defined, rather than being inner-defined. Inner-defined individuals do not get their cues as to what to think and what to do from others.

The ninth cause of insecurity is guilt—both appropriate and inappropriate guilt. Inappropriate guilt is often the result of criticism by an authority figure who is uses guilt throwing as a form of manipulation. Virtually all guilt occurring in this manner is inappropriate.

Appropriate guilt is always the result of words or actions that are non-virtuous and as a result are not altruistic at their core. For example, in Proverbs 6:16-19 we are told that there are seven things God hates. Modernizing the meaning of the Hebrew words, these seven things are arrogance, a lying tongue, murder, schemes—schemes of wickedness that take advantage of the innocent—easily-influenced individuals—those who can be easily led into committing acts of evil. The two last things on the list are lying under oath and a person who is constantly stirring up drama, trouble, and dissension in families, as well as among God's people. I'll comment on a couple of these only within the context of the subject of insecurity.

Let's face it. We know there are people, who are "bad news". We know there are those who are very dangerous. A person's physical safety is in jeopardy when he or she is around dangerous people. We also know that there are people who cannot tell the truth. These would not know the truth if it were a shark and bit them in the nose.

However, there is no question that the most common "headache" among us is the one possessing a critical spirit. Most individuals with a critical spirit are also guilty of being arrogant, which is nothing less than a self-serving inner-mechanism that projects an image that these individuals are better than everyone else. Ultimately, such people will be held accountable for so much. Unfortunately, such people are the last to realize a judgment of them isn't as far away as they may think.

Most of these people have become so accustomed to conducting themselves in such a manner that they have become completely blind to their critical spirit and their arrogance. Such horrible traits have, unfortunately, become intuitive in their lives. I truly believe that the reason they are this way is because they are militantly determined not to cultivate the virtue of self-honesty. They are haughty with just about everyone with whom they come in contact. Humility for such people is non-existent. They interpret *Godly humility* as *humiliation*. Arrogant individuals just do not know the meaning of humility. And the second verse to that declaration is that they do not want to know.

I don't have a problem going on record saying that those among us who are arrogant are also individuals who create more than their share of dissention in a group, organization, or even a church. Such character-disordered individuals for lack of a better metaphor, carry their "derriere on their shoulders". These people are also experts at strategically pointing fingers at you or me when we call them on the proverbial carpet for their behavior. Suddenly, they are not the problem. Instead, we are! Those with better sense simply say to themselves "Nice try, but counter-accusations are not going to stick because I am not guilty—you are." Cognitive people know that the "blaming strategy", does not work when character-disordered individuals try to use it on them.

o **Wisdom Principle:** *Arrogant people loathe being held accountable—for anything!*

The reason arrogance is listed first in this list of seven things that God hates is that it is the primary motivator for those characteristics making up the rest of the list (#s 2-7). For example, you have to be arrogant to lie. Most people who lie truly believe they won't get caught. You have to be arrogant to devise wicked schemes thinking all the while that bringing suffering to the innocent is okay just as long you get what you want. It also takes arrogance to believe that you can go along with those who have concocted evil schemes and that you won't get caught.

It is appropriate to point out that Proverbs 6:27 & 28 asks: *"Is it possible, for a person to take fire and press it onto his chest and not be scorched? Is it possible, for a person to walk barefooted on burning coals and his feet not burn to a crisp?"* Obviously, the answer is a big "No". A person can't do either of these two ridiculously stupid things and not suffer dire consequences. However, those, who go along with those who plot evil schemes to hurt the innocent are crazy if they believe they won't suffer the consequences for doing so.

What about those who are willing to lie under oath? Those guilty will discover that the deed will come back to haunt them. To think otherwise is simply foolish. Eventually, those who are so calloused that they would have the compulsion to lie under oath will suffer the consequences for such an imprudent act. The justice system may not catch them, but life will.

o **Wisdom Principle:** *Lying is an evasion of responsibility.*

Finally, what about people who are so insecure, so out-of-control and who consistently battle feelings of insignificance, that they have to always be stirring up trouble? What about when they always have to be the source, as well as be in the middle, of all kinds of never ending drama around them? These people are also arrogant. Everyone I have ever known has a relative with an undisciplined tongue that kept things stirred up in the family. Accusations are tossed against others like horseshoes in a game of toss. The anger these people can stir up is nothing less than wicked—senseless and evil. They enjoy being the tattletale of the family. It gives them an enormous amount of warped self-importance. Such individuals are determined not to be insignificant; even if they have to create dissention, drama, and unnecessary pain in the lives of innocent people, so be it. When it comes to these people, one thing you can count on is that they will not be ignored.

There you have it. What is the one common denominator that all of these kinds of individuals possess? All are naturally prone to exhibit relationship-destroying tendencies, and they don't seem to have a problem being so. This is sinfully tragic.

Any healthy person ought to be convicted of guilt when responsible of the acts described in the last several paragraphs. However, I know that the more you go against virtue the less sensitive you will become to being virtuous. The resistance to do what is right becomes weaker and the temptation to do what is wrong becomes stronger.

Once a person goes against what is right with prolonged consistency, his/her conscience eventually stops speaking. As the Apostle Paul states in I Timothy 4:2, a person's conscience can become insensitive to wrongdoing. When this happens, especially when it comes to certain sins for which they are consistently guilty, it's as if their consciences have been "seared with a branding iron".

Have you ever seen a cow that has been branded? When you look closely at the place where the branding iron was placed, the skin has been literally fried. It's horrible looking. Also, when you touch a cow around the branding area, the cow can't feel your touch because the skin is dead as are the nerves. This is what happens to a person's conscience when it goes against what it knows is true and right. Hebrews 10:31 says: *"It is a dreadfully frightening experience for the ungodly to find themselves at the mercy of a Living God!"* There are ultimate consequences in your life for being unrepentant of ungodly actions.

A healthy Christian who experiences conviction of appropriate guilt usually experiences insecurity. This is a good thing. Insecurity among those who take living a righteous life seriously is virtually always the result of getting off course. To get back on course and regain the confidence known only by having a viable relationship with Christ, these people simply confess their sins to God in prayer and move forward more illuminated, determined, and humbled.

Yes, some kinds of insecurities are brought on by appropriate guilt. Like failure, insecurities tell us things about ourselves that we can't know any other way. For instance, insecurities tell us what areas of our life need work and where we are incomplete. However, insecurities are the ultimate nemesis when they remain unresolved and plague us each day of our lives.

There is no question that insecurities are unresolved issues in each of our lives that we have failed to work through. They will always exist when a person is not giving the appropriate concern or consideration in resolving them.

Finally, such insecurities can be areas of life a person could have failed to acknowledge as being a real problem. More often than not, these have remained so simply because individuals faced with them were often militant in their refusal to address them. Perhaps this refusal to face insecurities is because of arrogance—thinking one is too good to have such flaws. Another reason could be a lack of courage—he/she is truly afraid of what might be seen in his/her own life that could possibly bring personal shame, embarrassment, or guilt.

- o **Wisdom Principle:** *Most adult insecurities are simply unresolved insecurities from adolescence.*

Now that I have given you the main insecurities, I want to give you the consequences of what can happen in the lives of those who do not choose to face their insecurities, but would rather continue to rationalize them and/or ignore them. I must tell you that it is not fair for our insecurities to negatively affect the lives of those with whom we associate, whether it is family, friends, or acquaintances when we are in a position to do something about them.

- o **Wisdom Principle:** *One of the greatest contributions one can make to the world is to NOT be a burden to other people.* —Dr. Wayne Dyer

Frankly, it is nothing less than pure selfishness a person to allow their insecurities to negatively affect the lives of those with whom they associate or live. For those narcissistic individuals who believe being an imposition is okay and that others should adjust to them, the only thing that can be said is that it will be only a matter of time before they find themselves all alone. No one intentionally wants to be a part of such a person's life!

Just because the Apostle Paul states in Romans 14:7, that *"No person lives only to themselves, and no person dies only to themselves;"* no one has the right to inflict inconvenience, suffering, and pain on others while flippantly saying life is a "give and take" proposition. Those who believe that being an inconvenience is just part of life are confused, if not patently self-serving.

Also, there are those who have no problem inconveniencing others to get what they believe they are rightfully entitled to receive. Just because there is a scripture in Galatians 6:2 which says that we are to "help bear one another's burdens" doesn't mean that it is okay to inconvenience others in order to achieve our own selfish ends. Those of us who believe this are grossly misinterpreting this verse.

As a rule, my experience has been that individuals handle insecurity in their lives one of two ways—passive or aggressive. The passive approach is predominately embraced by weak-willed individuals, while the aggressive approach is used by strong-willed individuals.

Weak-willed individuals usually seek to hide their insecurities by flying below the radar socially speaking. These people are often wall flowers; they are shy—timid and quiet when among people, especially those they don't know. Weak-willed individuals will not usually speak to someone unless they are first spoken to. Even then their responses will be brief ... almost cryptic. They suffer from deep inferiorities. At the same time, they don't possess volatile tempers; this part of their lives is usually kept under wraps and well-disciplined. When they do get angry, they do it so little that they actually feel guilty when they show it.

In contrast, strong-willed individuals are fighters, refusing to lie down and be run over by those who seek to intimidate, hurt, or control them. This tendency to stand up against the social "power brokers" is commendable. Strong-willed individuals fare better standing against those who pressure them to conform to expectations, as well as in the pursuit of achievements, in contrast to those who are weak-willed.

However, more often than not, strong-willed individuals are too aggressive in dealing with those who seek to get them to conform to what they—the social power brokers—want them to do. They are also too aggressive in how they respond to the teasing and put-downs that cliques hand out. In fact, they actually communicate to these cliques that the teasing and put-downs are getting to them by their aggressive response. Most of the consequences of strong-willed individuals being long-term victims of insecurity can be traced back to how such insecure-causing contexts were handled in the past. Those who suffer from terrible insecurities often compensate for it by projecting a superior attitude toward others. In other words, they have what is commonly called a superiority complex.

There are serious consequences to long-term exposure to insecurity, and these consequences have a direct negative bearing on our relationships with others.

One of these consequences is a person believing they are unlovable as well as unworthy of being loved. Long term, when a person is treated cruelly by others, is disrespected and made fun of, and is looked upon as unattractive, he/she comes to believe the negative messages of these horrible attitudes and verbal put-downs. Constant exposure to such abuse will eventually turn the victim into an ally of those guilty of abusing them. This victim also comes to believe that he/she is unlovable. Individuals believe such terrible things about themselves because of their being bombarded repeatedly and consistently with such horrible negatives from others.

Constant reinforcement of such negatives from peers and family members opens the door for the victims to believe that they are indeed not significant, special, and, as a consequence, unlovable. When a person truly believes that he/she is unlovable or insignificant, the damage has completed the cycle of destruction.

However, eventually such a person is smiled upon by God and is in the right place at the right time when someone enters his/her life who treats him/her as the most important person on earth. All of a sudden, a whirlwind of ecstasy envelops that person and he or she goes on a "magic carpet ride" of love and devotion never known before. Individuals who experience this understandably never want this romantic ride to end.

However, when the subconscious compliance—the belief of unworthiness—that has plagued such insecure individuals resurfaces, the "magic carpet ride" ends. Self-doubt and that sense of unworthiness raise their ugly heads. Rather than experiencing a sense of gratitude for the blessing of having someone in their lives who devotedly cares for them, they begin to allow the belief that they are unworthy of being cared for in such a fashion. This conviction reinforces their subconscious compliance of being unworthy.

What happens next is that these individuals do one of two things. They slowly begin to mistreat the individual who devotedly cares for him/her and will do and say things to drive that person out of their lives. This is their way of affirming their unworthiness of love, as well as acquiescing to their deep-seated feelings of unworthiness. Or, they will try to dominate/control that person's life and smother them right out of the relationship. This is their twisted response to their fear of losing that person, as well as fearing the pain of lost love. Doing either one validates that sense of unworthiness, which has plagued them in the past and remains unresolved.

The tragedy is that such a sense of unworthiness is only valid in the mind rather than being ingrained in reality. Reality has changed. Based on what is real—what is happening in his/her life at that moment—affirms that he/she is worthy. However, this unworthiness, which is nothing more than a subconscious compliance, has plagued them for so long that they don't have the strength to refute it. They have grown accustomed to the misery. The need to be right—the need to affirm this belief of being unworthy of love, which is embedded deep within the subconscious—overcomes the desire to be happy.

Also, it can be legitimately stated that insecure people often look for reasons for a relationship to fail. As stated, the failure of a relationship confirms such a person's own sense of unworthiness. In the end, he/she will deny that they are truly loved and that the person who has showered them with all of this love and devotion is not as great as originally thought, because if that person had been truly that great, he/she would not have chosen to love him/

her! And the *"beat"* of such horrible subconscious compliances tragically *"goes on"*. [15]

The only way one can overcome such a subconscious compliance is to stand up to this insecurity and decisively determine that such unworthiness shall never be allowed to haunt them ever again. They may even ask, *"What about the opinions of all of the people that have come in and out of my life who have deemed me unworthy and as a result unlovable?"*

My response is, *"Those people were shallow, more insecure than you and dumb as a brick."* Just look at those horrible people in your past as being graduates of *"Psychos-Are-Us"* Preschool … end of subject. With loving support from the one who loves you, and if possible, from others who love you, this insecurity can become a thing of the past … permanently!

Second, individuals by choice must believe that they have just as much right to be loved, cherished, and treated with dignity and respect as anyone else. When such individuals begin to treat themselves better, the shackles of unworthiness are broken away. These individuals begin to become the person they have always wanted to be.

o **Wisdom Principle:** *Insecurity is the principle cause of individuals sabotaging their own happiness. Insecure*

---

[15] This is the same cycle that a man or woman, for example, experiences when he has a job that is better than what he/she believes is deserved. Or, he/she is making a salary so terrific that his/her self-worth and self-respect are not equal to the money being paid. Either way, a person who struggles with the inferiority of unworthiness will continue to sabotage the success that he/she is experiencing.

individuals do more to sabotage their own happiness than anyone else.

o **Wisdom Principle:** *The greatest message of Christ dying on the cross is that every single individual is invaluable, significant, and lovable! However, this message is ineffective until it is embraced.*

Third, such individuals must allow the love, attention, and sense of importance conveyed to them by the ones who devotedly care for them, to nurture their hearts and positively affirm their significance. The proof that someone has done this is the mirroring back to the person who has shown him/her the admiration, respect, love, and devotion, initially given to him/her.

Fourth, fear is another consequence of experiencing some of the insecurities mentioned previously. There are five great human fears that exist in this world. Let's look at them.

The first is of rejection. I am convicted that being controlled or consumed by this fear is a complete waste of time. We can't control who ultimately genuinely accepts us or not. I know there are millions among us who leave their homes every single day expecting 100% acceptance by those whom they encounter in their work or activities. Such an expectation is extremely unreasonable. Total acceptance by others is just not there and never will be. This is true; the world is impersonal—it simply doesn't care!

The theory of cliques consistently bumps up against the reality that the 100% unconditional acceptance from others simply will not occur. This theory states that the greater the numbers of individuals in a clique the greater the possibility that a clique member will be accepted by others as a result of the pressure other clique members can put on a person if the acceptance of a member of their clique does not occur.

This acceptance is based on the premise that being part of a clique, and the significance of the number of individuals who are part of a particular clique, insures, almost to a certainty, that individuals can be pressured into accepting others in the same clique. The theory also states that this pressure occurs by the intimidating hand of the clique-hounds—clique members. This is not just a misconception, it's actually false.

You or I being unconditionally accepted by someone is one thing. However, to be conditionally accepted by someone because one fears rejection by the clique-hounds or someone else, is on the opposite side of the spectrum. Clique-hounds and leaders of cliques refuse to admit the reality that 100% approval is simply not there. For each of the clique members the end justifies the means. In other words, to get acceptance and conformity by any means is fine as long as acceptance and conformity to the clique's expectations occurs.

o **Wisdom Principle:** *The unconditional acceptance of an individual is completely opposite of the conditional acceptance. One is based on respect while the latter is based on* *conformity to the expectations of the social power brokers of any social circle.*

The acceptance or rejection of someone is primarily based on these five particulars: physical attractiveness, personality, religious affiliation, social/ economic status, character qualities.

Of these five, two are superficial standards by which most individuals determine whether to accept or reject someone. Those who determine with whom they will be friends on the basis of these two very shallow determinates demonstrate a lack of character as well as a pervasive shallowness.

The second great fear is of failure. I have already spoken about failure in the first chapter. Let me simply add here that failure for those who know and have experienced success is critical in achieving success. There are lessons to be learned in failure that cannot be learned any other way. Also, individuals who are successful are not deterred by failure, but rather use it as an opportunity to strengthen their character as well as collect valuable information, which can be used in formulating a more effective plan of success farther down the road.

There are four primary reasons for failure. Successful people will use any or all of these reasons to reassess their circumstances, correct their mistakes, and buttress their plan of achievement with greater and better means and methods in order to assure their success in the future. The primary components of failure are:

➤ **Poor planning:** Possibly didn't have enough research at the beginning of the task, therefore, miscalculations occurred. These miscalculations could have been in the areas of research or finance

➤ **Lack of determination or desire:** The cost of success was not correctly or accurately assessed. As a result, the price to be paid for success was too great for the individuals involved. More commitment was needed

➤ **Unforeseen legitimate obstacles:** This could be partners for the project dropping out. It could be government/legal obstacles. It could a be a political obstacle, poor sales for the service or product you were selling, or poor timing (a full-blown recession occurred when you started promoting your service or product)

➤ **Poor attitude:** Sometimes a project gets started off on the wrong foot. When it does it's usually because of one of two things—poor preparation or poor attitudes—which have infected the team working for success

The problem with most people is that they perceive failure as being a commentary on one's intelligence and ability. Not true! In fact, only in a very small minority of circumstances is failure a commentary on a person's intelligence or ability. No person's life should be defined by failure, even a particular failure, unless that person allows such to occur. The lives of each of us ought to be primarily defined by our character. My final comment on failure involves the four critical components for success in a particular project or endeavor. When commencing a project, one must have a firm handle on these four critical components: research, finance, preparation, sales.

The third great fear is the loss of love or something of personal significance. There is no question, at least in my mind, that individuals who seek a relationship with another individual for the primary purpose of terminating loneliness are haunted by the fear of loss of love, of companionship, or something else of any personal significance. These individuals seek a relationship for all of the wrong reasons. Relationships cultivated by those who are plagued by a sense of loneliness more often than not are subpar at best.

Those relationships seem to turn into an endurance test for both of the participants. Resolving loneliness through a relationship will always end in disappointment. A relationship is the wrong vehicle for resolving either loneliness or neediness. Any person who is haunted by the fear of the loss of love is not ready for any kind of a love relationship. There aren't any guarantees in life. Also, there is no such thing as absolute security in life. There is no question that needy individuals not only are unable to receive genuine love, because they are also unable to give it.

The fear of losing something of significance is an equal component to the fear of the loss of love. That significant something in most peoples' lives is either money, pride, or both. People who have money usually have a great deal of pride. Those who fear losing both live with a relentless fear deep within them.

Such individuals believe they would not have the wherewithal to replace what they have if they lost it. The same is true with the fear of losing something significant. This fear is caused by a belief that they are lacking ability or competence to be able to replace what has been lost.

The fourth great fear is of poverty. Some people fear being poor because of their perception of those who are poor. I spoke of this earlier. Most people conduct themselves and their affairs as if those who have less than they do, are less than they are. Others fear being poor because they remember the tremendous challenges poverty caused them in the earlier years of their life. Poverty, for them, was stigmatizing and painful. As a result, they never want to experience poverty again! Such individuals choose to believe that being poor is the problem rather than one's perspective of poverty. Also, such individuals have seen the treatment by others of those who are poor and never want to experience the same thing!

I made some statements earlier regarding poverty. I stated that the primary cause of poverty was ignorance. I stand on that statement because in today's world, it is true. However, what I have not said, until this moment, regarding this subject is that in the time of Christ, poverty was a political issue, as well as an issue of the uneducated society's ignorance. The overwhelming majority of the people in Christ's time were ignorant. Only a very select minority—primarily male—studied in what was considered at the time as the great schools of philosophy.

However, this is not true today. Poverty can be overcome. Educational opportunities abound for the poor through scholarships, grants, and student loans. There is obviously significant commitment and sacrifice, which any individual must make in order to escape poverty. Marvelous opportunities are there for individuals to improve their lives. Such cannot be denied. My admonition to anyone who is poor is not to believe that poverty or wealth has anything to do with either being fortunate or unfortunate. Wealth and poverty primarily have to do with the abundance or lack of: education, attitude, desire, and discipline.

The fifth great fear is of death. When I was a young man I was told that if a person wasn't ready to die, he/she was also not ready to live. This may sound simplistic, but it is nonetheless true. The subject of death is not something likely to be broached during an afternoon tea. Dr. Scott Peck speaks of having patients who actually would drive far out of their intended route in order to avoid driving by a funeral home or cemetery. I find it difficult to imagine, at my age, this preoccupation with the avoidance of the subject of death. Death is as natural as birth and an inescapable part of our human existence. Facing the reality of death is a prerequisite for living, because it helps us realize there is an ultimate deadline. And, as you may or may not know, we all work better when we have deadlines.

Our obsessions with our bodies looking younger and our desire for living longer are stark examples that a significant majority of the world's population is not able to wrap its mind and arms around this subject. Men and women collectively spend billions of dollars on surgeries and products that will hopefully help them look younger longer. It seems that the obsession that our image-driven society has with looking younger knows no bounds. However, death will not go away just because people don't want to be reminded of it. Death stands at the final intersection of each of our lives and forces us, sooner or later, to take its meaning for each of us into consideration.

No matter how rich you are, how famous, or how intelligent you are, eventually "Dr. Death" drops by. Usually unexpected, he says to each of us, "I'm here for our appointment." We may reply disarmingly, "What appointment?" However, we know what appointment Dr. Death is speaking about. It's useless to kid ourselves.

The best preparation for death is our acceptance of it. Again, I know this sounds simplistic. However, it's also true. Embracing death is essential to our integrity and wholeness. Don't bother running from death. You can't. Nor will you outrun it. Recognize the blessing of death. No, this isn't a morbid thought. Choose to work through your apprehensions of it deliberately and cognitively. No one has all of the answers when it comes to dying. Death is simply a hallway through which we must walk to get to the next level of consciousness.

Last, as the Apostle Paul says, we must "make the most of our time" (Ephesians 5:18). This means we must treasure time and make it count. We do so when we make positive and effective use of our time. There are many things of which we can get more. However, time is not one of them. Make your time count while you can.

o **Wisdom Principle:** *Possessing the energy to accomplish what you must is more important that having more time.*

One last thought about death and getting older: there is nothing more marvelous to see than a man or a woman who has embraced the inevitability of growing older. Such people have a marvelous rhythm and flow about them. They maintain a dignity and grace that few understand. No, Hollywood isn't going to serendipitously discover them and make them stars. The beauty about this reality is that such individuals know such a thing isn't going to happen and they are okay with that.

How many people are still chasing an unrealistic dream that Hollywood is going to pick them out and that they still have a chance of becoming a star? There are too many to count! Only a fool refuses to see the truth for what it is. However, those who have embraced the reality that all of us eventually pass away have been able to discipline their egos to accept the fact that they can't live forever. We were never meant to do so. All we can do is be the best we can be until that time arrives. This means that each of us needs to be kind, gracious, altruistic, decent, and thankful for the time we have.

o **Wisdom Principle:** *Death may be the greatest insult to the ego, but for Christians, death is the beginning of our heavenly journey—the greatest yearning of our redeemed soul.*

When individuals live their lives based on fear, it is safe to conclude that the thing they fear the most, will likely occur. Fear acts like a magnet and a goal in our subconscious. We are actually drawn toward its fulfillment. To understanding the power and destructiveness of inappropriate fear is pivotal. All of the fears I have mentioned are inappropriate. Most are fears that are a complete waste of time. No good comes to any person who becomes obsessed with any fear. Fear will eventually take you over and your life will diminish as a result. Every byproduct of inappropriate fear is a negative that will bring about living life on minimums and with self-imposed limitations.

For example, I have known parents who worried about their son getting into drugs, getting in trouble with the law, getting killed in a car crash, or getting a girl pregnant. I have known parents who worried about their daughter being raped and murdered, getting pregnant, drinking, or taking drugs. When it comes to their children, parents need to be very careful about their worries. Like I said in the previous paragraph, you can worry your greatest fears into reality by drawing those fears into your life. We must not forget that our fears work like magnets.

o **Wisdom Principle:** *We partly define ourselves by what we worry about.* —Dr. Gordon Livingston

Worry is a byproduct of fear. The Bible is filled with admonitions regarding worry. Christ tells us in Matthew 6:25-34:

> *"Consequently, I implore you not to worry about your life, such as what you will eat or drink, your*

physical attractiveness, or your clothing. Isn't your life more important than what you will eat, what you look like or how 'chick' your clothes look? Take a focused look at the birds in the air. Can't you see that they do not plant or harvest? Can't you see that they do not build barns and hoard a harvest? Yet, your Heavenly Father takes care of them. They find food and they have plenty to eat. Have you ever seen a bird die of starvation? Of course not! Yet, aren't you much more precious than they? Which of you can add 18" to your height or years to your lifespan by worrying? None of you!

"Also, why are you so worried about your clothes—how you look and the quality of them? Take a focused look at the lilies of the field. Look at them as they grow. These flowers do not work or produce any tangible thing. However, I promise you that Solomon, in all of his spectacular wealth and splendor, was not as gorgeous, as one of these flowers. If this is how God cares for the grass in the fields, which sprouts up today and is cut down the next day and thrown into a fire, let me ask you a question: Will He not be more conscientious of your needs? Will He not make sure you are clothed? Oh, goodness! You have such little faith!

"I implore you, don't get caught up in the vicious daily cycle of questions like 'What are we going to eat? What are we going to drink? What are we going to wear?' The uncouth, unenlightened, and unrefined people are chasers of the shallower things of life. However, your Heavenly Father knows what you need.

"Let me share with you a heavenly axiom: Seek the citizenship of God's kingdom first, and the righteous character of God. As a result, all of the things necessary for life and living will be provided for you, as a consequence of your seizing the opportunities of being of service to others. As a matter of fact, don't go around borrowing trouble, when it comes to tomorrow. Tomorrow comes soon enough and you will need to work through the challenges tomorrow presents when it arrives. Each and every day has its own challenges."

Earl Nightingale has said that worry is counterproductive. Worry robs us of energy, which can be used in creative efforts, problem-solving, and production. Worry steals from all of us opportunities we will fail to recognize because we are consumed with anxieties. Mr. Nightingale has broken down the percentages of worry and how trivial worrying about life and living can be. He says the following:

➤ 40% of worries never happen
➤ 30 % of worries already have happened and cannot be changed
➤ 12% of worries are needless worries about health
➤ 10% of worries are petty/miscellaneous/irrelevant
➤ 8% of the things about which people worry are legitimate[16]

Let me ask you this. When you look at these percentages, don't you feel a bit embarrassed or a little bit foolish? I have come to realize that there are two ways to eliminate worry from our lives.

---

[16] From Earl Nightingale's speech entitled "The Strangest Secret

One is to pray and the other is to effectively communicate with others. Praying is "venting vertically". Praying increases our confidence in God and increases our courage. Prayer gives us boldness to confront each challenge. Also, please make a note: Effectively communicating with those who are involved, directly or indirectly, in the things about which we are worrying will have a diminishing effect on our tendency to worry.

Finally, each of us must understand that fear is a prerequisite for courage. If we never feared we would never need to have courage. As I stated earlier, courage is not the absence of fear, but the mastery of it. Just as failure is a necessary component of success, failure teaches us how not to do something. Fear tells us that we lack the character, confidence, competence, faith, or knowledge necessary in order to face the challenge that lies before us.

Another consequence of the insecurities mentioned previously, is an angry and cynical attitude. This, more often than not, is projected from a base of what I call angry arrogance. I want to warn you that individuals who are afflicted with angry arrogance, are manipulative, hypocritical, and mean. What makes such people dangerous is that they have the ability to be kind, gracious, and considerate when it serves their purpose. Also, you will never see this attitude of angry arrogance in the beginning of the cultivation of a relationship with someone like this. Such individuals put their best on display when needed. However—and you had better read the following closely—the insecurities they have failed to work through, viciously haunt them and they fight these insecurities by being controlling, intimidating, confrontational, and uncooperative in relationships once they are comfortable enough expressing themselves.

When they reach this comfort level the real person is revealed and those who are more than knee-deep in a relationship with such individuals begin to "pay the dues and sing the blues". When we, as victims, are caught in the deadly web of such people we find that they will consistently look out for #I (themselves) at the expense of #2 (us). It is a zero-sum strategy on their part, but the angry arrogant are too dumb to know that this is true.

I happen to believe that in the lives of the overwhelming number of individuals who fit this description such people have never had a personal encounter with the Living Christ. In fact, those few who have had such an experience, and possess an angry and cynical attitude, are so far out of sight and mind in their daily walk with God that their lives can be described as secular, as well as spiritually cynical. I am of the conviction that a profound spiritual encounter with the Living God is the only hope of turning these people around.

Yet another consequence of the insecurities mentioned previously is the phenomenon of becoming invisible. People become invisible in many ways. Shyness is one. Being excessively quiet when around others is another, as is being a social recluse. The consequences of any of these strategies are the same. People become invisible to others and communicate, as a result of their aloofness, that they want to be left alone. When a person sends this non-verbal message out to the world, intentionally or unintentionally, such an individual will ultimately be left alone. How and why does this happen? Others perceive this type a person as not being interested in mixing with them—that he/she would rather be left alone. When others pick up on this nonverbal message, they will respect the wishes of the person who is withdrawn. If this is not the intended wish, no signal has been given by the aloof individual that this is not the case. In truth, a person chooses to be this way because of deep insecurities—possessing deep feelings of inadequacy, a low social IQ, or simply fearing rejection.

Still another consequence of insecurity is being sensitive to, if not obsessed by, the opinions of other people. As long as you are concerned about what other people think, you will always have a restless spirit and experience a lack of peace in your heart. Being sensitive to the opinions of other people is the second fastest path to mediocrity. The fastest path is an entitlement attitude.

The final consequence of insecurities is what I call *"masking"*. This involves individuals, who have become expert practitioners of self-rejection, taking on roles in life. Such individuals live an illusion. They talk about achieving things they have never achieved, getting educations they have never received, coming from families of wealth, power and influence, when the opposite is true, and having resources and relationships with others that, in reality, they do not have and have never had. Masking can also include trying to speak with a particular inflection. For example, a person may sound quite southern when speaking in their natural tone of voice, but want to sound differently. As a result, he/she will seek to put a different inflection in the way they speak, rather than to express themselves in their natural voice.

To be quite frank, every one of us has exaggerated something about ourselves. We have put a sensational twist to something we have said we have done, when in reality, we have not done anything of the sort. For most of us, such contexts occurred when we were very young. However, for some people the game of convincing others goes on, and on, and on, until all credibility is lost. The stories told are just too incredible to be true.

Let me illustrate: A few years ago, there was a fellow who pretended to be the star quarterback of the Pittsburgh Steelers—Ben Roethlisberger. He looked a little like Ben. He even said he was "Big Ben". But the truth was that he was not Ben Roethlisberger. In fact, the only way I heard about this story is that it got a terrific amount of press. I heard about this story first on ESPN. This guy thought he would be looked upon as special and important by portraying himself to be someone else. However, in the end he was exposed for what he was—a fraud.

There is no question that those who mask have significant unresolved psychological and emotional problems. With treatment, masking can become a thing of the past. However, very few such individuals ever conquer this very dangerous way of hiding insecurities and feelings of insignificance.

One of the great proofs that masking is a huge social problem in our country, is the success of tabloids such as *The Star* and the *National Inquirer*, magazines like *People* and TV programs like *Entertainment Tonight*. I remember one evening seeing an episode of the sitcom "The Office". In that particular episode one of the young women who worked in the office had been on vacation. Upon her return, she was asked by one of her co-workers if her vacation had gone well. She immediately launched into a report on the lives of Angelina Jolie, Brad Pitt, Tom Cruise and other celebrities. He responded to her by saying, "That's interesting, but I asked, how your vacation went." Her response was, "I just told you!" Unbelievable, isn't it? There are millions of teenagers and young adults just like her. Reality for them is boring because they are boring!

Insecurities cause great pain and suffering for the insecure, as well as those who are part of the lives of these insecure individuals. When it comes to dealing with these people it's a two-sided coin. On one side, there's compassion for what they have gone through and are going through. The other side of the coin shows the statute of limitations—being a continual victim of such insecurities very often has expired.

A few paragraphs ago, I spoke about those who were afflicted with angry arrogance. This is the result of a person not processing well the vicissitudes of life they were dealt. The angry arrogant individuals among us know in their guts what they truly are. They also know they will never have any kind of a relationship with anyone as long as they continue to project anger arrogance. However, the problem is this. They don't care enough to change. Therefore, they mask their anger with arrogance. People who hide the person they truly are for selfish purposes, are just dangerous. They are guilty of many things, but within the context I am writing about here, they are guilty of masking.

What we need is tolerance for those who are victims of insecurity. However, what we also need is for each of us to be an encourager to those who are insecure. We need to consistently communicate to them that they are valuable and each one of them matters. To those of us who have the greater illumination, we have the greater responsibility to be encouragers.

o **Wisdom Principle:** *The more we postpone having to deal with legitimate suffering, the more we suffer in the end.*

There are four things regarding insecurities that must be done.

One, insecurities must be faced. By faced, I mean that you need not run from them, ignore them, or rationalize them. Facing up to insecurities means to see them as they are, not the way you think they are. This requires self-honesty rather than self-rationalization. Self-rationalizing your insecurities simply will not get it! When one rationalizes insecurities, problems are often compounded.

Two, insecurities must be acknowledged ... out loud. Stand in front of a mirror and say out loud the kinds of insecurities that have haunted you. There is something about hearing yourself saying these things out loud that gets them out in the open, i.e., out of your heart and mind where you can see them. You will sense a peace come over you that you've never experienced up that point. There is something positive to be said of those who declare such things aloud rather than just repeating them in their minds.

Three, insecurities need to be confronted. By confronted, I mean that the insecurities that have vexed your life need to be personalized (taken ownership of), looked squarely in the eye and stated. From that point on they (the insecurities) will no longer victimize you. I advise you to say this over and over again. I would advise you to make a card that says that the insecurities are beliefs and feelings that have been imposed on you from your own ideas, thoughts, and actions; the media themselves; and others.

Also, put on that card that such insecurities will no longer sabotage your belief and confidence in yourself. I would put this card in your wallet/purse, the corner of your bathroom mirror or on your refrigerator door. Look at it every day and commit yourself to follow through on your declaration of being free from the stigmatism of insecurity.

Besides taking a card and writing down your insecurities, you need to make a commitment to live an ethical and virtuous life. There is no question that living right will do wonders for your self-respect, your self-confidence, and your character. I have written about this area of life adequately in this book so that you are able to organize your life, in order to chart a path toward excellence in your daily life.

You also need to accept yourself just as you are and make a commitment to tell yourself that you genuinely love yourself. You do this for the best reason of all because Christ loves you and gave His life so that you could receive forgiveness and eternal life. Proverbs 19:8 says: *"Individuals who make a commitment to becoming wise, are people who love their own soul and nurture it with God's love and wisdom."* Self-acceptance is paramount to your loving yourself. Also, affirming your love for yourself occurs by having positive conversations with yourself about yourself. What you say about yourself to yourself is more important than what others say about you, or will ever say about you.

o **Wisdom Principle:** *Loving yourself is wise. Falling in love with yourself is not so wise. The former is altruistic and the latter is narcissistic.*

Finally, insecurities that have to do with your competence or something about you that you have the ability to change must be worked on every day. Your intention to do something about the insecurities in your life that are within your power to eradicate, in contrast to doing something about their eradication, is like starting a car and putting it into drive. Starting a car does not get you where you want to go. However, putting the car in gear does! There is a huge difference between intention and action—intending to do something and actually doing it. Once you take action, insecurity will no longer be your ultimate nemesis.

o **Wisdom Principle:** *The only way to grow as a human being, is to turn weaknesses into strengths.* —Dr. Wayne Dyer

CHAPTER NINE

DIFFICULT PEOPLE / THIRTY MARKERS

o **Wisdom Principle:** *All of us have to come to terms with the monster within us. Either we allow ourselves to be controlled by it or we control it. Our misery or happiness will be determined by what we allow.*

Chapter Introduction

Because one third of the vicissitudes in our lives come from our contact with difficult people, I was compelled to write this chapter. I am not going to play games with you. This will likely be an uncomfortable chapter to read. I would rather write positive and uplifting chapters rather than write chapters that speak about the miseries and difficulties of life and the individuals who do their fair share in creating them. There are too many people who have been scarred as a result of associating and being in relationships with difficult people.

Life has taught me that the pain and suffering in our lives are divided into thirds: one-third from self-inflicted pains; one-third from the vicissitudes of life, to which all of us are vulnerable; and the final third from the contacts, associations, and relationships, we have with difficult people. Because of this I can't be silent about the damage these people do to others. It's needless! Fasten your seatbelts. This chapter is a "rough ride". The reason is that all of us will see ourselves in some of the markers I have listed that make up part of the lives of most difficult people.

The only individual who doesn't know that he/she is difficult to live with, work with, or associate with is the one who is difficult. Because we could better comprehend just exactly what the components of a difficult person are if we had a few examples to consider, I want to return to the story of the Prodigal Son in New Testament book *The Gospel of Luke*. Let's focus on the verses 15:25-32 at the end of the parable. These verses introduce us to the older son. If you recall, he was the one who stayed home, while the younger son took his inheritance and left home in order to find his true self. What we find out in this passage is that the son who stayed—the son who worked on the farm every day—was just as messed up, if not more so, as the younger son who left. You may ask, "How could the son who seemingly did the right thing, be the one who needed the most illumination?"

Let's look at the latter part of the "Parable of the Prodigal Son" found in Luke 15:25-32.

> *"All of the joy and preparations for a celebration were the result of the father and prodigal son being reunited. During this activity, the older brother was out in the fields*

working. When the day's labor had been concluded, the older son returned to the family home. As he approached the house, he heard music, dancing, and laughter. Curious, he called one of the house servants over for an explanation. The servant told him what had occurred and that his father ordered a celebration and feast as a result of his brother's return home, safe and sound.

"Not pleased, the older son became defiant and refused to go in and join in the celebration. When his father heard that he was outside and refusing to come in, the father went out to reason with him. However, his older son refused to listen. He began to make the case for himself to his father. Here is what this older son said: 'I want you to realize just how many years I have stayed here working and serving you. I have not given you (as far as this older son knew) one moment's grief. I have been faithful and responsible; yet, you have never thrown a party for me and my friends. All of a sudden this younger son of yours, who has squandered your money on prostitutes, returns home and you throw a magnificent feast!'

"The father remained calm. 'Son, you have been with me throughout your younger brother's absence, and because of this, all that I have belongs to you. But you don't seem to understand what is happening here. This is a very significant event and we had to celebrate it. Your brother was dead, as far as I was concerned. However, he is alive! He was lost, but now he is found!"

o   **Wisdom Principle**: *A person can be right but act in such an arrogant and self-righteous manner that others will be repulsed at his/her display of self-righteousness.*

Now, the events that followed the younger son's return are very clear. What is not clear are the reasons for the reaction of the older brother. Did he not love his brother? Did he not also miss his brother as his father did? Was he not grateful that his brother had returned home safe and sound? These are fair questions. Over the years of my ministerial work I have had scores of people tell me they have great issues with how this parable ends. To them, it looks as if the younger son escapes the consequences of his irresponsibility, while the older son is condemned for being responsible. On the surface, it may seem that way, but it isn't.

The obvious question is: What made this older brother difficult to work with, live with, and associate with? He had a terrific father. He seemed to have a terrific home life. Therefore, what made him the difficult person he seemed to be? The succinct answer is that he chose to be this way. I believe the scripture is very clear about this. I believe the older son misconstrued the love of his father and the quality of the home life, of which he was a part. He saw such graces as entitlements and opportunities that he could take advantage of by manipulating them to his own ends. There is no question that he believed he was entitled to the privileges he had. I am deeply convicted that he became the person he was by choice. Somewhere in his life, he decided that a person's life consisted of the things he possessed. He had decided to sacrifice relationships for material possessions and power. He had a "checklist mentality". For him, relationships were a means to an end. To the older son, economic strength led to power and control over others. As a result, he "viciously" protected those two "assets" of his life. As far as he was concerned, the end truly justified the means.

Like our children, we must realize that this older son, after a period of time, was responsible for his decisions, no one else—not his younger brother or even his father. The younger son, although for different reasons, had an entitlement mentality as well. One son found himself in the proverbial "pigpen" (as well as a real one!), and the other among the self-righteous, in other words, having the attitude of the Pharisees. One was repentant and one believed that this experience called life was all about him.

The attitude of the older brother makes it clear to me that he likely had a great deal to do with the younger brother's exit from the home. When looking at his behavior under such "special circumstances" we see his character revealed. He obviously didn't give his father the benefit of the doubt. In fact, he made the worst assumptions or insinuations that he could make about his father and his brother. He was arrogant (he thought he was better than others), judgmental (loved finding fault with others), and unforgiving (he kept score). He had no interests other than his own. He put wealth above relationships, and made no apology for doing so.

I am convinced that virtually all behavior is learned. We learn from how we have lived, from our beliefs, and from what we have experienced. As a result, difficult people are primarily nurtured and developed. You may ask, "How are they nurtured, and developed, and by whom?" Overwhelmingly, difficult people are developed by other difficult people who, in turn, were developed by other difficult people. The odds are stacked against someone who has been raised by authoritarian individuals who, in turn, are difficult. Not everyone handles the vicissitudes of life the same way. Difficult people are difficult as a consequence of their inability to process the vicissitudes of life effectively.

I think it can also be said that parents do their fair share by cultivating the breeding ground for their children to become difficult people. They do this by either abusing their children or ridiculously spoiling them. Regarding the latter, I am speaking about parents who wait on their children hand-and-foot with the result of raising their spoiled children to grow up to become narcissistic adults possessing an entitlement mentality. As you know by now, danger is always at the extremes. It's the spoiled and the abused among us that wind up in the same place, although for different reasons. Difficult authority figures, as well as unintelligent parents, produce difficult children who, in turn, become difficult adults. I think that it is safe to say that we can, unfortunately, count on difficult people to produce difficult people, and this includes children from the current generation of our children.

As I have stated, difficult people can be raised in environments that are on opposite extremes. Difficult people are either raised in environments that are highly critical and abusive—psychologically, emotionally and physically; or they can be raised in environments, in which they have been given what they wanted, when they wanted it and how they wanted it. This latter environment gives children an enormous amount of unmerited and unearned power. To those who say that becoming a difficult person just happens, my response is, "Sorry, in 95% of cases, you will be wrong."

It is safe to say that affirmation, encouragement, and legitimate praise are, for the most part, virtually absent in the abusive environments. Children who are treated this way will, in turn, grow up to be difficult adults. Remember that difficult people are most often victims of difficult people and the compassion we should have for them is justified. However, the other side of the coin states that the "statute of limitations" has run out on difficult people being excused for being difficult, when they are well into their adult years. They can only use the excuse that they were raised in a family filled with difficult people, abused by difficult people, or suffered bad breaks in their life, for just so long.

It has been my observation that only a very small percentage of individuals have become the personification of what I describe as difficult simply by choosing to be so. However, the majority became difficult primarily because such behavior was modeled by someone whom they admired, who got what he/she wanted by being ruthless and intimidating. It isn't difficult to understand, why an individual would think that using the same methods would guarantee that he/she would get his/her way, too. Difficult people only care about getting what they want.

Let's begin looking at the components of exactly what makes a person difficult to associate, work, and live with.

1. Difficult People Do Not See Themselves as Difficult

It is astonishing to me that people can be as difficult as they are, and at the same time believe they are not difficult to associate with, work with or live with. However, this is unfortunately the case. The reasons they don't perceive themselves as difficult is because they are character disordered to begin with. All character disordered people blame others for the challenges they face, as well as the unresolved difficulties with which they wrestle daily.

When difficult people have conflict with the world at large, from their perspective the world is responsible for whatever conflict exists. Those with this point-of-view, 24/7/365, are either ignoring the truth, or have simply chosen to practice self-deception on the highest level. When Dr. Gordon Livingston says that the greatest deceptions are those we practice on ourselves, I believe he had such a scenario in mind. By the way, if you do not have his book *Too Soon Old, Too Late Smart,* your library is incomplete.

To me, difficult people are not difficult primarily because they are unlucky or genetically predisposed to this behavior. Becoming a difficult individual, as pointed out earlier, is primarily a consequence of three things.

The first is being raised in an abusive environment by adults who are themselves very difficult. The second is an individual being given virtually everything their heart desires. The third is the result of being roughed up by life's vicissitudes. It is obvious that difficult people ironically become so when raised in environments that are on the opposite extremes.

When individuals grow up in a home filled with difficult people, it isn't hard to see how they can intuitively become unintentional experts on them. I have seen the consequences of this, in the lives of members of my immediate family. There came a point in each of their lives that they had a choice in who and what they would become. Because I understood the flaws in my family environment, I begin to consciously refuse to be like those members of my family I had concluded were difficult to associate, live, and work with. The only exception was my grandmother. She was the antithesis of the rest of the bunch.

Those who have grown up in similar environments and found the challenges of living with difficult people to be enormous, want no part of being like them. However, although we don't want to be like those difficult individuals, we must understand that just growing up in such an environment makes possible the fact that we will likely reflect certain *markers* of these difficult people. Over the years, many have told me how surprised they were to discover they had many of the same tendencies as those difficult individuals they lived with. Those with those "markers" will spend their lives working to divest themselves of these subconscious compliances.

2. Difficult People Intuitively See the Worst in Others in Virtually Every Conceivable Context

Difficult people usually think the worst of any person or situation because they have a poor view of humanity in general and they refuse to give others the benefit of the doubt. As a result, they have an intuitive distrust and disrespect for people. Because of this distrust and disrespect, I think it is also fair to say that anything that is said to them that is critically observant either of their personality or their performance, is taken in the worst possible way by them. Difficult people, while projecting an incredibly arrogant attitude, are horribly insecure. They carry a persecution complex—24/7/365—believing everybody is out to get them. Since they consistently cause havoc in the lives of others, this isn't all that difficult to understand. Deep within most difficult people is an angst they sense, which is the result of their intuitive conviction that they deserve to be the target of the displeasure of others.

However, when difficult people are cognizant of such a conviction, they ignore it and push such conviction deeper into their subconscious. Over time, their being difficult ceases to be a cognitive reality and instead becomes completely subconscious.

They not only can be sensitive to the point of paranoia, but they can also make everyone else's life as difficult and miserable as theirs in such contexts. I spoke about insecurity in the previous chapter. What I want to state unequivocally here is that difficult people are not private about their insecurity. By this I mean that they reveal their insecurities in non-verbal ways as well as by their defensive reactions in certain contexts. They may individually pay the price for their insecurity, but everyone else who has to associate with them does, too. There is no question that having to associate with, work with, and live with difficult people is nothing less than a "zero-sum game" for everyone concerned.

3. Difficult People Must Be Accommodated in Order for the Life-Environments of Which They Are a Part to Remain Amicable.

Difficult people have a preconceived idea of how things are supposed to go. All of us have had individuals in our lives who've had to be coddled, catered to, and accommodated in order to keep any semblance of peace and tranquility in the environments they are a part. When not accommodated all kinds of problems emerge. Immature reactions on the part of the difficult individual involved begin to occur. Whatever guilt-throwing, criticism, or anger is expressed, these difficult people do it with an attitude of entitlement.

Those victims who have to relate to such people literally have to walk on eggshells when around them. Pouting, complaining, aloofness, and treating others as if they don't exist are all part of the difficult person's strategy to force others to get with their program. I'm always amazed that difficult people exude an attitude that they have the right to define the program and others are expected to comply. There is no collaboration, dialogue, or discussion. It is their way or the proverbial highway.

The older son in the parable had a program—a strategy. He wanted the younger brother out. He got his wish when the younger brother left. When this occurred, he knew the farm would eventually be his. He likely worked much harder than ever before, because he had all of the confidence in the world that his plan had succeeded. By working hard on the family farm, in reality he was protecting his investment. Part of his personal program protecting what would eventually be his was to make sure everyone had to follow his program/plan. He probably thought it would only be a matter of time before the family estate would all be his and he would rule with an iron fist. In his eyes, he had earned it. Let me add here that as a rule, difficult people believe that working hard, at any endeavor, covers/justifies any relational problems that may occur in their lives. I will address this point more thoroughly in a few moments.

However, the strategy or plan of the older brother developed a hitch. His younger brother came back. The plan was now threatened. He ought to have realized how mercenary he was in his attitude, but difficult people, as a rule, are virtually void of self-honesty. Difficult people are, psychologically, blunt instruments.

His reactions showed how he fearful he was regarding the return of his younger brother. This was the cause of his anger—that he had an innate fear of losing what he believed was rightfully his. I you will remember, this is one of the five greatest fears—the fear of the loss of something significant ... the family farm. He feared losing a significant portion of the farm to his younger brother.

Therefore, as most difficult people do when they are fearful and angry, the older son created havoc. When he discovered his beloved world had been disturbed by his younger brother's return, He became incensed and was ready to do whatever was necessary to get his environment back to where it was once his younger brother had left. The older son was so determined to do this that he was willing to make life miserable for all of the people who lived with him and who worked around him until he got his own way. What a jewel this guy was, don't you think?

4. Difficult People Are the Consummate Guilt-Throwers

The next thing we observe is that the older son shows another side of his character-disordered personality. He throws guilt at his father. Guilt-throwers are insecure, selfish, and manipulative. The older son couldn't have cared less that he was quenching his father's joy for the safe return of his brother. All he cared about was himself and his interests. So much so, that he was willing to ruin the evening of celebration for everyone by creating conflict in order to keep control. You will notice that until he showed up there was no conflict occurring. From the older brother's perspective, if he wasn't going to be the center of attention then nobody would be!

5. Difficult People Expect to Receive from Others What They Refuse to Give to Others

Difficult people are so needy in their insecurity that they are incapable of giving to others that which they want to receive from them. Consequently, they believe they are entitled to receive from others what they are unwilling to give. Also, they are unwilling to give what they are not prepared to give. As you know, I have spoken to this one issue in my essentials in Chapter One. What difficult people all have in common is that they are not qualified to be in any kind of a relationship with anyone. Difficult people are too immature, too demanding, too shallow, too needy, and too difficult to deal with. Again, their lack of self-honesty, as well as their behavior, gives them away.

Here is the key to this point: The insecure want everyone else to resolve their insecurities and deficiencies for them by accommodating them and giving them what they want. This gives difficult people a false sense of security. Difficult people do not want to work on this task themselves but erroneously believe that if others accommodate them their insecurities can be resolved and eradicated. In other words, if others willingly fulfill their needs and expectations, they must be OK or the fulfilling of their needs and expectations would not have occurred. This is really backward thinking, isn't it?

However, just as one nation cannot truly gain another nation's freedom for them; or another individual raise another's self-worth, others cannot create or bolster an insecure person's self-respect and self-acceptance. This is the job for the insecure and un-self-accepting themselves, not anyone else. However, difficult people don't seem to "get it" as the young say. When it comes to this, as long as a person has serious insecurities, he/she will be difficult, if not impossible, to work with, live with and associate with. Unfortunately, the last individuals on earth who understand this are the difficult people themselves.

There would be fewer broken and/or difficult relationships if there were a world-wide law which stated that difficult, immature, and insecure individuals could not be in relationships without proving they have made significant progress in resolving these issues. However, such a law will never happen. Why? Because the "wolves" are in charge of the "hen house".

- o **Wisdom Principle:** *Those who are married and still harbor deep-rooted insecurities, are difficult, if not impossible, to live with.*

- o **Wisdom Principle:** *The last people in the world to know they are difficult are the difficult.*

6. Difficult People Are Arrogant

- o **Wisdom Principle:** *"It is impossible to defeat an ignorant man in an argument."*—William G. McAdoo

- o **Wisdom Principle:** *The confidence of ignorance will always overcome indecision of knowledge.*

Difficult people truly believe that they are superior to others. If you don't believe it, give the difficult in your presence a little space and in a few moments, they will communicate this, if not by implication, then verbally. Arrogance, as I've said throughout this book, is a definite sign of insecurity and of ignorance. I have known scores of difficult people in my life, and without exception, all were arrogant and believed they were entitled to the fulfillment of their demands and expectations through and by the efforts of others.

There is no question in my mind that the older brother believed he was better than his younger brother and smarter than his father. If you noticed, he didn't even give his father a chance to talk before he interrupted and began to tell him how much more superior he was to his younger brother. In fact, he wouldn't even call his younger brother, his brother. He described him, to his father, as "this son of yours". Unbelievable, don't you think?

7. Difficult People Are Consistently Poor Listeners

Difficult people are poor listeners. They don't believe others have anything of any significance to say to them. How can one know this? By listening to difficult people complain about how dumb other people are in contrast to how intelligent they are in comparison.

I have experienced the vital role "active listening" plays in the development of effective relationships and intelligence. I have also said that listening is a necessary component of a terrific attitude. Listening is a key component of authentic intelligence and a loving spirit. Most difficult people are poor listeners because of their arrogance and their lack of spiritual and relational intelligence. If difficult people were truly intelligent, they would be better listeners. They just don't believe that anyone has anything interesting or intelligent to say except themselves.

8. Difficult People Are "Task Intelligent" Yet Relationally Ignorant

There are many difficult people who are task intelligent. In fact, it is because of their task intelligence that many of us put up with them. How many times have you said that a certain person was difficult to deal with or work with and heard someone respond, "Yeah, but they sure know their stuff."? In the "Parable of the Prodigal Son", the older brother was task intelligent. There is no reason to believe that he was not excellent at what he did when it came to his work on the family farm. However, he was relationally ignorant. His relational IQ was not even as big as the size of his feet. He simply did not value relationships, primarily because he saw people, in general, as a means to an end.

One example of a difficult person was the fictional character Dr. Gregory House in the medical drama *"House"* (Fox Television Network, now in syndication). Here was a character with a definitely low relational IQ.

Another example, a real person this time, is business mogul Ted Turner. I dare say that this television icon could also be considered a difficult person. The fact, that he has been married three times ought to be a huge clue, as to how difficult a person he possibly is to live, work and associate with. We also know, based on his unbelievable success, that he is extremely task intelligent. However, in spite of such success, I believe that his emotional, spiritual, and relational intelligence is very low. What I am amazed about regarding Mr. Turner, is how similar a personality he has when compared to the character Hugh Laurie plays in the medical drama "House". I do not believe this is a coincidence. Difficult people, very much like terrific people, have personality patterns. However, and get this clear: the negatives in the lives of difficult people, when it comes to their relationships, often far outweigh the positive contributions of their task intelligence.

9. Difficult People Have Unrealistic Expectations of Life and People

Because of their entitlement mentality, difficult people have unrealistic expectations regarding life and relationships. These expectations are not only unreasonable, their expectations are often unethical and unfair, as well. One of the seven causes of conflict in the world is unrealistic expectations. Those who have them are consistently dissatisfied and disappointed with life, circumstances, people, and the lack of the results they expect. Why? Their expectations are unrealistic.

I can assure you of one thing in regards to expectations: the amount of conflict in your life will be in direct proportion to how unrealistic and unreasonable your expectations of life and others are. When a difficult person's expectations are unrealistic, he/she is going to be a <u>thorn</u> in the side of most people with whom he/she associates. This is because the unfulfilling of their expectations gives difficult people the so-called right to get angry at people they believe are responsible for their expectations not being fulfilled.

I also said that the expectations of difficult people are unethical and unfair because I see these kinds of expectations that difficult people consistently have regarding others, as a strategy to set others up for failure. This set up as I call it, gives difficult individuals the so-called "right" to point out and criticize other's failures in order to justify their control and superiority over them.

The failure to meet the "unreasonable expectations" of difficult people is tailor-made for the strategy that difficult people commonly use. That strategy is to be able to put those who have failed to meet their "reasonable" expectations on the defensive; communicate to those who have failed to meet such expectations that they are also incompetent, and finally, such failure gives difficult people the so-called "right", to throw guilt at those, who have failed to meet such "reasonable" expectations. This is a ruthless and abominable strategy that is completely absent of fairness, kindness, benevolence, or love.

o **Wisdom Principle:** *You will rarely have a second chance with difficult people. But if you do, be careful in accepting that second chance. You may spend the rest of your life paying for it.*

Another fictional character that can be appropriately used in the making of this point is the character Meryl Streep played in the movie "The Devil Wears Prada". In this movie Meryl Streep plays Miranda Priestly, editor of the #1 fashion magazine in the world called *Runway* (*Runway* is likely a metaphor for *Vogue*). This role is a perfect example of a person who is extraordinarily task intelligent yet impossible to work with. To put it mildly, she has enormous, as well as unreasonable, expectations of her employees whom she treats as if they were slaves for which she, herself, bought and paid for. She throws guilt at people as a means to manipulate them, and she expects "the moon" at every turn.

Ms. Streep's character is not only rude and inconsiderate, but cruel, void of understanding and compassion and is as loyal as a Mafia hit man. She expects the impossible from her employees and also expects them to sacrifice their relationships with their children and spouses to meet her expectations. You know why she has such expectations? It is because she sacrifices her relationships with her spouse and children. It isn't lost on me how in the movie her marriage falls apart. I'm sure you can believe that I was surprised about that! Yeah, right! Above all, what is almost incomprehensible is the arrogance of the character Miranda Priestly. She is truly an example of what it's like to make a deal with the devil.

To illustrate my point regarding unrealistic expectations, Miranda Priestly asks her first administrative assistant—Emily— to get her twins a pre-publication copy of the new Harry Potter book that had not yet been published. Ms. Priestly wanted her twins to have the book to read while on their vacation. Through professional contacts, her assistant is able to get the copy of the manuscript and have three copies printed and bound, and she accomplished all of this in just a few hours. What is amazing is that Ms. Priestly expected this to occur. In real life, you and I know that there is no way such an achievement would have been possible. Fiction or not, this was an unbelievable and unrealistic expectation. However, such did not stop Ms. Priestly from imposing this expectation on an employee—an expectation that was both illegal and unrealistic.

I believe the behavior of the older brother indicates that his expectations in regards to his father's compassion upon the return of his youngest son, were unreasonable and inappropriate. Because difficult people, as a rule, are the "Ice Kings and Queens" of the world, any warmth, compassion, and forgiveness shown by anyone, regardless of the context, is seen as a sign of weakness. Since it is likely that they never received warmth, compassion, or forgiveness in their formative years, they do not believe it is necessary to give it or that anyone else should receive it. They surmise that they didn't receive these three things from others and they survived, therefore others can survive without them, too! Any reasonable person would find this attitude inappropriate, unreasonable, and unjustified. There is no question that individuals who consistently have unrealistic expectations of others are difficult to associate, work, and live with.

10. Difficult People are Unreasonable and Inflexible

Difficult people are the antithesis of what it means to be reasonable. They are also inflexible. In contrast, people of character are reasonable. Reasonable people are truth-driven and fact-driven. Nothing hurts a reasonable person more than to make a wrong judgment about a person or about anything significant in their lives. This is why reasonable people are determined to be benign. On the other hand, difficult people do not see themselves as unreasonable or inflexible. They see themselves as simply being right. I also believe that another reason they do not see themselves as unreasonable and inflexible is that they must be comparing themselves to the Antichrist, and of course anyone can look better when making such a comparison.

Part of the difficult person's inflexibility is their being resistant to change. Dr. Scott Peck tells about a patient, who spent his savings coming to therapy for nearly two years. While in these therapy sessions, the patient complained about how long the trip was to and from Dr. Peck's office. Dr. Peck not only suggested a short-cut to his office that would save this man ten minutes each way, but he also gave him a map. In future sessions, the patient continued to complain about the long round-trip to his therapy sessions, and upon inquiry, Dr. Peck found out that this man had also lost more than one map that had been given to him. Finally, Dr. Peck stopped a particular session and insisted that this patient make the trip with him. Afterward, the patient finally admitted that the reason he didn't try the shortcut was his resistance to change. My thought upon reading this was what an expensive lesson to learn. Individuals who are this resistant to change are virtually impossible to communicate with, either logically or factually.

Was the older brother in the parable unreasonable, as well as inflexible? If you have to wonder, think again!

11. Difficult People Are Committed to Control, Not Co-operation

Difficult people, as a rule, do not primarily have relationships with people who are interesting, but rather with people they can manipulate, control, and over whom they can maintain a sense of superiority. Difficult people cannot maintain relationships with individuals who are secure and assertive. Such people drive difficult people literally out of their minds. As a result, they avoid those they can't manipulate or control. In fact, not only do they avoid such people, they insatiably search for reasons to tear them down and invalidate them.

What is their goal in doing this? They want to show such people as actually being difficult, incompetent, and unintelligent, thereby justifying just why they do not cultivate relationships with them. In other words, in the minds of the difficult among us, fully-functioning people are inferior. Independent-thinking people are also inferior. For difficult people, the need to *feel* superior to others trumps what is true. Difficult people are so self-absorbed that they intuitively seek to gather their own cliques that can serve the purpose of telling them just how great they are.

Because the older brother was into manipulation and control, we are told in this passage of *Luke* that he walked back to the house alone. Notice that identifying someone or others walking with him back to the house after the day's work, can't be done. There was no one with him. Why is this important? It is likely that the older brother was a pain to work for and to be around. Those who worked for him probably couldn't get away from him fast enough. If this were not true, I don't think the older brother would have been alone when he arrived home and heard the music and laughter.

People are basically the same all over the world. All of us want to be around those we like and enjoy being with. People were no different in the day of Christ than now when it comes to being liked and accepted by others. If the older brother were a genuinely likeable person, he wouldn't have been walking from the field back to the family home by himself.

12. Difficult People Are Distrusting and Disrespectful of Others

By being distrusting and disrespectful of others, difficult people choose to think the worst of other people. There are three reasons for this.

One, their distrust and disrespect of others is based on fear— especially fear of being taken advantage of. The code word in our society for such traits is *cautious.* As far as difficult people are concerned, this word cautious justifies their distrust and disrespect of others.

Second, this distrust and disrespect of others justifies other negative strategies, which they use in order to maintain a sense of superiority and control. Difficult people thrive on keeping others on the defensive, and they do this by subtly sabotaging others' self-confidence and competence, bringing both into question through their condemnation and criticism.

Difficult people just love it when the worst expectations they have of others are actualized. When others fail in any endeavor, difficult people are quietly ecstatic, because the mistakes that others make, open the door for them to criticize. This, in turn, reinforces their belief that they are superior to those whose efforts and failures they are criticizing. And difficult people live to criticize.

Obviously, such feelings are not valid. However, that does not, nor has it ever, stopped difficult people from believing that their feelings of superiority are appropriate and justified.

Third, difficult people are distrusting and disrespecting of others because they would rather think the worst of someone, rather than give him/her the benefit of the doubt ... until proven

otherwise. I believe it would be appropriate to state here that difficult people give few people the benefit of the doubt because they find it virtually impossible to be trusting and respectful of most people—especially people they don't know.

Now, do I have to point out that the older brother thought the worst of his younger brother, as well as their father, for putting on this inappropriate (?) celebration? Do I need to point out that the older brother was also distrusting and disrespectful of his younger brother and their father? And finally, do I need to point out that he did not give either one of them the benefit of the doubt?

13. Difficult People Are Committed to Conflict

One thing you can be sure of: there is a consistent and constant agitation in your life when you associate with a difficult person. The problem is that no one knows when the agitation will begin or when it will end. Just know that it will raise its ugly head on a regular basis.

Difficult people are not only committed to control, they are committed to conflict rather than co-operation in their relationships. They would rather talk conflict and create conflict than focus on resolving conflict. Think of this: there was no conflict in this part of the story of the prodigal son until the older brother showed up. Sadly, difficult people can truly be counted on to ruin any positive situation. It's like they ooze negativity. I have never understood why the lights don't go out in a room when a difficult person walks in. I think their difficult persona ought to drain the energy out of all electrical circuits!

When I observe conflict following certain people everywhere they go—their homes, their work environments, their relationships with others—I see people who are committed to conflict. This is more than just a coincidence. These aren't people who simply have the bad luck of conflict following them everywhere they go and in everything they do. Haven't you noticed that where ever there is conflict around the lives of certain people you find them in the middle of it? Difficult people are determined to get their way and have no problem creating the conflict necessary to do so. If they believe that they have lost control of something significant in their environments or in their lives, they will do whatever is absolutely necessary to regain that control.

Conflict is an integral component in the life of a difficult person who wants to maintain control. This is because they can't distinguish between mountains and molehills when it comes to the everyday issues and challenges of life. To the difficult among us, every issue is a mountain. They perceive any issue or event that does not follow their personal script as a potential loss of control and power. This is something they cannot nor will not tolerate.

It is important you and I understand that conflict is a means to an end in the lives of difficult people. Decent and benign people practice cooperation and peace. Difficult people see such traits as weaknesses, and a compromising of integrity. Now, this last justification is major baloney. As a result of seeing a cooperative and peace-loving attitude as a sign of weakness, difficult people seek to capitalize on these perceived weaknesses. They do this by using conflict as a weapon to break others down to the point where they throw up their hands and tell the difficult people, "Okay, have it your way." The difficult among us, by their demeanor, say, "Okay, I will. Thank you very much," and carve another notch on their gun signifying that they have "won" another confrontation.

o   **Wisdom Principle:** *The difficult may win many battles over their lifespan, but they will ultimately lose the war!*

14. Difficult People Would Rather Be Right Than Be Happy

o   **Wisdom Principle:** *Difficult people are better at arguing for their stupidity than anyone else in the world.*

As far as difficult people are concerned, they are never wrong. In fact, they have a motto: "I may not be right all the time but I am never wrong!" Difficult people are not beyond saying that they are not perfect, but their attitude communicates an arrogance that says that they believe they are perfect. How do I know difficult people believe they are rarely, if ever, wrong? I know because I never hear them apologize ... for anything.

The need to be always right is a byproduct of a need to pre-serve a false sense of integrity and dignity. It is the need to cloak one's self-image in what Dr. Scott Peck calls their assumptions of righteousness. Such people just can't let go of their simplistic thinking.

I had a friend some years ago who told me that while he was married to his first wife, close to twenty years, she never admitted that she was wrong about anything. Individuals like this are every-where! Such people believe that admitting wrongdoing is tanta-mount to admitting a weakness. Difficult people loathe looking weak or timid and will do whatever is necessary not to come across looking this way. So, don't expect them to be apologetic. This is an enormous blind spot in the lives of difficult people.

You will recall, in the story of the prodigal son, that when the father tried to reason with the older son, the young man did not calm down and admit that he overreacted. No, he stuck to his guns, as they say in Texas, and refused to admit any wrongdoing in his attitude, his perspective, or in what he said. From the perspective of this older brother, he was perfect. If we could have asked him, I am confident that he would have declared such. He was especially perfect when compared to his younger brother, or so he thought. Realistically, you and I know that he thought wrong!

15. Difficult People Are Nice Only When It Serves Their Purpose

o **Wisdom Principle:** *Difficult people have a pleasant side that is occasionally revealed, but seldom do they have an endearing side.*

Altruism is completely absent, in the life of a difficult person. You can count on this unmistakable fact: difficult people are occasionally nice, while reasonable people are consistently nice. I don't see anything nice about this older brother. He had a terrific work ethic, but, as we've seen, his work ethic was self-serving. Difficult people possess an unforgiving spirit/attitude and they are rarely nice. You may ask, "When are they nice?" Answer: When they want something, they can't get any other way, difficult people can be marvelous social performers. This is so because they have found that being nice is a means to a desired end.

Why do you think that men who are found to be abusive with their wives, as a rule, have been perceived, prior to such a revelation, as being the nicest guy anyone could ever meet? Difficult people know how to be socially charismatic. They have the ability to behave opposite of what they truly are, in order to accomplish their own purposes.

Just keep in mind that more often than not, when difficult people get their way, it's an expectation to which they believe they are entitled. This being so, difficult people will rarely be grateful for the proverbial "dominoes" of any life situation falling the right way ... their way! Obviously, the right way is the way they believe such dominoes should fall. When the dominoes do not fall as they believe they ought, usually all hell literally breaks loose.

Isn't it amazing that when the dominoes didn't fall the way the older brother had set them up that he was not very nice about it? In fact, he was very ugly about it and he showed himself being so by losing his temper over the party his father gave his younger brother.

o   **Wisdom Principle:** *Difficult people are rebels who have grown up, but only chronologically.*

16. Difficult People Have a Vicious Temper

Difficult people usually have a very volatile and vicious temper. My grandmother used to say, *"You can tell the size of the person by the size of the things which make them angry."* The only people who disagree with this saying are difficult people. When difficult people don't get their way, the strategy to turn things around so they do get their way is anger. Brutal anger is the intimidating tool used to keep control and get their way. I don't think that I have ever seen an exception to this.

As I have said many times already, difficult people are committed to control and as a result will use their capacity to get brutally angry in order to keep it. They do this without apology. I want to point out here that there is nothing that can cause me, personally, to lose complete respect for someone any quicker than when he/she uses anger inappropriately including at the wrong time.

About thirty years ago, a group of young men left an evening activity at the church where I was a youth minister and went to a pizza parlor to have fun on their own. Because I was responsible for those who were supposed to be there I was obligated to inform the parents of these young men about what they had done. Most of the parents who had come to pick up their teenagers handled had what occurred with understanding and calm dignity.

There was one young man—blond, very nice looking—whose father came to pick him up. I was standing in the youth recreation lounge when this man came in. In front of me and a few others he asked his son if what he had heard was true. To this young man's credit, he responded, "Yes, sir." Immediately, and I believe without thinking, this father stretched out his right arm and slapped his son squarely on the left side of his face. It was a brutal slap. The father told the son to come with him and the young man left, crying loudly.

As I recall this incident I see myself as being disappointed in me because I didn't come to the aid of this young man when this occurred. The treatment he experienced from his father, in my presence, was uncalled for and this father ought to have been told so by me right then. If I had this to do that evening all over again, I would have told the father that what he had done was uncalled for, and that he ought to be ashamed of himself. Had I done so, I may have risked this father coming after me at that moment. I can only say, right now, that I would have welcomed such an action on his part. He showed what he was and it was not a compliment to him. I hope such a tragedy did not ruin his relationship with his son, but I would be shocked if it didn't. Difficult people have no qualms regarding the use of such brutality when they are angry or when they think it is necessary.

Someone very close to me a very long time ago, didn't like something I did. I hadn't done anything immoral, unfair, or unethical. It was simply something this person believed that I shouldn't have done. I am putting it mildly when I say that this person came after me verbally with a vengeance. When it was all said and done, if his/her words had been a sword, I would have been drawn and quartered. Something happened in my heart and to my heart that day, and I have never been the same since. The lacerations left on my heart have healed but the scars are still there. I force myself not to think of this incident because, at the time, I loved this person with all of my heart. I still love this person very much, but it is not the same. It never will be the same simply because it cannot be. This outburst was the result of a difficult person becoming extremely angry and determined to make their point, no matter what the cost or the expense to my heart. This experience, for me, was unbelievably brutal. It was forgivable but not easily forgettable.

17. Difficult People Gather Information to Use It to Hurt Others

Difficult people are information gatherers of the highest order. What do I mean by information gatherers? A few pages back, I mentioned the character Hugh Laurie played in the medical drama "House". In one episode, House begins gathering information on the people who work for him and with him. The information he gathered was not the kind that employers normally obtain on their employees, but goes way beyond those parameters. He said he wanted this information in order to learn more about those who worked with and for him. However, the truth was that he wanted it to exert more control over his staff.

This is why difficult people are information gatherers. They want to use it against those they want to keep under their thumb. Such control is essential for them to keep their insecurities at bay. Difficult people falsely believe that in order to keep control, it's necessary to have certain critical information, which can be used against someone, when their control is being threatened. To these difficult people, whatever means is necessary to get such information is fine because again, the end justifies the means.

o **Wisdom Principle:** *In order to get control, we must learn to relinquish control!* —Dr. Gordon Livingston

Most difficult people do not have the money to hire a private investigator to gather information on those who are part of their lives. However, this doesn't stop them from using any means necessary to get that, which gives them the assurance that they are still in control. They will use relatives to do their spying, even friends. They will go through the purse or the wallet of the person about whom they are seeking information. They will check cell phones to see who their target is talking with. There are even occasions when they will risk their spouse being fired by calling him/her numerous times a day, in order to make sure he/she is where he/she is supposed to be, and actually doing his/her job. Just like Gregory House in the medical drama, difficult people will use any justification for their uncooperative personality and outrageous, distrusting and disrespectful behavior.

By the way, there are two things that difficult people must control—their home environment and the people who are consistently part of that environment. Without exception, difficult people who seek to control both of these areas of a person's life, believe they are unquestionably qualified to do so. Without exception, they also believe that if they don't control these two aspects of their lives, they in turn will be controlled by someone else. It is always an either/or, win/lose thing with them. From their perspective, it is better to control than to be controlled. Difficult people are dangerously paranoid, when it comes to control!

To my knowledge, these people have never had the gall to explicitly state that they are qualified to control their home environment, and the people in it. In reality, however, we know that in order to be qualified to control both of these aspects of another's life; one has to be nothing less than a genius. In no case can any person, much less a difficult person, qualify for being in control of these two aspects of another's life. There isn't anyone on this earth that is actually smart enough to do so. Yet, in the lives of the difficult among us, such qualifications are unquestionable.

18. Difficult People Are Consummate Criticizers

Difficult people are criticizers of the highest order. In fact, they are intuitive criticizers. They criticize without even thinking about it. Being critical of others is as natural as breathing to them. In fact, most difficult people, who often look like they're unconscious, come alive when they begin to criticize others. Their eyes even light up and their interest in the discussion at hand intensifies. They seem to literally love conversations that involve the criticism of others. It's as if they possess a sense of power over those they are criticizing. The diminishing of the importance of others is a key to their critical attitude because it contributes to their illusion of power. I don't know exactly how their possessing a power over people by criticizing them is supposed to work, but difficult people behave in a manner that says the existence of such a power is fact.

Difficult people will not hesitate, within certain contexts, to criticize anyone about anything. Why do they get such satisfaction in criticizing others? Again, it gives them a sense of superiority. Control and superiority are everything to them. Only individuals who are enormously distrusting, disrespectful of others, eaten alive by insecurity, and consumed by bitter anger can believe in this king of superiority.

19. Difficult People Are Completely Blind to Their Own Flaws

Difficult people are completely blind to those things in their lives that irritate others. Why? Because the subject about which most difficult people are the most ignorant is themselves. Of all of the things they know, they know the least about themselves. As a rule, they don't have the ability or the capacity to be introspective or self-honest. Also, they don't have the courage to risk being personally embarrassed by seeing themselves the way they truly are.

When a difficult person hears a description of negative behavior by another difficult person, he/she will not recognize his/her own negative behavior in the scenario. In other words, the difficult person is militantly blind to these same traits in his/her life.

Why is this so? Difficult people are double blind—blind to how difficult they truly are, and blind to the fact that they are blind. In other words, they don't know, and they don't know that they don't know!

20. Difficult People Believe Their "Hot Buttons" Are the Same as Everyone Else's

Difficult people believe the things that bother them ought to bother everyone else, as well. This is because they are *will-driven* rather than *solution-driven*. For instance: difficult people think that if others would do what they ought to do, as well as be what they ought to be, then they themselves wouldn't have to be upset with those other people. Now, how arrogant is this concept? It's unbelievably arrogant. If a difficult person is upset because someone said something or did something that they did not like, they believe anyone else in the same situation that is as *normal* as they are, would react the same way. This isn't true. What bothers one person, may not bother another. Our temperaments are not the same and as a result, our hot buttons are not the same, either.

However, difficult people see themselves as the bell-weather, of normalcy. I don't need to tell you that this is absolutely absurd.

The older son in the parable became angry at what was occurring inside his father's home—keep in mind that his father still owned the homestead, even though the older brother acted as if he owned it. He couldn't understand why his father didn't agree with his anger. It's obvious, within the context of what occurred in this story, that the older son was perplexed, if not dumbfounded, in regard to his father's reaction to his anger.

Notice that his father did not acquiesce to his son's anger, his forceful condemnation of his brother, nor did he apologize for the festivities in progress. The older son simply could not believe it. In fact, the older son remained completely unfazed by his father's affirmation that everything he owned would one day belong to his older son. How perplexed the older son was that his father couldn't understanding that he was upset! The older brother had an absolute need to control his home environment and the people in it.

o **Wisdom Principle:** *Hot buttons are danger signals that tell us there remain unresolved issues in our lives we need to bring under discipline.*

21. Difficult People Are Extraordinarily Narcissistic

o **Wisdom Principle:** *Narcissists take from life and add nothing positive to it. What they do add is virtually all negative.*

There is no question that individuals who are comfortable being as difficult as possible are self-centered. Life is all about them ... all about their desires, their wishes, and their expectations being fulfilled. As far as the difficult among us are concerned for others not to acquiesce to, and fulfill their expectations, is unfair and unreasonable.

They are so self-centered that they can't see their own flaws, even when they are staring them in the face. They suffer from a militant self-blindness. Difficult people run from truth, especially about themselves. Remember that self-honesty and self-evaluation are completely absent in their lives. This is why such people are so immature, temperamental, and narcissistic. Difficult people rarely grow up but usually remain psychological and emotional adolescents all of their lives.

Finally, their narcissism causes them to believe that relationships are an entitlement, rather than a gift. Consequently, they have no problem using relationships for their own end. This is what we see in the older brother. He saw relationships as a means to an end. He did not see relationships as graces to be treasured and respected.

22. Difficult People Are Impatient and Resent Being Inconvenienced

To say that difficult people are impatient is an understatement. It doesn't take much for them to become irritated when someone has not responded to their demands as quickly as they believed they should have. When they become irritated at another's lack of urgency in meeting an immediate need, they show this irritation in a dramatic fashion. They give the one who hasn't responded appropriately, *The Look*—an icy, hateful glare. Difficult people want to send a message with *The Look*. That message is: "I am not pleased with how you are attending to my desires/needs. Snap to it!" Wouldn't you love to be married to someone like this?

Difficult people not only have *The Look*, they also have a definite *pace*, about them. When others don't conform to that pace the difficult among us get very irritated with them for basically holding up the show. Difficult people do not adjust to others … others must adjust to them. This is one component about their personality that makes them almost impossible to live, work, and associate with.

Difficult people are also resentful when inconvenienced. Anytime the proverbial dominoes do not fall as they have anticipated, their next move is one of displeasure for being inconvenienced. This displeasure is often shown in a dramatic fashion as well. The emotional immaturity of difficult people can't be illustrated any clearer than when they are inconvenienced and their lack of patience is revealed.

When life is all about you, everyone is expected, to cater to you. When this doesn't happen in the life of the difficult person, everyone involved will know it. Narcissism is nothing less than someone seeing themselves as the center or their universe. Others, who are part of it, serve to fulfill their wants, desires, and needs. The ultimate result of such unbridled narcissism is prolonged psycho-spiritual illness and ultimately self-loathing.

23. Difficult People Are Maskers

Socially speaking, difficult people behave on the opposite side of the spectrum than what they truly are. The best among us have been fooled by them. The reason we are so easily fooled is because they are very proficient at masking the person they truly are. Those who have been taken in by a difficult man or woman, usually are not aware this is happening until after they find themselves knee deep in a relationship with one of them.

Shortly after one marries, the struggles in the relationship will become centered on the need for the difficult person to be in control. Within a matter of a few months the difficult person usually manages to get control of the finances. The next goal is the development of a strategy to keep tabs on his/her spouse. Where the partner goes and with whom he/she associates, becomes the difficult person's focus in the relationship. Questions are asked in abundance to make sure the information the difficult person has or knows matches the answers the other spouse is giving. It is the classic "M & M Strategy"—the same used by local, state, and federal governments. If he/she can control/trace the money, and can control/track the mobility of his/her spouse, then, proverbially speaking, the difficult person can control that spouse. You may ask, "Are these people that cold blooded?" Yes!

When I lived in Texas, I met a couple I thought got along great, and were very much in love. In my conversations with the husband, I remember telling him how impressed I was with his marriage. He responded to me that he was a much better man having married his wife. (Of course, this is what every man who desires to have the best marriage possible, wants to be able to say in regards to his wife.) But there a "catch" regarding how he phrased this.

Some time passed before I saw this man again—and I didn't know then that this would be the last time I would ever see him. His countenance was sad and he seemed troubled. I spoke to him for a few minutes and mentioned that the sparkle in his eye that I was accustomed to seeing was missing. He told me something I shall never forget. He asked me if I recalled his telling me that he was a better man for having married his wife. I told him I remembered. He said that what he really meant by his statement was that he was so challenged in his marriage he had to dig very deep within himself to muster up the necessary character to be able to stay married to his wife.

I told him I did not understand. He said that his wife was the most difficult person, whom he had ever known. In reality, she was the antithesis of the woman she projected herself to be in the beginning of their relationship. Prior to marrying her she was the kindest, most cooperative, loving, and considerate person he had ever met.

However, after three months of marriage he saw a completely different person. She revealed a side of herself that was insecure, demanding, controlling, and confrontational. He told me that all of the tough times—the pain and misery that he had experienced in his life prior to marrying her—had been multiplied tenfold since they had married. The only benefit, he said, in being married to his wife was that he had gained enormous self-discipline and cultivated, with all of his might, all of the virtues necessary, in order to keep the relationship viable.

I must tell you that this is one of the saddest stories about a marriage that I had heard up until that point in my life. I venture to guess, however, that this man is not alone. Also, I am sure that there are women who can say the same thing about their husbands when it comes to being difficult.

How many people do you know who are married to a difficult, if not an impossible individual, while quietly enduring the misery such a relationship is giving them? I have known individuals who have difficult spouses and the amazing part is that each of these difficult spouses believe they have a marriage that would be envied by most. How in the world could a difficult person not know that their spouse was miserable in their marriage? This is beyond comprehension. Most difficult people are oblivious to how bad things are in their marriage. As long as they are in control and the dominoes of life continue to fall as they believe they ought, difficult people will assume all is well with the world. Don't you find this incomprehensible?

24. Difficult People Are Not Sharers of What Belongs to Them

There are two things that difficult people have problems sharing—resources and relationships. Both are perceived by them as endangered in their lives.

Resources: Difficult people don't share resources because they are primarily distrusting of others, believe that they have some kind of ownership of the people in their lives, and they fear losing control ... especially when it comes to sharing relationships. They don't necessarily have a valid reason for distrusting, they just simply are. Their distrust is intuitive. It is simply easier to be stone-cold dead than being sensitive to the needs of others.

Relationships: Difficult people also have a twisted idea about relationships—especially marriage. They believe that the relationships in which they find themselves are to be led and controlled by them. No exceptions! Relationships are not privileges to be enjoyed but rather rights to be exercised. In other words, the difficult among us believe they have a right to define their relationships.

Of course, difficult people, in the initial stages of any romantic relationship or friendship are not going to put individuals on notice and let them know that when such relationships develop that they, by personal proxy, become the definers, of those relationships. Such a revelation will be subtly revealed after an individual becomes immersed in a relationship with them.

As a consequence, the difficult resent having to share their spouses with friends or the spouses own relatives. Of course, when it comes to sharing their spouse with their own family and friends, the spouse being shared all of a sudden is not being fair if he/she does not enthusiastically conform to the difficult spouse's expectations regarding his/her family's needs and desires.

When a spouse is with his/her difficult spouse's family and friends, there had better not be any clock watching. However, the difficult spouse usually is a clock-watcher when with his/her spouse's friends or family. The difficult individual believes that attention that is being given to others is attention he or she is not receiving. In essence, the difficult believe they are being robbed of time they believe legitimately belongs to them. Unbelievable, isn't it?

Unfortunately, tens of thousands of spouses who have had to seriously adjust their relationships with friends and loved ones in order for any semblance of consistent peacefulness to be part of the home environment. Brutal, isn't it? But many good people live with such brutality in their marriages 24/7/365. It is only the idiots among us who choose to believe this is not true.

A gentleman I know loved his brother very much and was very close to him. Both were avid golfers and loved playing together as often as possible. Once he married, his wife did all she could to turn her husband against his brother. She did not succeed, but what she did do was make her husband's life a living hell every time he saw his brother. Over time, his resistance to this conflict wore down, as I explained earlier in this chapter would happen in such scenarios. Predictably, he eventually acquiesced to his wife's wishes. Of course, all of us know that if his difficult wife had had the integrity to express such intentions to him while he was only a future spouse, then obviously he would no longer have been the future spouse in that difficult woman's life.

The difficult among us know this will happen, so they wait to perform the proverbial relational bait and switch until after they said "I do". Spending time with each other's families is pivotal to determining just how healthy the relational interaction will be after marriage. We must all do this in order to protect the relationships we enjoy and the people we love.

o **Wisdom Principle:** *One third of the suffering and pain experienced in this world is caused by difficult people.*

25. Difficult People Have an Incomplete Understanding of Love

This point isn't very surprising, is it? As much as we want to think the best of people, when it comes to the difficult among us, it's very hard to do. It never ceases to amaze me what difficult people think love is in contrast to what the mature among us believe it is. These two views are on opposite sides of the spectrum. As a rule, difficult people substitute the giving/providing of material things in place of extending themselves for the well-being of others. They also give with strings attached. Their giving is nothing less than a quid pro quo system. When they give, they expect something of equal value, in return.

I stated in another section of this chapter that difficult people never give in to something they would not normally give in to unless they badly wanted something in return. Absent such a scenario, difficult people will, more often than not, get what they want by first using their own abilities/resources. However, they will not hesitate to use other people to get what they want if they can't get their wants/desires fulfilled through their own efforts. Since most difficult people have an entitlement mentality, doing this does not bother them at all. Anytime a person has to work to obtain love, respect, and admiration from a difficult person such an individual is headed for a crash of major proportions; it just isn't going to happen.

People in a relationship with a difficult person are rarely treated with love. Difficult people have bursts of benevolence, but being consistently loving with others is not one of their character traits. To treat people lovingly, one must know what love truly is and the ways it is exemplified and communicated. Absent of such knowledge, as most difficult people are, people who associate with them will rarely know what it is to be loved or to be treated lovingly. As a result, those who are married to or live with difficult people truly do not know when the benevolent side of that person will show up. Those who have to live with and associate with the difficult continue to hope against hope.

26. Difficult People Rarely Show a Sense of Humor

Laughter is something that, at best, is inconsistent with the difficult who live and work among us. It is their lack of laughter that indicates their misery to others. Difficult people I have known usually laugh at whom they've aggressively teased or laughed in a manner that diminishes others.

One of the ways these people will reveal themselves is when someone tells a witty or genuinely funny joke. You will see a difficult person barely crack a smile because he/she doesn't know when something is genuinely funny or witty. They are so serious about their mission to control and define others, as well as environments, that they have lost their capacity to be light-hearted. It is believed that consistent laughter adds 12 years to one's life. I believe this is true except in the life of the difficult.

To create humor, they aggressively tease others by making fun of the vulnerabilities of their victims. They tease their victims about what they—the difficult—perceive as weaknesses. Such attempts at humor are both cruel and crude. Tragic!

27. Difficult People Physically Deteriorate Faster Than Others

Another thing I have noticed about the difficult among us is that they begin to show signs of physical problems that often don't have an exact medical explanation, genetic link, or even an environmental link. Instead, they are usually psycho-spiritually somatic, or in other words, self-made and self-induced.

The pressure difficult people put themselves under and the stress they endure in order to control environments and other people has to be enormous. How would I know? I am under an enormous amount of pressure to be the best I can be and I am cognitive of the pressure of the discipline that is necessary to accomplish this. I have all I can handle just keeping up with me. I cannot imagine the stress and worry created in the lives of the difficult when they are compelled by forces within to control the environments, as well as the people, in their lives. This has to be physically tiring, as well as mentally and emotionally draining. The consequence of such unhealthy needs is nothing less than the deterioration of one's health and relationships.

28. Difficult People Do Not Adjust to Others; They Expect Others to Adjust to Them

One of the traits of difficult people that I've spoken about is their inflexibility. This inflexibility shows itself in how difficult it is for them to adjust to others. Unquestionably, one can count on difficult people to be unaccommodating of others. They are so very inflexible that even any willingness to adjust to others is a virtual impossibility. This is directly due to their attitude and temperament—their attitude is drenched in arrogance and their temperament is testy and saturated with impatience.

This innate inflexibility to adjust to others is the reason we must be wise if confronted with the necessity to associate or work with a difficult person. Any adjustments necessary to make the relationship work will have to be made by the most flexible person—you or me. Difficult people don't have the relational skills to make such adjustments in their daily relationships. Those skills were never cultivated, because the difficult believed relational skills to be unnecessary. Why? Because difficult people were taught by their authority figures that relationships outside of family were overrated—not of any value.

The inflexibility factor is readily seen in the area of leadership. Difficult people rely on their position power to excuse them from having to adjust to others. They expect others to adjust to them because they—the difficult—are in positions of leadership, thus their inflexibility becomes the primary cause for the low morale and poor performance of people they lead. Remember, morale starts at the top—the leadership—and sifts to the bottom—the followers. There is no such thing as raising morale in an organization. It definitely must be possessed by those at the top. If it is it will sink to the bottom. If it is not, it won't.

o **Wisdom Principle**: *An organization attitudinally divided cannot survive.*

29. Difficult People Are Isolationists—They Intentionally Stay Away from People, Whenever Possible

Difficult people prefer staying away from others with whom they do not have to associate. The traffic of people coming into their lives is very limited, probably because their relational drawbridge is perpetually up. Oh, they may briefly converse with others, but because they basically do not like people, their contact with them will always be extraordinarily limited.

Another part of the picture is that their social I.Q. is low, thus their comfort zone with people they don't know is non-existent. They prefer to stay to themselves and have around them only those over whom they have firm control. Predictability in relationships is pivotal to the contentment of difficult people. Those whom they cannot control are expeditiously removed from their environment. This is true of family members, as well as acquaintances. No one is immune to such a possibility happening. The difficult person's absolute control over their environment—especially their own home—is critical to their contentment.

30. Difficult People Will Not Discuss Sensitive Critical Concerns with Anyone Because Resolution Would Usher in Necessary Change

Let's face it, difficult people absolutely loathe changing, adjusting to, or accommodating anyone. I believe they would rather take a beating from Mike Tyson, than give in to anyone. Accommodating or adjusting to someone else, is, to them, a sign of weakness and difficult people will not allow themselves to look weak to anyone. It is paramount for a difficult person to create the image of being tough and uncompromising, a no-nonsense individual, and as-tough-as-nails.

I've spoken to scores of people throughout my adult life who have described scenarios of wanting to speak to a relative, an immediate family member, a spouse, or a friend regarding a critical concern. Without exception, the attempt to discuss the subject with an individual they described as difficult, either escalated into an argument, or the person they were talking to stood up and walked away mumbling incoherent words ... in some cases mumbling words of profanity.

Difficult people see others as the problem, rather than themselves. Their attitude is that if all of us would conduct ourselves and our affairs the way they believe we ought to, then they wouldn't have to be upset with us ... they wouldn't have to nag us when we don't do what they think is best. This makes for an impossible situation that we must work through and accept. As long as difficult people see others as the problem, nothing will change ... most of all, them!

There you have it ... the 30 markers of difficult people. If you want to know how difficult you truly are, take the number of markers that remind you of you and divide them by 30. You then need to take that percentage and multiply it by 365. The result will give you the number of days out of the year you usually behave in a manner that would categorize you as being difficult to either live, associate, or work with. If you consistently have more than 20% of the markers, you are likely very difficult to live, work, or otherwise associate with.

You need to be more cognizant as to how you affect others. If you have the discipline to do so, think of those times and certain contexts when people didn't like you and didn't want to be around you. If you are honest with yourself, you will recognize that you were exhibiting the traits of a difficult person.

Now, ask yourself: "Why is it important to know the characteristics of difficult people?" One very clear reason is that difficult people create all kinds havoc in the lives of the people around them simply because they believe life is all about them—especially in getting their own way and always at the expense of doing the right thing. Relationships, with difficult people, have three unmistakable ingredients: chaos, control, and pain. Insensitive is a term that appropriately describes difficult people in this context. Their lack of sensitivity makes difficult people expert distributors of pain, brutal anger, misery, and relational tragedy. Most of all, by the time difficult people become mellow and soften, they have left a trail of relational debris in their wake. By then, the damage has been done and relationships have been irrevocably damaged.

Another reason you should know the characteristics of difficult people is to ascertain the extent of the damage done by them to their victims. The individuals, who are the most vulnerable are those who live with them. Knowing what I call the cycle of invalidation is critical in not becoming a victim of it.

Here is how this cycle works. Difficult people seek first to control those in their environment. They have a compulsion, deep inside, to do so, primarily because of their insecurities. They use the threat of anger, guilt-throwing, or other punitive actions against anyone in their environment who is not completely compliant with their desires, wishes, and expectations. Over time, a difficult person will have successfully cultivated individuals who believe not that they are the victims of their treatment but that they themselves are at fault when there is a conflict between them and the difficult person who is an authority figure within the home. In other words, the victim becomes neurotic, believing that when there is a conflict between them and someone else that they are at fault.

As with any abusive relationship, after a while the abused get tired of the abuse and decide to fight back. This fighting back has a remarkable resemblance to the exact same strategies the difficult person has used on them. By now, based on what I have already written, you know the drill regarding the abuse—i.e., the guilt-throwing, the anger, and other punitive punishments. On closer scrutiny, what the victim mirrors back to the difficult authority figure, is the same. What all victims do who are at this point in a relationship with a difficult individual, is start mirroring back to the difficult person what they have been receiving. What you start seeing is the abuse that difficult people have been throwing at others boomerang. The abuse, as you can see, has turned the corner, coming back to the difficult individuals who initiated the abuse to begin with. In the end, victims of all difficult people, in order to protect themselves from further abuse, become diffi-cult with the difficult people in their lives. The victims have now become exactly like the difficult people who initiated this horrible abuse on them. In the end, the once abused have truly become character disordered individuals themselves.

It is important that you are able to identify such people before you ever get involved with them in any way. I can't begin to tell you the people who married someone they thought was terrific, kind, and sympathetic only to discover that the person they did marry was the Antichrist him/herself. Many people find them-selves trapped in such relationships and find no easy way out. For these, the only option they believe they have is simply to endure. Therefore, they endure such relationships, usually to an early death. It is rare that individuals in this kind of situation ever have more than an area smaller than a jail cell in their life in which they can experience true peace and contentment.

In order to live with, work with, or associate with difficult people, we must do some difficult but necessary things.

One, we must stand up for what is right as well as true and not apologize for doing so. A truth-seeker of the highest order will not be on the Christmas List of a difficult person. You won't be one of their heroes or favorites. However, to be true to yourself you must stand up for what is right.

You may find your convictions regarding what is right, decent, and true being deflected by the difficult person in the relation- ship, which may include your spouse. Even so, stay the course and stand up for the right as well as for what is important to you. Do not expect the difficult person or your difficult spouse to accept or respect your positions. The definition of character and the meaning of integrity are over the heads of the difficult among us.

o **Wisdom Principle:** *We perpetuate people's weaknesses in direct proportion to our accommodation of them.*

Two, we must endure anger when we stand with integrity regarding what is true, ethical, and descent, because the diffi- cult person involved is going to lose his/her temper. My advice is to back off and let them. Don't respond in kind. Keep calm and do not lose your composure while in the face of their fiery anger. You will play right into the hands of that difficult person in your life when you react with anger. Your anger will further justify his/ her own actions, at least in his/her mind.

There is nothing you can do to change difficult people's perspective on this. They will never hesitate to start a conflict and if you capitulate, i.e., get down on their level, when it is all over you will be blamed for what in their minds started out as a conversation and ended up escalating into a screaming match.

There is no question that you will need to be prepared for their anger, guilt-throwing, and manipulation. Difficult people use anger first. They will communicate that you should also fear the loss of privileges, like loss of their co-operation, loss of a peaceful environment, or even the loss of intimacy. They will use manipulation such as tears, playing the role of the victim, and drama (exaggerating the hurt or pain being caused to them). Let them do whatever they have to do, but from your end keep the confrontation firm but benevolent (kind, not hurtful).

Three, we must see dealing with difficult people as an opportunity to improve our weaknesses. I know you would like to have every difficult person in your life drawn and quartered, however, many times God allows us to endure the trials of dealing with such people to show us our deficiencies—what comes out of us when we have to deal with these people. Difficult people can be winds of adversity that blow through the lives of all virtuous people. But believe it or not, we become better people when we can be kind, even compassionate to those we would normally find impossible to be kind and patient toward. This is part of the arduous work of the discipline it takes to become the best we can possibly be.

Four, we must keep our tongues disciplined. This is probably the most difficult thing to do when an unreasonable and difficult person is in your face saying terrible and hurtful things to you. I can tell you from experience, you will always lose when a difficult person gets in your face and you fall to the temptation to respond in the same manner they have conducted themselves with you.

You and I must understand that we cannot win when dealing with a difficult person. He/she knows all the tricks and doesn't play by the rules. This is why we must take the high road. Difficult people will bring you down with them if they can get you to lose your composure. Let the difficult person rant. As Christians, we have the whole armor of God. Christ is our strength and our shield. We are not alone when we are being attacked by the difficult among us. We have a higher calling that must take precedence over our ego-centric pride. It is Satan's strategy to use difficult people to break our spirits and lose hope in the wonder and goodness of life. These situations are some of the toughest defining moments of our lives. We must be prepared for them because they will come.

o **Wisdom Truth**: *"A person with a healthy spirit can meet any adversity with dignity; however, when one's spirit is wounded; how can one survive?"*—Proverbs 18:14

Five, we must pray for the difficult among us. Why should we? I believe the Bible teaches us to do so. Think of this. Praying for the difficult people in our lives is for our benefit more than it is for theirs (See Matthew 5:43-48). Prayer keeps us balanced—knowing when to turn the other cheek and not become a human doormat, to the difficult people, in our lives.

Six, we must work with the difficult among us with an attitude of lovingkindness. They are the way they are because they have not handled well the pain and suffering in their lives. The vicissitudes of life visited upon them have hurt them and difficult people have a big problem when trying to let the winds of pain and suffering blow through them. Pain and suffering make them bitter rather than better. If we are a healing ointment in their lives, it is possible that God can use us to turn them toward a better way of living and being. It's worth it, isn't it? This is a defining moment for any individual who has to deal with difficult people. You have to decide … are you going to fight difficulty by being difficult. Are you going to deal with problem people by being a problem? Only you know the answer to these two questions. Don't hope you will do what is best … decide that you are going to do what is best.

Last, the church must speak out. As I see it, the church must do two things: One, speak out against relational abuse and teach that it is sinful to the core. Two, be supportive of those who are enduring such abuse. For a minister or church congregation to say that such contexts within personal relationships are none of their business, is kin to the German people in WWII turning their backs, while Jews and others were being gathered and placed into concentration camps, saying all the while that it is none of their business. It is my very deep conviction, that to turn our backs on those in our congregations, who are suffering as I have described, is nothing less than spiritual treason, as it is applied to the spirit of the Christian faith.

CHAPTER TEN
LIKEABLE PEOPLE

In Chapter One I introduced to you a young man by the name of Joel Swanson. Joel had most of the components of what it means to be a likeable person. I mentioned a few of these then. I would like to expand on these components now and add others not mentioned earlier.

The largest number of likeable people I've been around have been members of the churches I served in. I shouldn't be surprised that I found so many legitimately likeable individuals in one particular church. These likeable people carry within them an inner magnet and, as a result, are drawn to other likeable people.

I took note of the components in the lives of people I found likeable. As time has progressed, I've continued to take note of certain components that keep reoccurring in their lives, as well as in the individuals with whom I have associated in my personal life. I have studied these notes, organized them, and written comments beside each of them over the past several years. Here they are for your consideration.

One, likeable people, as a rule, are unconditionally accepting of others.[17] This is possible because likeable people are self-accepting. Likeable people are comfortable "in their own skin". They simply like themselves. They like who they are. I have spoken about self-acceptance in several chapters in this book. This is the context in which I spoke of Joel Swanson in that first chapter.

I have no doubt that Joel truly liked himself, and I have to say that to have met such a young man with this marvelous quality in the 9th grade even today absolutely astonishes me. Without question, liking ourselves is one of the three greatest gifts we can give ourselves. Self-acceptance is a prerequisite to liking oneself. Without self-acceptance and liking oneself, it is simply not possible for one to be accepting of others consistently. For truly likeable people, who also possess sagacity, their self-acceptance is based

---

[17] Special Note: When I state that likeable people are unconditionally accepting of others, I think it is only fair to define what that means. How someone projects him/herself to be, it is obvious that he/she will either be accepted or rejected by others based on that projection. Being unconditionally accepting of others on a consistent basis, means that when a person presents him-/herself in a particular manner, if such a persona is not literally off the radar screen socially speaking, he/she will be welcomed, as well as socially embraced, by those who are truly likeable individuals.

However—and this is a very big however—if a person eventually proves him/herself to be the antithesis of how he/she originally projected him/herself to be, that person will find out that hypocrisy is not a character trait that likeable people tolerate very well. Likeable people have their hot buttons just like everyone else. The difference is that likeable people have very few hot buttons. They are not going to associate with those who are hypocritical. Call this being judgmental if you will; but you are wrong if you do. None of us can run from the principle of attraction that authenticity gravitates toward, or attracts authenticity. To willingly associate with individuals who are not authentic in how they present themselves to be, is to eventually be dragged down to the level of living life where such individuals live. Such is not one of the goals of authentic and likeable individuals.

on God's love and His unconditional acceptance of them. Likeable people who are spiritually smart, are very cognizant of this.

Also, liking oneself is a prerequisite to possessing self-trust and self-respect. The basis of an individual possessing an attitude of distrust and disrespect is the direct result of a person having an innate rejection of him/herself. Individuals who do not believe in themselves find it difficult to be self-trusting and self-respecting. You see, if a person does not like him/herself, he/she will not see him/herself as trustworthy or even worthy of respect. And, if a person such as I am describing is not worthy of trust and respect, his/her attitude will reflect that neither is anyone else!

o **Wisdom Principle:** *An individual who truly does not respect him-/herself will likely not respect anyone else. You just can't give anything away to others that you do not have to give to yourself.*

Have you ever wondered why Christ was always at odds, with the Pharisees? When you examine the New Testament closely, you will see one huge difference between Christ and those religious leaders of the day. Christ made acceptance the basis of change, while the Pharisees made change the basis of acceptance. All other differences between Christ and the Pharisees are peripheral in comparison to this one difference. It was pivotal.

When we are loved by someone, one of the key components of the proof of that love is that we sense we are accepted just as we are. There are no hoops we have to jump through and no particular criteria to meet. We are OK just as we are. There is no more powerful elixir than this, with the exception of having a personal encounter with the Living Christ, which the Bible calls salvation.

You may wonder why likeable people are so accepting of others. It is because they genuinely like people. The basis of acceptance of others is liking people. If we do not like people there will always be an issue with unconditional acceptance of others, especially those we perceive as radically different.

There exist in our world a sizable number of people who simply do not like people; and without liking people acceptance of others simply does not exist. The reason is because those who dislike people have an ingrained distrust and disrespect of others. As I have said before, distrust and disrespect are kissing cousins. Where you have one, you have the other. [18]

_____

[18] I have been asked, on some occasions, why is it that a good percentage of people simply do not like people? The answer is clear. People who do not like people struggle with relational intelligence. They simply do not know how to cultivate positive and effective personal and professional relationships. For them, it is simply easier not to seek such relationships, than to have to learn the relational skills necessary to be able to positively cultivate them. These people will say, on rare but candid occasions, that their experiences with others have been overwhelmingly more negative than positive.

On closer scrutiny, you will find that these same people, during their adolescent years, had some difficult and painful experiences in their relationships with their peers. These experiences have justified their view. However, you can ask 1,000 people and 950 of them are going to say that their adolescent years were very difficult, as well as challenging. Virtually everyone has had rough going in their teen years. Yet, most of these 950 managed to cultivate the necessary relational skills in order to have positive and effective relationships with a number of individuals. Therefore, my conviction about those who don't like people, and who use this argument as the reason for not cultivating positive and effective relationships with others, is that they don't like themselves. Or perhaps they are using their adolescent experiences as the basis for believing that cultivating such relationships is not worth the time or the trouble. In many cases, it could be both of these reasons.

It must be said, on both counts that they are misguided and are succeeding in boxing themselves into the proverbial corner when it comes to having meaningful and positive relationships. However, when the time comes that they truly need relationships, these will not be there to assist in carrying them through whatever challenges they are facing.

o **Wisdom Principle:** *You cannot give to others what you have not first, given to yourself!*

Two, likeable people are good listeners. This is an absolute key. Without exception, individuals who have sat with me over the years and genuinely listened to me are people whom I grew to like very much. One of the highest compliments we can pay someone is to sit and listen to them. It has been said that a good conversation requires a good listener. True! If you or I want to become a good conversationalist, we are going to have to become very good listeners.

Listening communicates value and respect to the one who is speaking. That person may not be able to articulate this, but there is no question that those to whom we listen without interruption sense such value and respect from us. Trust me when I say that when they do sense such value and respect they never forget it.

We live in a white-hot world. People go everywhere as fast as they possibly can and it seems they are always running to catch up. Catching up with what I don't know; but they seem to be chasing something that is always just out of reach. People are so busy going fast in their endeavors, while arriving at their destination out of breath, that at the same time they talk more about less and less.

We live in a world that has become a soap opera. We see a great deal of movement and activity on a soap opera but very little happens in each particular episode. For every problem that is resolved on an episode, there are two more that take its place. The lives of many people are the same way. There is a great deal of activity in their lives, but nothing significant ever seems to occur; and it is rare if any significant problem ever gets resolved.

One consequence of such a fast-paced lifestyle is that we only partially listen to people. We consistently fail to give them the time and attention due to them as individuals. One proof of this lack of listening is how often you hear someone respond "whatever" to the one who's been speaking to him/her. This contemporary response is so distasteful. I can state, without reservation, that we are never going to be liked the way we would wish if we do not significantly improve our listening skills, especially in our conversations, with those in our family, our associate at work, or in our social lives.

Another reason likeable people are terrific listeners is that they understand that men and women communicate differently and for different reasons.

It is my observation that men are more direct—linear. They verbally go from point A straight to point B as quickly as possible in making their point.

Women are more global when saying what they want to say. Perhaps this is because they are more interested in connecting to the individuals with whom they are communicating.

Men think before speaking, while women speak and think as they are speaking.

Men speak to make a point. Women speak, often discovering the point they want to make while they are speaking.

Since men speak to make a point, they will always be more direct, in their communication, while focusing, on a specific point. This point is what I call, the micro-view. Since women speak to relate, they will always be global in their communication style while focusing on what I call the macro-view.

One last comment on this point: Being a terrific listener comes from having a heart characterized by loving-kindness. No, you are not reading this wrong. Without exception, those who exude loving-kindness toward others are excellent listeners. Likeable people listen without correcting, criticizing, condemning, or counseling.

A few years ago, I was visiting with my brothers and their families during one particular holiday weekend. My favorite niece happened to be visiting. We sat down together and had a terrific conversation for about 20 minutes. After we moved on to speak with others, she came back and asked me how I did it. "How I did what?" I asked. She said, "How are you able to listen the way you do and the person to whom you are speaking be aware of it?" I gave her an answer that I believed was true. However, her comment reverberated in my mind for quite a while. Finally, it occurred to me why I gave her such rapt attention. It was because I love her very much. Likeable people listen with rapt attention because they possess a loving heart.

Three, likeable people are transparent. When you see them, you see them! I have spoken about transparency throughout this book. I truly believe that transparency is critical to effective leadership, effective communication, and others being at ease with an individual. You do not have to wonder if those who are transparent are sad, mad, or glad. Their countenance shows it. You need to write this on your forehead—likeable people are transparent, easy to read, easy to communicate with.

If someone says anything different than what I have, ignore them. They really don't know what they are speaking about. They are simply justifying why some people choose to be aloof and difficult to read—nonverbally stating that such behavior is out of an individual's control. The truth is, unless there is a medical reason for not being able to control how one comes across to others, a person has absolute control as to how to communicate with others, as well as how transparent he/she chooses to be.

> o **Wisdom Principle:** *A lack of transparency is indicative of a lack of self-acceptance.*

There is no question that one who is easy to read and, as a result, is transparent, has some things going for him/her that those who are difficult to read do not. For one, this person is comfortable with who and what he/she is as an individual. For another, he/she likes people—both associating with others and working with others.

Finally, likeable people are not only transparent but are also considerate. I am convinced that those who are not very considerate are also not very transparent. Without exception, I see non-transparent individuals consistently struggle with conversational etiquette, as well as being kind and considerate to others.

> o **Wisdom Principle:** *In the world of the difficult-to-read, one must earn the right to see them. Few ever do!*

Transparency in an individual's life communicates self-acceptance, possession of a healthy self-love and, in general, an intuitive fondness for others. No one can justifiably be uncomfortable in the presence of such individuals. If they are, it is much more a commentary on their flawed world-view and character, than on the truly likeable individual who is in their presence.

Four, likeable people are reasonable. A likeable person is flexible rather than rigid. He/she has a sense of goodwill toward others. Being reasonable makes this possible. If you recall, in the previous chapter I described difficult people as being rigid. Likeable people are the antithesis of that.

Reasonable people are open-minded and willing to consider points-of-view other than their own. They are not threatened by those who may have more insight into a particular subject than they. Reasonable people know that no matter how much they know about a particular subject, or how knowledgeable they are about how to do something, there are always other, better ways of accomplishing anything worthwhile.

Reasonable people possess empathy. Notice that empathy and sympathy are different. Sympathy is sensing what an individual is going through and having the capacity to identify with what that individual is experiencing. Empathy is having the capacity to see something through someone else's eyes and feel at heart what another heart is feeling. It is having the ability to be able to actually put oneself in another's place. When you are speaking to a reasonable person, he/she has the capacity to put him-/herself in the other person's place in order to sympathize with that person as well as empathize.

Reasonableness is a virtue and is a critical component of character. I have never met anyone who had a problem relating to a reasonable person. Of course, there are individuals who do not gravitate toward reasonable people. They obviously see reasonable people as weak and people-pleasing. Such individuals often suffer from character disorders, which alienate most people, and as a result they have the limited capacity to relate to only a few individuals. The individuals, to whom they can relate are usually as equally off the radar screen as they are. Also, such people do not understand nor value reasonableness as a virtue.

By being reasonable, likeable people are comfortable around others who are different. I have a wonderful friend who lives in Mobile, Alabama. Tad and I go way back. He owns his own advertising firm and over the years he has made some changes in his looks and his demeanor. Since he is a very creative person he is not conventional, not as society would define conventional.

However, even though Tad wears a ponytail, an earring, consistently has a five o'clock shadow, and dresses casually, I have never allowed that to get in the way of my respect, love, and admiration of and for him. There are very few individuals with as great a heart as Tad's, and his appearance does not affect me negatively at all. However, the austere and difficult among us would totally judge Tad by his appearance and would likely never give him a chance to show what a terrific person he is, as well as how smart he is, in his profession. Reasonable people don't overreact when an individual presents him-/herself to be, in appearance or personality, different than they are.

About a decade ago, my wife became quite ill. After seeing several doctors, it was concluded that she might have a serious pancreatic disorder. She was referred to Medical University of South Carolina, which, we discovered, was one of the world's finest for pancreatic disorders. After the appointments were made and the protocol of the University Medical Hospital followed as to other requirements, we arrived for the initial appointment. We found ourselves facing a man who had unusually long hair, a shirt and pair of pants that looked like he'd slept in them for a week, and he wore an old worn pair of Sperry Dockers. Honestly, my wife and I both said to ourselves, "Oh, no! What are we doing here?"

However, after we sat down with this man, we found him to be much more than we could have hoped for and one of the finest experts in his field. Here was another indication that you cannot always judge a person by their appearance. This man may have looked like a refugee from a hippy commune, but he was one terrific doctor! We were so fortunate to have found him. I believe, without a shadow of a doubt, that he saved my wife's life. If we had been unreasonable—judging him by his appearance—and not given him the chance to show us that he could help her, we might have been burying my wife a few months later. Being reasonable can make a huge difference in your life at a particular defining moment in your life!

Five, likeable people possess a high social IQ. They have a social elegance about themselves. Likeable people are comfortable in social settings. They move gracefully in and out of groups standing/sitting together and simply enjoying small talk. In possessing a high social IQ, a likeable person is also polite, kind, patient, gracious, and considerate.

There comes a time in all of our lives when life calls us to be socially elegant. Being knowledgeable about etiquette, and demonstrating that knowledge in an elegant manner, is critical to possessing a high social IQ. When that time comes, we must be ready. Every person who is strong in social intelligence is prepared for these moments. Such times call for individuals to be competent in the knowledge of dress, table manners, graceful behavior, and in the use of the English language. Nothing less than excellence is acceptable in such a context.

Likeable people have a distinguished manner about them in such contexts that truly captivates others who value social intelligence. In such a scenario, the likeable person has the capacity to consistently treat others as if they are the most important people in the room. Likeable people can do this without being patronizing or pretentious. The only way you can be such a person is to commit yourself to being the best you can possibly be in this kind of context and be willing to work at becoming nothing less than a class act.

Six, likeable people live above and rise above the negatives of life. The situations and circumstances which irritate and drive others crazy are not much of an issue in the lives of truly likeable people. They don't complain about the inequities of life. In fact, they use those experiences as opportunities to grow in grace. In Job 13:15 it says, *"Even though God may slay me and wipe me off the face of the earth, yet I will everlastingly place my hope in Him."* Likeable people are truly graceful, as well as grateful, when experiencing the common vicissitudes of life that all of us experience.

Genuinely likeable people are also not sensitive when others are blunt, hurtful, inappropriately teasing, condescending, exceedingly difficult, and inconsiderate. Likeable people are calm, polite, and have a marvelous inner discipline. They are neither emotional nor dramatic in style and demeanor. They possess a peaceful soul and they have also learned to live without the good opinion of others. These two component virtues are absolutely necessary in becoming a truly likeable person.

This living above the negatives of life can only be possible because likeable people are emotionally self-disciplined, and not visibly sensitive about offensive or inappropriate behavior and/or conversation. They know that social settings will occasionally draw the difficult, the uncouth, and the socially inept. Individuals who perceive themselves as being much better and higher than others who have experienced a little tangible success (money), have also failed to cultivate any class while accumulating their modicum of success and new found social status.

More often than not, such misbehavior occurs more with men than women. However, there are women who also have gained a modicum of professional and social status who have over-invested their self-worth in such things and, as a result, believe that they are above others, who have not experienced similar success. These men and women confuse being better than others with just being better off.

When it comes to men, this can occur when their compulsion is to present themselves as macho and manly. These men don't realize that manliness is shown by possessing the character qualities of meekness, considerateness and gentleness. The macho among us very often can't comprehend this. Give them enough rope and they will eventually hang themselves, socially speaking.

Because many difficult people are task intelligent, it's not uncommon for them to experience tangible success and thereby assume they have achieved authentic classiness as a result. People who believe this are usually those who consistently embarrass themselves socially, as well as in their extended family relationships.

I would like to add that the easiest part of classiness is looking classy. However, the thoroughbreds, socially speaking, display their class through their behavior, their character, their presence, and their use of the English language. These four qualities are much harder to fake. No one cannot consistently fake these four critical qualities. Competence in these four personal/social qualities requires knowledge, commitment to excellence, and discipline.

The more truly knowledgeable one is of social etiquette and the more truly grounded one's character is, the more graceful one will be in any social setting.

Having said this, the ability to live above the fray is further defined, by one's ability to maintain a discipline of living above the negatives of life every day. Class never takes a day off. It is part of who and what a person is when it's the real deal in one's life. Class is intuitive, among those who are truly classy. When you are a class act you don't have to think about being classy, you simply are.

The last point I want to make about living above the negatives of life is that likable people have a consistent absence of complaining. I am convicted that those who complain a great deal about life, circumstances, and people believe that life's inequities never ought to befall them. Such inequities of life ought to be the lot of the so-called other people.

In the life of the likable person, complaining is absent because such a person knows it's a waste of time and also a sign of immaturity. After hearing a constant complainer for a period of time, most people go out of their way to avoid him or her. Complainers wear people down and change the environmental focus from the possibilities of success to the unfair impossibilities of life. Constant complainers rob others of hope, and, as I've previously said, where there is no hope in the future there is no power in the present.

Seven, likeable people are trustworthy and dependable. Trustworthiness and dependability are component virtues. When you look up what it means to be trustworthy, you get words like solid, tried and true. When you look up dependable, you get words like responsible, reliable, safe, sure, and solid. So, as you can see, you can't be one without the other.

404

Likeable people can be counted on to always do the right thing. They are not perfect, but they are examples of excellence. The key component to being trustworthy and dependable is virtuous discipline. Likeable people are liked by others because they can be trusted to do what is right, as well as stand for what is truly true. Also, they can be depended upon to do or not do what they say they will do or will not do.

Eight, likeable people are encouraging. They have the commitment and compassion toward others to be comforting, inspirational, hopeful, and helpful. Likeable people are hopeful with others and will always say something encouraging to them. They know that to be guilty of robbing people of hope is to risk taking all they may have left.

Likeable people know that God never gives up on individuals. God always remains hopeful that people can and will make the decision to turn their life around, to change. Because God is merciful and is the giver of grace, likeable people are aware that giving someone a good reputation to live up to is never a mistake. A "pat on the back" and a recognition of a "job well done", are two ways of encouraging people every day. No one gets tired of being told how important they are to a family or organization. Likeable people often say such things to others. It is easy to like people who lift you up rather than tear you down.

Nine, likeable people are self-nurturing. They take care of themselves by treating themselves with respect. I have always believed that individuals who enjoy spending time alone, as well as spending time in the contemplation of life, goals, relationships, and service to others know how to be self-nurturing.

Dr. Scott Peck, as a military officer stationed at the Pentagon, was part of a team that brought together individuals from all

branches of the armed forces who were exemplary in their performance. Once gathered, the reason was explained as to why
they were summoned and given tasks. The first was to list the
three most important priorities in their lives. They were given an
allotted time to do this exercise. Some took all of the time allotted,
and some finished in half the time. Their priorities varied. However,
what did not vary was the inclusion of one particular priority. Each
in essence said, "I am the most important person in my life."

Think about it! How can you be depended upon to be there
for your loved ones, if you do not take care of yourself and be
responsible in your endeavors? The answer is, you can't! One of
the great lessons of life is that every individual in this world works
either from a base of strength or a base of weakness. Those who
consistently excel in personal and professional endeavors, treat
themselves with importance and respect. They know that if their
base of strength is depleted the strength, energy, and determination needed for a particular challenge or task will not be there.

As a result, they take very good care of themselves. They don't
mistreat themselves. Instead, they nurture the critical areas of
their lives. Individuals who truly have a healthy self-love know
how to nurture themselves to keep performing at their best. Such
individuals know that if they fail in the endeavors for which they
are responsible, others whom they love will be adversely affected.
This is something they will not allow!

Ten, likeable people rub-off well with others. No matter how
much time you spend with a likeable individual you really don't
get tired of him/her. The time you spend with them is what is
commonly called easy time, enjoyable time. Likeable people are
like a positive virus. I know is sounds odd to put positive and virus
in the same phrase, however, likeable people have the ability to

be positively infectious. This is possible only because of the eight qualities I have listed above.

I can promise you with complete assurance that if you are unconditionally accepting of others, a good listener, transparent, reasonable, possess a high social IQ, rise above the negatives of life, are trustworthy as well as dependable, encouraging and are self-nurturing, you will rub well with others.

Be aware that there are times when genuinely likeable people do not rub well with others. This happens when they are in the presence of those who are self-dishonest, insecure, self-rejecting, and truly difficult. Those people are the antithesis of who and what likable people stand for. In these instances, likeable people have met their enemy. They don't have a chance with insecure, difficult people who will never give them a chance to be accepted, even though the likeable will be reasonably accepting of them. This is because difficult people have an agenda and likeable people do not.

In conclusion, I must point out that likeable people are not people-pleasers, nor are they self-promoting at the expense of others. Likeable people first seek to be the best. Once this occurs, whether or not others are pleased with them is simply irrelevant. I truly believe that any individual who is a people-pleaser is not well-liked by many.

o   **Wisdom Principle:** *When one tries to please everyone, one usually pleases no one!*

CHAPTER ELEVEN

THE GREATEST HUMAN ENEMY: THE EGO

One of my mentors, Dr. David Richo, in his marvelous book *The Five Things We Cannot Change and the Happiness We Find in Embracing Them*[19] taught me many wonderful things. Among them is that our ego has a face—F-A-C-E. Dr. Richo used the word "face" as an acrostic to illustrate how the ego seeks to dominate our lives and how its inherent flaws seek to negatively affect the most important and worthwhile endeavors in life. I was moved, as well as enlightened, as he explained how the ego worked against our happiness and fulfillment.

I am going to only borrow the acrostic he used in the book, but my explanations are my own. However, before I begin I want to say that those among us who are not cognitive of how powerful the ego is are likely to be ego-driven, though blindly. The ego sets the tone of their personality—how their personality is publicly expressed, as well as the basis of their decision-making.

---

[19] Richo, David. *The Five Things We Cannot Change and the Happiness We Find in Embracing Them.* Shambhala Publications, Inc. (Boston, MA, 2005)

It is extraordinary to see this in those who are in show business and professional athletics. Most individuals in either of these endeavors are enormously, if not completely, ego-driven. I recall seeing a well-known football player perfectly illustrate this. I remember his scoring a touchdown on a Sunday afternoon. When he did, he threw his arms open and look heavenward. He had this expression on his face, as if he had accomplished something God-like. However, nothing could have been farther from the truth. Based on the applause and cheers he received, one could not help but conclude that there were many thousands in the stadium who believed as he did—that what he did was almost God-like, heavenly.

For the most part, it is understandable that young people in show business and professional athletics are not all going to conduct themselves and their affairs as responsibly as someone exceptional such as Peyton Manning. Many of us forget that most of the individuals in either of these two endeavors are in their twenties to mid-thirties. They are still very young. Do you remember when you were this age? I do. I wasn't nearly as smart as I thought I was. As these individuals in these professions aptly demonstrate, neither are they.

o **Wisdom Principle:** *The more we are ego-driven, the more our personal purpose and meaning are diminished in heart and mind.*

o **Wisdom Principle:** *Ego-driven people are constantly afflicted with boredom. Nothing is more boring than to be self-consumed.*

The same is true of our American teenagers. As much as I love them—their energy, their creativity, their enthusiasm, and their optimism—I cannot help but admit that there are very few teenagers who are not primarily ego-driven. I would say only about 5% of our teens are not. As I look back at the teenage generations that followed mine, that percentage, in my mind, has remained consistently low.

There is no question that there are enormous insecurities and gaps of maturity in the lives of those who are primarily ego-driven. Everywhere they go, they must be the center of attention; they must be the main attraction. Based on their behavior, the attention they crave is equal in importance to the air they breathe. When someone's ego has this much control over one's life, serious problems are in store for such individuals in the future. What can be done?

First, we have to learn that we are not the only show on earth. There are other people on this earth besides us—billions, in fact! Also, God loves them—the rich, the poor, the haves and the have-nots, the crazy and not so crazy—just as much as He loves us. I know that is very difficult for the ego-driven among us to embrace, but nonetheless, it is true.

Second, we can learn that we are here on earth to add to life rather than take from it. Most ego-driven people are very narcissistic. Narcissists take from life with no intention of ever giving anything back. This lends credence to the truth that such narcissists really suffer from a lack of genuine, authentic self-worth. Dr. William Glasser once said that all psychological problems, from the slightest neurosis to the deepest psychosis, are merely symptoms of the fundamental need for a sense of personal worth. He says that self-respect is at the core of the health of any human personality. Ego-driven people are much more afraid of life than they are of death.

Third, we must learn that the ego is primarily emotionally-driven. The battle of life today is fought on the battleground of truth vs. feelings. This battle pits the ego, which is primarily emotionally-driven, against the soul, which is primarily wisdom-driven. If the ego is allowed to call the shots, a person will go with how he/she feels virtually every single time. If the soul—which was breathed into each one of us by the breath of God in order that we may commune with God—is allowed to decide our words and behavior without any interference from the ego, then truth will reign in every word action or decision. I have spoken on this subject of emotionally-driven decisions, throughout this book. I am not going to repeat myself here. What I will say is that if we have the courage to discipline our emotions, then the ego will have enormously less influence in what we think, say, or do.

Therefore, let's look at our egos—this significant yet deadly part of ourselves. Let's see why this is the greatest enemy we face—every day.

David Richo's Face of the Ego[20]

F—A—C—E—
Fear—Attachment—Control—Entitlement

"F"–Fear

The ego fears all of the five great fears I spoke of in Chapter __ on insecurity: rejection, failure, loss of something significant, loss of love, and the consequences of being poor.

The ego is the throne of our pride, and we will do anything to preserve this pride. A person's ego is determined that others think well of him/her. It's the part in all of us that is into people-pleasing and being significant—that is, being known as someone quite special.

The ego is obsessed with the opinions of other people. In fact, the more the ego is obsessed with the opinions of others, the more it will defiantly declare that it is not. However, what do you believe is the one thing that tips all of us off that a person is obsessed with others' opinions? The answer is behavior that conforms to the social norms or expectations of the peer group represented by the person in question

In our everyday lives, our egos are fearful of being embarrassed of being hurt, of being ridiculed, gossiped about, or shortchanged. The ego of the insecure is constantly and consistently tied up in emotional knots. I have known people who live this way and it is not an attractive sight. You see it in their eyes and in their behavior; they are scared to death of life. As Henry Thoreau

---

[20] , Ibid.

prophetically declared, *"People live their lives in quiet despera-tion."* The ego-driven among us are the personification of this.

The only way we can significantly diminish the effect our ego has on our lives is to subdue it, discipline it. I gave you three answers a few paragraphs ago that would help in this endeavor. What I need to add here is that the stronger the control in our lives, which the ego covets, the more desperate it is. Desperation is always a byproduct of fear. To diminish fear, we must embrace faith and cultivate an attitude of loving-kindness. We must realize that we cannot predict how others will respond to us, nor pre-dict the outcome of everything in our lives. There is an enormous amount of insecurity to life.

Those who embrace this insecurity, fare much better than those who run from it, who must have absolute certainty in life— both in their relationships and in their endeavors. Such absolute certainty in life is a myth. It is amazing that the more we are willing to embrace the fact that there are no absolute guarantees in life, the more secure in our relationships and endeavors we become.

o **Wisdom Principle:** *The antithesis of fear is love.* — *Epistle of I John*

"A"–Attachment

The ego attaches itself to anything and everything that will boost its position, influence, and power in our lives, as well as in the lives of others. Spiritually speaking, the "ego" is the carnal side of our lives. Some would call the ego the sensual side. If something cannot be heard, seen, touched, smelled, or tasted, the ego is not interested in it. The ego is in this life for itself. It is #l in its own mind. To remain so is its daily mission. This is why the ego attaches itself to anything, which it believes, can give it meaning. By meaning, I'm talking about anything that reinforces its importance.

This is exactly why the ego is not and cannot be a spiritual component of our lives. The ego is the primary self-centered component of a person's life. Our soul is spiritual, while the ego is primarily emotionally-driven. For this reason, the ego is a very dangerous part of our being. It is illogical precisely because it is emotionally-driven. Remember that emotions are not logical. Since the ego does not care for the spiritual things of life, it only cares for the things that comfort it and give it the attention it desires. This is why the ego is into acquisitions, things. The ego loves things and when it is given sway will use people in order to get things. In essence, the ego believes that a person's life consists of what he/she possesses.

- o **Wisdom Principle:** *You can never kill the ego. You can only discipline it.*

- o **Wisdom Principle:** *Depression results, in most cases, in continually accommodating the ego at the expense of the soul.*

To the ego a beautiful home, chic fashions, expensive automobiles, physical attraction, fulfillment of the senses, and sensual appetites are what matter. All of these are superficial as well as emotionally-driven. When these are lost or taken from us, the ego loses complete meaning. We can lose ourselves as we lose the ability to acquire these things. Tragic!

Christ calls us back to reality when He says, *"A person's life does not consist of his/her possessions—what he/she owns."*

Attachment is a weakness. It ultimately has no permanent meaning and purpose, in our lives; and, in the long run, can't deliver what it promises. Attachment seeks to fill a void in one's life that only God can fill.

We have a hole in our soul, which is God-shaped. No matter how much a person owns, enough will always be a little bit more than he/she has. For the ego, enough is never enough. When the ego gets all it wants, the only satisfaction it has, is to get more. I spoke about this when I discussed the *IFD Syndrome*[21] developed by Dr. Wendell Johnson. The question begs to be asked, "What will we leave behind when we die?" The answer is everything, except our character!

"C"–Control

By control I mean the personification of control. The ego has an enormous hunger for control and believes that if it does not control others or its environment it will be controlled by someone else. The ego is into control. The soul, in contrast, is into surrender. These are opposite sides of the spectrum. For the soul, wisdom says that we gain control in direct proportion to our willingness to relinquish it. For the ego, one gets control by seizing it.

I spoke a good bit about control in the chapters on insecurity and difficult people. The main point I need to make here is

---

[21] Wendell Johnson in a Series of Lectures in 1976 by Wayne Dyer

that control is a myth. None of us can control everything in our lives. There are billions of people who believe otherwise to their detriment.

There are some things over which we have control. However, there are more things in our lives, over which we don't have control. We have no control over people—their affection or lack thereof for us; their attitude toward us or their perspective about us. We have no control over whether others will like us or unconditionally accept us. When it comes to our health, we don't have complete control over it. A portion of our health is dictated by our family background—our genetics.

We don't have complete control over the well-being of those who are important to us. If you disagree with this, take a trip to Memphis, Tennessee, go to St. Jude's Children's Hospital and look at those precious children who have been stricken with various kinds of cancer. Then, tell me that we, as human beings, could have prevented their becoming ill with these horrible cancers. I doubt you can truthfully do this.

We don't have control as to whether we will live as long as we would like, and ultimately, we don't control when we die. We can take good care of ourselves as best we know how. We can respect our bodies and treat them appropriately. However, if we do so, we still have no iron-clad guarantee that we will live to be a hundred.

We have no control over the decisions our children make as they grow older and begin the process of individualization. We have no control over vehicles driven by other people on the streets, roads, or highways we travel every day. We have no control over the weather—whether tornadoes will strike and when, or where hurricanes will hit.

We don't have control over whether our garbage will be picked up as promised, or whether our televisions will be working when that special program comes on. Most of all, we can't control people against their cooperation.

The ego says that we can know all. Reality says we can know very little. The ego says that we have the power to define our ultimate meaning and purpose in life. Wisdom says that only God has the ability to define man's meaning and purpose. The ego says that man can begin with man and solve all of the problems with which he has been perplexed over the centuries. Wisdom says that the ultimate questions in life are found in finding our God-ordained purpose in life.

The reality is that man controls very little. As an example, we have in the last 12 years experienced a hard, economic recession as a nation. Some analysts say that we are finally over this and the economy is growing. Other prognosticators are predicting that the recession will continue. If we could control anything, most would want to have the ability to control our nation's economy so that hard recessions would never occur, but we don't have control over this state of affairs. During the recession news broadcasters trotted out one expert after another, asking them what the answers were to resolving the economic dilemma. The responses were the same: *"We can try yada-yada-yada, but we don't know for sure if it will work."* When asked how long it would be before we could climb out of that hard recession, the answers were still speculative. No one knew for sure. If this one reality does not burst the bubble of the ego in thinking that it can have complete control over anything that affect us, nothing will.

Listen, complete control is a myth. Don't let your ego convince you otherwise!

o   **Wisdom Principle:** *Ultimately, we live by faith and we walk by grace.*

"E"–Entitlement

By strict definition, entitlement means "to claim a privilege". The ego believes it is entitled to be first in line for all the things it wants in life, and that the world was put here to fulfill its wishes, demands, and needs. All of us have been afflicted from a little to a lot by this flaw of the ego.

We have enormous examples of this ego-driven character-istic. People who rob and burglarize believe they are entitled to invade people's homes and take what does not belong to them. Those who commit all kinds of crime do so primarily because they believe they are entitled to do so. We are told that rape is a crime of hate. I am sure there is validity to this statement. However, would I be out of place if I suggested that men who rape women also believe that they are entitled to take from women what they wish, even if these same women say, *"No, you cannot."*?

In Genesis 3:1-7 we read about the temptation of Eve, and eventually Adam, in the Garden of Eden. There have been hun-dreds of thousands of messages brought by ministers on this pas-sage and some terrific insight has been brought to light. One insight I've garnered is that Satan implied in its response (verse three) to Eve's statement (verse two) that she was entitled to eat the fruit from the *Tree of Knowledge of Good and Evil*. Satan convinced her of this by telling her that what God said was not what He meant. The ego's right of entitlement, along with other dynamics, was a key factor in Eve's being tempted to doubt God's instructions and to trust her own feelings. Bad move!

If the ego could get its way in every context of life, it would seek to get a college degree without proving it could do the work. It would demand that the knowledge necessary to get a degree be imputed rather than learned. It would demand its paycheck on Monday instead of getting it after the work was done on Friday. It would demand that it be given a pass every time it chose to do what it wanted when what it wanted did not work out as it thought it would. It would demand that others acquiesce to what it wants, rather than expecting it to do the right thing. It would demand control of all aspects of its existence, which directly affects its happiness and contentment.

An entitlement mentality is rooted in narcissism and all narcissists lack self-discipline. An entitlement mentality is also rooted in a misconception that everything in life, is about what the ego wants. Make no mistake about it … you cannot have an entitlement mentality and a responsibility mentality at the same time. If the ego had its way, it would choose entitlement over responsibility every single time.

The ultimate entitlement to which the ego believes it is entitled is to be exempt from all of the vicissitudes of life. In other words, the ego believes it ought to be exempt from all legitimate suffering. This is why all ego-driven individuals will do everything in their power to circumvent legitimate suffering. Any individual, who gives into his/her ego on this point will remain a child psychologically, emotionally, and spiritually all of his/her life. An individual in this condition is in for a long, hard life.

There you have it, the *F-A-C-E of the Ego*. Thanks to Dr. David Richo, we are much more enlightened to the danger of our egos being the decision-making component of our lives. Everything the ego embraces is against all biblical teaching, as well as against any demonstration of spiritual common-sense. When we allow our lack of self-discipline to put our egos in charge of our lives, we will never know the meaning of peacefulness—fulfillment and what it means to be fully-functioning.

- o **Wisdom Principle:** *"Don't indulge your ego at the expense of your soul."* —Rick Warren

- o **Wisdom Principle:** *The ego-driven among us are the most immature, insecure, and shallow.*

CHAPTER TWELVE

SUCCESS FACTORS

Chapter Introduction

As I write this chapter, I am well aware that there are many Christians who don't believe that it is right for a Christian to be concerned about career and success. They believe this because none of us will take these two components of life into eternity. The fact that we will take our character into eternity further emphasizes the critical truth that an indomitable character cannot be attained without self-discipline and a burning desire to become the best you can be. I have yet to meet a successful individual, both personally and professionally, who was not self-disciplined. It is difficult to be self-disciplined in life and at the same time not be successful in your personal and professional endeavors. Those who hold to the view that Christians shouldn't be concerned about careers and success, are, more often than not, militantly ignorant regarding the success factors for living a fully-functioning life.

They are also likely guilty of living their lives by doing the minimum required. In the chapter on the Five Critical Lines of Life, I have given a solid counter-response to their pseudo-spiritual posi-tion. This position, which many emotional and ethereal Christians embrace, is not only pseudo-spiritual, but is also, I believe, a justi-fication for mediocrity and living one's life on minimums.

We are allowed to live in the world, but in the Epistle of I John we are also admonished not to become <u>of</u> the world. I Timothy 5:8 tells us that anyone in charge of their own home who does not provide the necessities of life as best they can for those within their household, is worse than an apostate. A Christian is com-pelled to live a disciplined life as well as live a fully-functioning life. This is difficult to do without a daily commitment to becoming the best you can be. For those who live life in the real world, believing pseudo-spiritual mumbo-jumbo will not get them where they need to be in life.

There are many components to success that I have already discussed in this book. It is important to me, however, that I give you a brief overview of what I believe to be the key success fac-tors that propel any of us toward a level of excellence that only about 5% of the world's population achieves. This chapter is the shortest chapter in this book because much of the material you need to read, comprehend, and digest has already been given to you in previous chapters. What I want to do here is to review these components, briefly describing each.

You may not know the name of Joseph Sugarman. However, he is a remarkable individual. He wrote the book called *Success*

Forces[22]. It did not get a very wide reading. I found it on a bargain shelf at a book store several years ago, and I recently read it. I ought to have read it the first week I bought it. However, I may not have comprehended key parts of this book if I had. The adage that no one can learn anything, until he/she is ready, is absolutely true in my case.

Joseph Sugarman developed, organized, and led the largest mail-order company in the United States from 1975-2000. His book was written in 1980. In it, he details his "bumpy" ride to success and is quite candid regarding his failures. He specifically gives the key lessons he learned from each one.

What I enjoyed in this book was the marvelous honesty Mr. Sugarman demonstrated in how he sought to correct his mistakes and failures. I have never met him, but someday I hope I do. In this book, he gives the key components to both personal and professional success. I learned most of these concepts thirty years ago. However, he gave a couple in the book that I'd never considered, especially in the manner he presented them.

Mr. Sugarman's components for success do not differ very much from the components that other "success gurus" have on their respective lists. But his style of presenting his success factors is refreshing. The list I am going to give you is a compilation of a list I have made over the past three decades. I have adjusted it some, as well as added to it. When I come to a point that Mr. Sugarman also had on his list, I will point out how his presentation was refreshingly different.

The first component for success is deciding to be successful. There are too many people who take life as it comes and never

---

[22] Sugarman, Joseph. *Success Forces*

make a consistent, long-term, concerted effort to passionately pursue a worthy and successful endeavor. This is because they never decide to do so. They spend too much time hoping and wishing but never doing the things they need to do. First, a person must decide to be successful.

o **Wisdom Principle**: *"If one advances confidently in the direction of his dreams, and endeavors to live the life he has imagined, he will meet with a success unexpected in common hours."* —Henry David Thoreau

The second component is that you have to be the success before you achieve the success! Another way to put it is that a person must be successful within before evidence of that success will occur without. You simply have to become what you want to experience daily. I have spent a lengthy amount of time explaining how becoming internally successful occurs.

The third component is to have a determination to be the best. You must be determined to be an expert at what you want to do professionally. Too many people depend on "lotto luck" for success. Too many waste time wishing they were better at their various endeavors. Too many wait for a miracle. Too many choose to believe that fate is the final determinate. Too many are simply lazy. Such beliefs, assumptions, and attitudes will always end in disillusionment, disappointment, and failure.

The world is impersonal. The world doesn't care who is successful and who fails. Factually and realistically, it is up to each individual in this world whether he or she will be successful or unsuccessful. It's not really complicated. It has to do with you, me and, what we decide to do about our lives.

I have heard people say that they just haven't had the breaks that others have. This is an excuse not a reason. I have seen people who've been lucky. I also know that if such "lucky" people lost what they had they wouldn't be able to reproduce it. Those who have been "lucky" have neither the knowledge nor character to be successful at any significant endeavor because they have never done something that was legitimately successful before. They also don't have the discipline to be successful. Would you rather cultivate the skills and character to be successful, or would you rather try "Lady Luck"?

Commit yourself to being the best at that for which you have a passion. You will never regret committing yourself to being the best you can be at such an endeavor rather than settling for a kind of "that's good enough" level of competence.

The fourth component is focus. The most common reason for failure, though not the only reason, is a broken focus. Everyone who has achieved something of any significance will eventually mention the necessity of possessing a powerful and undistracted focus. The areas in which a person must be nothing less than excellent must be given an unbroken focus. Also, by focusing on the select areas in which your expertise must be exemplary, you accelerate your success. All endeavors result in failure when an individual gets off target, is distracted, or goes on a tangent. Don't go off on tangents! Tangents are dangerous! Also, don't allow yourself to be distracted.

The fifth component is do it differently.[23] I can relate very well to this one point. All of my life I have seen young people in athletics mimic their athletic heroes in how they stand in the batter's box in baseball, throw a baseball, shoot a basketball, dribble a basketball, or throw a football. I have also seen young people mimic their heroes in their behavior after they score a run, make a basket, score a goal, or make a touchdown. However, upon closer examination the most successful athletes, musicians, or actors have been those who did it the way that helped them become the most effective in what they sought to achieve. Being authentically themselves helped them to become the achievers they became. Mimicking others is a failure force.

Do it differently if you want to be successful in your endeavors. While you are doing it differently why not seek to do it better? I think it is worth a try. Don't you? Pull yourself out of the system. The more innovative you are, the greater your success. The more you copy something that has already been done, the greater your chances for failure! When you innovate, you are doing something that no one else has done in exactly the way you are doing it. Remember the principle of conformity: When you are like everyone else and you act like everyone else, you lose your uniqueness. Your uniqueness is your most important asset!

The sixth component is cherish your failures.[24] Joseph Sugarman is the only individual, who has put this one in the components for success, of all of the books I have read. In the movie *Batman Begins* there is a scene in which the young Bruce Wayne

---

[23] One of the components of Joseph Sugarman's **Success Forces**

[24] One of Mr. Sugarman's success forces.

falls into a dry well and breaks his arm. When his dad rescues him, he asks, while carrying him up the stairs, *"Bruce, why do we fall? So we can learn to pick ourselves up."* This is a great scene in the movie and it is a memorable line. I have heard this line most of my life, but not as succinctly as how it was given in this movie.

We ought to cherish our failures for many reasons. I have already given you some reasons in chapter one where I say that "failures are stepping stones which point you toward success."[25]

What I want to add to this point, regarding failure, is that you will learn much more from your failures, than you will your successes. Failures teach us where we went wrong and what will not work. Failure helps us to become stronger, at the "broken places".

Also, there is information needed that can only be learned from failure. Properly applied, this information propels us toward success. I am deeply convicted that it is much better to take action in an endeavor and fail, than to simply do nothing and hope for the best.

The third thing I want to point out is this. You must understand that to be risk-averse—to hesitate to extend yourself in the achievement of a worthy endeavor—is to admit that you have too big of an ego to fail. The fear of failure and the size of your ego are the two components that contribute to an individual being risk-averse. I didn't share this point in any other section of this book in which I have spoken about failure. However, our opportunities to fail increase our opportunities to succeed in the future if we effectively process the information we gained from our failures.

---

[25] This is one of the fifteen essentials in this volume, Chapter One, page 39.

o **Wisdom Principle:** *Setting out to achieve a worthy goal, while facing the fear of failure, is to succeed in the greatest endeavor of life. That endeavor is attempting to succeed when failure is staring you in the face and saying, "You can't."*

There are those, who attempt only the things they believe they have a well-above average chance of succeeding. In those endeavors, according to Mr. Sugarman, the individuals he knew who managed risk in this fashion were minimally successful.

Go after what is important to you. The greater the risk, the greater the effort will be required, and the greater your reward will be. It is healthy to attempt to accomplish endeavors in life with an attitude that if you fail you will embrace such failure because the information you gain in failing will propel you toward success faster than if you had played it safe.

o **Wisdom Principle:** *Your resilience grows stronger in direct proportion to your willingness to risk failing in order to succeed in any endeavor.*

When it comes to failure, it is to your disadvantage to have an ego that is timid when facing risk. If you allow your ego to get in the way when you consider taking a necessary risk, you will never be uncommonly successful. Therefore, keep in mind that your unwillingness to risk is a sign that you have too big and too fragile an ego. Letting this happen is foolish.

My perception of people who always play it safe, is that they are gripped by the fear of failure, as well as the fear of losing something of significance. Fear freezes them into being risk-averse.

Besides this, you will find that such people are critical of anyone who has taken a risk and failed. By criticizing someone who has taken risks and failed, they are justifying their own lack of action. They seize upon such failure, using it as a reason for not taking any necessary risk. You and I know that if our forefathers had taken the same attitude, the United States would be primarily located in what is now New England.

o **Wisdom Principle:** *"I don't like people who have never fallen or stumbled. Their virtue is lifeless and it isn't of much value. Life has not revealed its beauty to them."*—Boris Pasternak, Novelist

o **Wisdom Principle:** *Failure is a temporary condition. Giving up is permanent.*

o **Wisdom Principle:** *"I would rather be a failure at something I love; than a success at something I hate."*—George Burns / Entertainer

The seventh component is relish your problems! Henry Kaiser once said, "Problems are opportunities in work clothes." The sages of history spoke in concert regarding problems. We all know, for example, that problems are part of life. People who resent problems are mainly the ones who believe life ought to be easy and problem-free. This is not only a misconception but an unintelligent view of life.

There are three kinds of problems: Those you cause, those that occur by simply living life, and those that are created by others. Everyone has problems. The only individuals who do not are dead! The greatest success stories, according to Joseph Sugarman, are those in which someone recognized a problem and turned it into an opportunity. The one who succeeds in an extraordinary way, the one who embraces problems, defines them, and looks for the opportunity that is hidden within them.

o **Wisdom Principle:** *Looking at problems as just problems will create the seeds for failure that cause you to want to give up.*

How do you turn a problem into an opportunity? Good question! Here is an exercise for you to do:

1) **You must define the problem**. What is the problem and what caused it? What were the mitigating factors? Were individuals involved in creating the problem? Would there have been a problem even if the smartest individuals in your group had been involved in the project? If you answer these questions you will have defined the problem.

2) **Restate the problem**. Mr. Sugarman says that you should do this in a creative way that will give you a fresh perspective. Rewrite the problem in several different ways. It doesn't matter how many, you just need to rewrite the problem enough until something clicks inside your head and you say to yourself, "Got it!"

3) **Take a yellow legal pad and write SOLUTIONS in caps at the top of the page**. Next, begin writing ideas/solutions that will aid in resolving the problem you are facing. Write ten solutions. When you finish, reread your suggestions for resolving the problem. If none of them are viable, stop the exercise and do it again the next day. If you are under a deadline and a solution must be found by the end of the day, take a break for about an hour and then do the exercise again. Brian Tracy, the marvelous performance psychologist, is credited for developing this exercise. Those who have used it in problem-resolution swear by it and have testified that it has never failed them.

4) **Finally, look your problems squarely in the face and decide that you will not allow yourself to be defeated by them.** I love the saying: *"God is greater than any problem I face."* Never fear your problems. Inside each one you lies a seed that if properly nurtured, can propel you toward success.

The eighth component is always be honest. Mr. Sugarman has a list of six "success forces". Of the six, this one is by far the most profoundly explained. The discussion of honesty is the best chapter in his book. I like how he begins the chapter: *"Don't over-sell, don't over-promise, but always over-deliver."*

Throughout this book I've emphasized that honesty is engrained in an indomitable character. As a nation, we have experienced an unusually harsh recession, and during that time we witnessed instances, and heard stories, of some very unscrupulous and dishonest business dealings that resulted in the need for the US Government to spend trillions of dollars to keep our economy afloat. We have discovered it is possible to be dishonest in your business dealings and yet not be illegal.

It is easy to believe that those who walked away with ill-gotten wealth got away with it. However, just as it takes time for a hurricane to gather strength before making landfall and creating havoc, over time most of these dishonest businesspersons are getting their just due. No amount of money will get them out of their self-made prisons, or the federal ones either, when such a hurricane hits their lives.

As a result of the horrible example these stars of Wall Street have set, it's easy for someone who is young and naïve to believe that in order to come out ahead in business, you have to lie, cheat, bribe, and steal. Such beliefs are nothing but misconceptions. The belief that a person who is honest and has integrity is at a disadvantage in a business environment is simply false. Truth is ingrained in the universe. Think about these points.

1) Those who embrace honesty and live accordingly will come out ahead. Those who don't respect honesty and truthfulness will create a failure factor in their lives that will be difficult to overcome.

   Mr. Sugarman says that every dishonest businessperson is eventually found out and from that point on travels under a dark cloud. *"The dishonest businessperson doesn't see the cloud, but everyone, who deals with him, does."*

2) Only deal with honest people. I have always heard that you never do business with those who have more problems than you. Not doing business with dishonest people needs

to be added to that admonition. Dealing with dishonest people can come back to haunt you. They are always looking out for themselves, most often at others' expense. There is only one way to protect yourself from dishonest people; and that is to not do business with them—period!

3) Always have a paper trail regarding agreements. Even an honest person can have a poor memory. As a result, have contracts. Make sure these agreements spell out what is expected from your vendor and what your vendor expects from you. If you are getting special pricing from your vendor because you have committed to selling x-number of dollars' worth of products over a 12- or 18-month period, that needs to be in the agreement, as well.

Anything that has been discussed and agreed to needs to be in the agreement. Anything that can put "sand in the gears" of the agreement to keep it from working at a level of excellence, needs to be in the agreement. Agreements avoid misunderstandings, as well as helping to prevent dishonesty.

4) Finally, pick the people with whom you will do business before you pick the product. If you want to know why I say this, you need to refer to the second point of this particular success factor. Honest people relieve you from the enormous stress you would be under if you had chosen to work with dishonest people.

Example: Several years ago, I met a gentleman I'll call Jay. He was much younger than I and I perceived him to be quite a special somebody in the company where I was working at that time. For quite a while I only knew him only from a distance. Eventually, I had the opportunity of working with him. As I got to know him, I admired his honesty and that he didn't play favorites when it came to the truth. It gave me a tremendous amount of peace to know in my gut that I could trust him. This alleviated an enormous amount of stress in my life and also helped me give greater focus on my purpose for working in that particular company. I've never forgotten the benefit and affirmation that his honesty contributed to my life, both professionally and personally. He was a prince of a gentleman and I'm confident that he still is. The reason I say this can be summed up in one word—character. Character trumps any other deficiency a person may have, and it always will.

Within that same company there were some dishonest people who were absolutely lethal. They were experts at managing perceptions, in contrast to delivering results. I, unfortunately, did not recognize soon enough that the stress I endured while working with them was a signal from my intuition that they could not be trusted to do the right thing.

I hate to think the worst of people. In fact, I try to think of everyone as having a good reputation to live up to when possible. However, what I failed back then to realize was that there are people who only want to get ahead using the least amount of effort. If you are in the way, you will, as they say, eventually be toast. Working with dishonest people will drain you of the energy you could be using to help improve the company's success as well as your own. Therefore, if you have the opportunity to work with someone like Jay you should be intuitively comfortable. Pick the people with whom you will do business first, then pick the product.

The ninth component is always set sensible and realistic goals, and the effective strategies to achieve them. People don't have problems achieving goals; they simply have a problem in setting them. Setting goals is not as easy as most think. I have been in meetings when goals were being discussed and more often than not those who were leading the meeting were off the proverbial radar when it came to setting them. In some cases, I truly believed that they may have been born without a brain. How can one trust those who have set ridiculous, unachievable goals? Outrageous goals lead to failure 99.99% of time!

I mentioned in the first chapter that we have become a society of words. What I meant by this is that we now live in a culture that believes if something is said it has been done. As you and I know, such a belief is insane. However, we have millions of people who believe that intention is the same as action. Those you know who have this perspective cannot be trusted to make good decisions much less set common-sense goals.

1) **Goals must be achievable**. Earlier in this chapter, I said that we've been in a long and difficult recession. I personally know of individuals who are working for companies that have set sales goals that would be difficult to achieve in a healthy economy, much less in a recession economy. Why senior managers throw unrealistic goals at their people in such an economic climate is beyond my comprehension.

I cannot believe that these managers didn't realize they were sacrificing their credibility as well as their trustworthiness, when they conducted themselves in such an illogical manner. However, this doesn't seem to stop them.

I have read every book I could find on sales success. I have read scores of books on how to be successful. I am telling you, unequivocally, that goals must be realistic. If they are not, demoralization of your organization is just around the corner. When your team is demoralized, the company/organization for which it works has literally lost everything. Goals must be achievable.

2) **<u>Goals must also be believable</u>**. I don't know of anyone who has reached a goal that didn't believe it could be reached. I spoke to this point earlier in the book. Believable goals are imperative to success, because you must have a target that not only you can visualize achieving, but that you truly believe you can achieve. If you don't have a believable target, you don't know what you are aiming for. Without believable goals at which to aim, all you have is nothing. When you aim at nothing, you will always hit it. You must be clear on this point. Your target must be believable, as well as realistic.

In the movie "The Shooter", the lead character (Mark Wahlberg) is a man trained by our military to be a sniper. He honed his talent so well that he could hit a can of stew virtually dead-center at 1500 yards. The catch is that he was only one person of about a dozen individuals in the whole world who could make that shot. Here is where sales managers go wrong. They assume that the members of the company's sales team, are as much of an expert at selling as an expert sniper is at shooting a weapon. Truthfully, most sales people are not even close to being such experts in their respective sales fields. For your people to be sales-persons with the skill of a sniper, they must have extraor-dinary training, which in turn has produced extraordinary ability. There are only a few people in the United States who can provide training in sales at such a high level of expertise. Brian Tracy used to be one of those individuals.

Those who believe that such incredible sales ability is easy to obtain and without much sacrifice, are misguided. If you are an owner of a company or in upper manage-ment of a corporation; and you have such incompetency in your sales leadership, you need to do something about it, before you are let go for being dumb enough to have hired such individuals in the first place. Bad sales managers can sink a company faster than a laser-guided missile can level a building.

3) <u>Goals not only must be sensible, achievable, and believ-able, goals must have a plan for achievement</u>. I am sure you have been in meetings, where goals were set and an ambiguous discussion as to how to achieve them occurred. Ultimately, as a result of such a nebulous conversation, a definitive plan was never set. It was assumed that everyone involved would devise their own plan to achieve the goals. This is a very bad assumption, as well as a huge mistake by the sales management. Goals cannot be achieved, without

having a strategy to achieve them. If you have had trouble achieving your goals, you likely have had two problems to overcome. One was your inability to believe you could reach your goals; and the second was failing to develop a plan for achieving them.

o   **Wisdom Principle:** *A goal without a plan is only a dream.*

o   **Wisdom Principle:** *"It takes as much energy to wish as it does to plan."* —Eleanor Roosevelt

o   **Wisdom Principle:** *"When you reach for the stars, you may not quite get them, but you won't come up with a handful of mud, either."* —Leo Burnett

The tenth and final success factor which I want to mention is be a believer in you. As I close this chapter, there are times when I think about this and tears come to my eyes. Why do I cry? Because I was a fool to allow others to decide my worth, define what I was becoming, and also determine just how much I should believe, in myself. For me, it was the three greatest mistakes of my life. What I allowed other people to do was sabotage my belief in myself rather than enhance it.

All of the work my grandmother did in helping to instill confidence in me, went for naught at times once I got out into the world. I truly wish that I had remembered her words and had turned a deaf ear to those who knew less than she and were even less intelligent than I. How I wanted to please others and be liked by others. But over time, I found out that in order for that to happen I had to betray myself. Once I found out what I'd done it broke my heart. I also became very angry—at myself—for allowing this to happen.

In time, I found the grace, with God's help, to forgive myself for not having more sense and more courage. What is so tragic about all of this is that I allowed people, who truly did not really know me at all, to strongly diminish my belief in the person I was, and was becoming. I wasn't perfect, but I was faring better than most. This was the greatest self-inflicted pain of my life.

You and I are on a pilgrimage. We are to be learners. We are to be doers. We are to be encouragers. There are too many people out there who want to redefine us. Frankly, they are not qualified to do so. You and I must set very high standards for those who seek to influence us and seek to "remold" us. People who seek to redefine us are likely to be extremely unqualified to fill the role, because if they were qualified they would be setting an example rather than talking one.

God created you. You were in His mind before you were in your parent's mind. He saw you, when you were in your mother's womb and He loved you with all of His heart. God would not have created you if He hadn't believed in the person you could become. You are God's handiwork; you and I need to reflect it.

o **Wisdom Principle:** *You must believe in yourself before anyone else will believe in you.*

o **Wisdom Principle:** *"No one rises to low expectations."* —Les Brown

CHAPTER THIRTEEN

FINAL THOUGHTS

There are obviously many more issues that deserve a whole chapter. However, I must allow you to think on what I've written and give you space to work out the critical issues I've discussed in this book with yourself and the Heavenly Father.

Before I close this volume, I want to highlight some of these important issues. I don't have a particular order for them. I wrote them down over a period of time and decided I'd would write something about each concept or admonition that you can take further yourself.

1. Affirm God's importance of you by how you live your life

The world is impersonal. For this reason, what you and I do is important. People will ultimately ignore what we say but will pay attention to what we do. You must embrace the fact that you matter ... more importantly, that you matter to yourself. Don't worry about what the world thinks. The two most important opinions we need to be concerned about when it comes to us, are

God's and our own. All other opinions are inconsequential compared to these two. Elizabeth Elton Smith once said, "There is an applause superior to that of the multitude—God's and one's own about oneself."

I've read that Oprah Winfrey has said that there is nothing that can equal the knowledge of contentment that comes from being the person you are meant to be. Amen, Oprah! You are a beautiful person when you can say something in so beautiful a manner. All of mankind is loved by God and each of us in this world is the object of His everlasting love. When you affirm God's importance to you, the longer you live, the more beautiful life becomes. God does not love us because we are beautiful. We are beautiful because He loves us!

2. Half-hearted commitment is no commitment. – Dr. Bill Self

Make up your mind that you are going to give everything you have to whatever you commit your life to. Operating your life on minimums will get you minimum results. I admonish you not to settle for less than your best. It takes enormous discipline over a lifetime to stay the course and continue to pursue excellence. However, those, who have not done so over their lives, very often live to regret it. I can tell you from personal experience that no amount of money can buy back your regrets.

Wayne Gretzky, the great ice hockey player who is now retired, once said, "You always miss 100% of the shots you don't take." I could not have said it better. Whatever you choose to do, you must give it your whole heart.

3. If truth is not part of your life, it will be difficult to recognize.

One of the great tragedies of living life from day-to-day is getting used to lying about who and what you are and living the lie you have become. When you do this, a portion of the eyesight of your heart becomes blind to what is true. Cut it anyway you like, you can't know truth when you won't first confront the truth about yourself.

o   **Wisdom Principle:** *Our ability as individuals to grow and mature is in direct proportion to the exact and true knowledge we each have of ourselves. The more ignorant we are as to who and what we are as individuals the more immature we remain.*

Also, you need to commit yourself to being a truth-seeker of the highest order in every area of your life. This requires that you stop rationalizing the limitations and flaws about yourself, family, friends, and even about life itself. It isn't worth it. Again, your continuing to lie about these areas will have a diminishing effect on your ability to ascertain what is true in the simple, everyday aspects of life and family. One's inability to ascertain what is true in life leads to a person being consistently confused as to what to believe in critical contexts of life.

o   **Wisdom Principle:** *The less a person embraces what is true, the more a person will seek to rationalize what is* *untrue. He/she will eventually "couch" what is not true as being true.*

When you refuse to be truthful regarding these criteria, your ability to know and understand what is true becomes a frustrating and confusing endeavor. Just as you have to have a hammer to effectively hit a nail, you have to have a definitive, uncompromising commitment to truth to be able to clearly recognize it and to effectively process it into your life.

This is a much bigger issue—this uncompromising pursuit of truth—than most in this country realize or admit. There is so much rationalization going on in the trenches of life that most people would not know the truth if it were a shark and bit them in the nose. Make your life the embodiment of what is true.

Dag Hammarskjold, Secretary General of the United Nations in the 1960s, wrote: *"You cannot play with the animal inside you without becoming wholly animal. You cannot play with falsehood without forfeiting your right to truth. You cannot play with cruelty without losing your sensitivity of mind. He who wants to keep his garden tidy doesn't reserve a plot for weeds."*

4. Never stop dreaming!

When someone stops dreaming, something terrible happens deep inside of the heart, and it isn't good. Where there is no hope in the future, there is no power in the present. We must dream. Every achievement begins with a dream. Why are dreams so important? Three reasons: One, we have the ability to become what we dream. Two, dreams become achievements when we believe and act on them. Three, as Eleanor Roosevelt once said, *"The future belongs to those who believe in the beauty of their dreams."*

What is necessary to make dreams come true? *One is self-discipline.* I have read several biographies over my lifetime. In all of them I found that the first victory for each was conquering the inner space of the self. *The second necessity is drive coupled with passion, which is nothing less than an unwavering commitment.* Call it what you will, but to fulfill a dream you need to be driven, as well as be moving in a specific direction.

Sometimes you are going to experience smooth sailing, and sometimes you will be sailing against the tide and the prevailing winds. Regardless, you must sail your ship. The fulfillment of dreams will never occur while drifting aimlessly on the sea of life, or anchored in the safe *harbor*. Dreams cannot be achieved by playing it safe. There are billions on this earth who believe they can, but this is either a misconception or nothing less than militant stupidity. Carl Jung once said, *"Those who look outside, wish and those who look inside; awaken!"* Look within you to find what you are passionate about. Never fear dreaming. If you do, you will never reach the potential that God has for you.

5. Never stop learning and growing!

o **Wisdom Principle:** *"Growth is the only evidence of life."* — Cardinal John Henry Newman

o **Wisdom Principle:** *"The only way we can grow is to turn weaknesses into strengths."* —Dr. Wayne Dyer

Quite frankly, I don't know what people are thinking once their kids are grown and out of the house. It seems that psychologically and spiritually, they atrophy. As we grow older, I don't understand why we believe our usefulness, our ability to learn, and our need to continue to grow are not as important as they used to be. Some of the greatest achievements in this world were accomplished by people over the age of sixty. In fact, some of the most significant growth of my own life occurred after age fifty. I don't believe my hunger to grow in virtue, knowledge, and effectiveness has ever been greater. We must keep our minds open. We are never going to learn what we don't want to know. We must face the truth that ignorance, more often than not, is intentional! We ought never to be guilty of intentional ignorance.

o **Wisdom Principle:** *"There is always room for improvement. It's the biggest room in the house."* —Louise Heath Leber

I know that our society, as a rule, sees the older generations as impositions. However, those who share that perspective are making a huge mistake. That kind of attitude results in the development of an ambivalent attitude of one group toward another. This is not what becoming the best you can be is about. The most enlightened and insightful minds are possessed by the older people who live among us. They can give us an enormous amount of insight into life and living that would take most of us decades to learn. To discount the elderly as useless is to make one of the biggest mistakes of life.

If I were a youth minister or a minister of religious education, I would have a senior citizen in every youth Bible study and young adult Bible study give a 10-minute talk every Sunday on subjects such as:

> ➤ What is the most meaningful experience of my life?
> ➤ What is my most memorable vacation?
> ➤ What is the greatest defining moment of my life?
> ➤ What is a legacy that is worth leaving?
> ➤ What are the key components in my relationships that contributed to my happiness?
> ➤ What is the greatest thought I have ever had?
> ➤ What is the greatest surprise/curve life has thrown at me?

These questions are important, as well as insightful. We all wonder, after people have lived their lives, what they have to say about it. We could have such an opportunity every week if we utilized the resources in our senior citizen groups. We should all be ashamed for not utilizing these wonderful people better.

For example: When I was in college one of the senior members of the church I attended, spoke to our college group. "The Greatest Challenge of My Life" was the topic for that Sunday. After this terrific lady spoke, she turned the question toward us and asked us to share the greatest challenge each of us was currently facing. One of those attending had moved on campus from a small town in Louisiana. Somehow the paper work for a student loan had been processed incorrectly. This person arrived on campus thinking the financials for attending our school had been completed only to find out that there was a problem. It looked like they would not be able to stay in school and would have to go home and reapply for student aid the next semester.

We were all quiet in the room and the lady standing in front of us said to this student, "Get me the bill for your tuition, books, and board and I will write the school a check." We all applauded. I was absolutely stunned. If that lady had not been our speaker that Sunday a marvelous opportunity for service would have been missed. God used her to resolve this challenge in the life of a college student.

We need our senior citizens to be a vital part of our lives. If they are not, all of us will greatly miss the illumination for life and living that is right at our disposal. In fact, a general perusal of the Bible will clearly show that individuals who were often used by God were well past middle-age before God called them for a specific assignment. Moses is a primary example.

Matthew Kelly, in his book *The Rhythm of Life*, has an exhaustive list of the names of world-renown individuals whose talents or abilities were not recognized until they were well into their senior years. I have seen similar lists before, but his was the largest. The achievements of some of the following individuals on that list, as well as others I have read, did not occur or were not noticed until these people were well past the mid-century mark.

> ➤ Henry Ford—50 when he started Ford Motor Company.
> ➤ Ray Kroc—52 when he bought out Mac and Dick McDonald and officially started his McDonald's Hamburger restaurants.
> ➤ Pablo Picasso—55 when his renown as a painter began to grow.
> ➤ Oscar Hammerstein—64 when he wrote the lyrics to *The Sound of Music*.
> ➤ Winston Churchill—65 when he became Britain's Prime Minister.

- ➤ Nelson Mandela—75 when he became president of South Africa.
- ➤ Michelangelo—70 when he designed the dome of St. Peter's Basilica.
- ➤ Ben Franklin—79 when he invented the bifocal lens.
- ➤ Frank Lloyd Wright—91 when he completed his work on the Guggenheim Museum.
- ➤ Abraham, the father of the nation of Israel—90 when his life's purpose was revealed to him.
- ➤ Moses—80 before he was chosen by God to lead the nation of Israel out of Egyptian bondage.

If you believe that your best days are behind you, you have seriously underestimated the effect of God's power in your endeavors, as well as your value to Him and the rest of the world. The world may not know it, but it is waiting for your assignment from God to become known to you so you can actualize it in your life and to the world.

- o **Wisdom Principle:** *"Knowledge is a responsibility for the integrity of what we are—primarily of what we are as ethical creatures."* —Jacob Brorowski, Scientist

- o **Wisdom Principle***: "It is what you learn after you know it all, that's important."* —Jimmy Williams

6. It's impossible to stumble when you are sitting down.

Ships were not made to stay in the harbor, any more than we, as human beings, were meant to be statues. I have spoken enough about those who are risk-averse. However, just in case you didn't get the message, you need to realize that you will never become what you were meant to be, unless you are clear, about what you were meant to become.

o   **Wisdom Principle:** *Only the cowards, the doubters, the wishers, and the lazy play it safe.*

To accomplish your purpose, you must stay away from those who try to belittle your ambitions and your dreams. Small people have a talent crushing ambitions and dreams. But the truly great among us draw us toward the light so that we can see the possibilities of what we can become.

Therefore, live your life; not as your acquaintances, friends, family members, or even spouses who doubt what your dreams tell you, but as the Heavenly Father leads. It is the only way to live a life that is truly worth living. You do this and you will find yourself whispering the words spoken by Franklin Lloyd Wright, the great architect. *"The longer I live, the more beautiful life becomes."*

Yes, we are all going to make mistakes. Mistakes are events in our lives, but they don't necessarily define our lives, if we don't allow them to do so. Most importantly, you need to remember that it is what you do after you have made a mistake that counts. James Joyce said, *"Mistakes are the portals for discoveries."*

He was right, you know. Even Benjamin Franklin said, *"The man, who attempts endeavors of significance will make mistakes.*

However, those who are fearless in attempting such endeavors will never make the biggest mistake of all—doing nothing!"

o **Wisdom Principle:** *It isn't what you start that is important, but what you finish, that is.*

I spoke in the chapter *Success Factors*, about having too much pride to fail. Don't be guilty of this. When you have too much pride the world can become a lonely place. There is a dignity—pride, if you will—that is humbling, demanding, and uncompromising. All of us need to embrace that kind of dignity. Don't have too big of an ego that you find it impossible to succeed. The fear of failure freezes all big egos. People who are afraid to fail are being guided by their egos. People who are willing to risk failure in order to succeed are most often being guided by their soul. Becoming the best we can be is a sacred responsibility.

o **Wisdom Principle:** *"A man must be big enough to admit his mistakes, smart enough to profit from them, and strong enough to correct them."* —John C. Maxwell

7. Learn to cultivate your own garden.

I'm not sure if many people can grasp this concept. I have said throughout this book that the mediocre among us tend to confuse managing perceptions with delivering results. The militantly lazy among us are unbelievably talented at this ploy. This ability serves to avoid accountability and management scrutiny regarding the results individuals are getting in their personal and professional endeavors.

The reason I brought this up again is that those who are adept at managing perceptions are also notoriously guilty of giving unsolicited advice and of telling others how they should be living their lives. Their conversations with others are filled with "you should have", "you need to", "you could have", "it would have been better if", and one particular overused, accusatory phrase, "it is your fault that".

I have found that those, who are notorious for telling spouses, brothers, sisters, friends, and professional associates what they ought and ought not to do, are often out-of-control in certain areas of their own lives. There simply is not enough time in a day to be advising the world and taking care of your own life at the same time. Those who are always dispensing unsolicited advice to others are almost always guilty of neglecting the cultivation of their own garden.

There is an interesting section of verses in the Gospel of John, Chapter 21:15-22. Christ had risen from the dead a few days earlier. He was having breakfast with His disciples, and when He finished, He looked at Simon Peter, who, the evening before Christ was crucified, had denied ever knowing Him. Then He asked, *"Peter, do you love me?"* Twice more He asked this question and all three times Peter gave Him the same response, *"Yes Lord, I love you."* After predicting Peter's ultimate fate (verse 18), Peter turned around and looked at another of Christ's disciples, John, then asked Christ, *"What about him? What's his assignment?"* Christ responded definitively to Peter saying, *"If I want him to remain here and simply live his life out in this village, what does his assignment have to do with yours? You just follow me."*

This scripture, more than any other in the New Testament, testifies to the necessity of cultivating your own garden—focusing on your assignment—rather than constantly focusing on other's lives and making sure that everyone else is doing what you think they ought to be doing and marching to the drumbeat of your expectations of them. When a person's focus is on others, their focus is completely off of what they ought to be doing. Frankly, I have always believed that those who are focusing on how others are cultivating their garden, rather than on the cultivation of their own garden, are often the most guilty of judgmental thinking—the redefinition of others, the criticism of others, and the gossiping of others.

If you focus diligently on becoming the best you can be, you will not have time to focus on what others are doing. I think you can trust me on this. Those who have time to focus on how others are cultivating their own garden, have lost the meaning and purpose of their lives and chosen to do the least to secure the most. Such people consistently live very frustrating and dissatisfied lives. Instead of getting their bearings and moving in a constructive direction, they choose to focus on how others aren't doing much better than they are. In turn, they criticize them in order to justify their own deficiencies, and their lack of discipline.

Learning how to "cultivate our own gardens" will propel us toward an unparalleled focus in the direction and effectiveness of our lives. When the challenges of life afflict us, our lives will have a serenity that cannot be found any other way. Cultivating our own gardens will give us the strength to encourage and help others in their endeavors, when the opportunity presents itself.

8. Defining moments are moments of decision!

At the end of his message each Sunday, my beloved pastor, Dr. Bill Self extends an invitation for those who need to make a defining decision regarding their relationship with the Heavenly Father. He invites people to come forward and share their decision. I find this to be the most critical time in our worship service. I have always believed that "pew decisions" are "poor decisions". There is something about coming forward and taking a minister by the hand and saying, "God is leading me to …". Whatever the commitment it settles your soul and seals that commitment in your heart.

Now you have read this book I hope that you found the message is clear. There is a definitive path to excellence. You can take it, or you can ignore it and believe that a successful life is mostly the result of luck. It's your call. God loves you. He has a plan for your life and if you will trust Him you will discover a life you only dreamed could be possible. Don't look at other people in order to determine the quality of your faith. Look at Jesus Christ. Now He is a person worth emulating.

Keep in mind that there isn't a mistake God can't forgive. There isn't a sin He won't forgive. No one is so bad that God can't redeem them, and no one is definitely too good to be redeemed on their own. You may ask, "What am I being delivered from?" You are being delivered from your sin and from your selfish, destructive self.

Listen to your soul, not your ego. Your ego is too proud to ask forgiveness. Your soul isn't. Your soul was made for God. Only God can fill the void in your soul and in your life. To be the best you can be you must embrace the best there is. Nothing better exists, or is more critical than embracing Christ. You will be at the heart of my prayers! God's best awaits you!

###

THE LISTING OF SUBJECTS & SCRIPTURES IN PROVERBS

-A-

Accountability (The Consequences of Actions) (3) 5:21; 6:28; 6:33

The Adulteress (14) 2:16-19*(definition), 5:3-6; 5:8; 5:20; 6:24; 6:26; 6:29; 7:5; 7:10-21; 7:24-27; 9:13-18; 22:14; 23:26-28; 30:20*(Adultery, to the adulteress, is as ordinary as eating a meal.)

Adultery (5) 5:14; 5:16; 6:32; 7:22-23; 23:26-28

Alcoholic Beverages (6) 20:1; 21:17b; 23:20-21; 23:29-35; 31:4-5; 31:6-7 (This scripture refers to the benefits, in ancient times, to the medicinal use of certain alcoholic beverages.)

Anger (Deflection of) (5) 15:1; 21:14; 25:15b; 29:8b; 30:33

Anxiety / Stress (1) 12:25a

Arrogance (An Evil Trait) (6) 17:19b; 21:4; 21:24; 28:14b; 29:1; 30:12 *

Attentive (Paying attention) (5) 4:1; 4:20, 5:1; 7:24; 22:17

Avoid (Things to) (5) 4:15; 20:3; 20:19; 16:6; 16:17

-B-

Base of Strength (Depletion of) (2) 5:10; 6:1-5

Beauty (Seduction of) (1) 6:25

Being Teachable (5) 10:9a; 11:9b; 13:10b; 18:15; 20:18

Blameless (The Blessing of Being) (9) 2:7; 2:21; 11:15; 11:20; 19:1; 20:7; 28:6; 28:10; 28:18

-C-

Challenges (2) 17:12; 20:22

Character (Loss of) (5) 5:9; 10:9b; 12:3a; 25:9-10; 30:7-9

Common Sense (Thinking & Behavior) (10) 4:26; 10:11a; 10:14a; 10:19b; 10:20a; 11:12b; 19:16a; 20:11; 21:29b; 27:17

Compassion (Generosity) (5) 11:24-25; 18:16; 19:6b; 22:9 (Speaks of kindness to the poor); 24:11

Confidence (Keeping of) (1) 11:13b

Contempt (3) 14:31; 17:5; 18:3

Contentment (2) 13:25; 19:23.

Control (1) 29:11

Correction (9) 5:12; 10:17; 12:1; 13:18; 15:5; 15:10; 15:12; 15:32; 29:15

Corrupt Talk (Evil & Profane Language) (23) 4:24b; 6:12; 8:13b; 10:11b; 10:14b; 10:18b; 10:19a; 10:31b; 10:32b; 11:9a; 11:10b; 11:11b; 12:6a; 12:8a; 12:13a; 13:3b; 15:4b; 16:27b; 16:30b; 17:7b; 17:20b; 26:24-25; 30:14a*

Co-Signing a Loan (5) 6:1-5; 11:15; 17:18; 22:26-27; 27:13

-D-

Deceit (Devious Behavior / Mind) (7) 2:15; 12:8b; 12:20a; 14:2b; 14:17b; 26:24; 26:26

Discernment (12) 3:21-24; 10:9a; 10:13a; 14:6b; 14:33; 15:14a; 16:21a; 17:10; 17:24a; 18:15; 19:25b; 28:11b

Discipline (Of Children) (4) 23:13-14 (The term "rod" is not necessarily a stick); 29:15; 29:17; 29:1 (Words alone will not result, in discipline.)

Discipline (Correction) (18) 1:3; 3:11-12; 5:12; 5:23; 9:8b; 10:13b; 10:17a; 12:1a; 13:24; 15:5a; 15:10; 15:31; 15:32b; 19:18; 27:5-6; 29:15; 29:17; 29:21

Discipline (Being Tested) (2) 24:10; 27:21

Disciplined Speech (26) 10:9b, 10:20a, 10:21a, 10:31a, 10:32a, 12:6b, 12:14, 12:18b, 13:2a, 13:3a; 15:2a; 15:4a; 15:7a; 15:23; 16:1b; 16:13; 16:23a; 16:24; 17:27a; 17:28; 18:20-24; 20:15; 21:23; 22:11; 25:9-10; 25:11*

Discretion (Tactful & Profound Insight) (5) 1:4b; 2:11; 5:2; 8:12b; 11:22

Dissension (Strife) (7) 6:14; 16:28a; 17:1; 17:14; 22:10*; 28:25a; 29:22a

Dreamers (4) 12:11b; 25:14; 27:1; 28:19b

-E-

Encouragement (2) 25:25; 27:17

Envy (5) 3:31, 14:30b; 23:17; 24:1-2; 24:19-20

Evil Desires (3) 11:6b; 17:5b; 26:25

Evil (Avoiding the Influence of) (1) 25:4-5

Eyes (Haughty) (1) 30:17

-F-

Failure (Fear of) (5) 10:24a; 21:20b; 24:12; 24:30-34; 29:25a

Faithfulness (4) 3:3a; 17:2; 20:6; 25:13

False Witness (Lying Under Oath) (15) 12:17b; 12:19b; 12:22a; 13:5a; 14:5b; 14:25b; 18:5; 19:5; 19:9; 19:28a; 21:28; 24:23-25; 25:18; 26:23; 26:28

Family (8) 11:29a; 17:6; 17:17; 18:19 (Family disputes); 18:22; 20:7b; 20:20; 24:27

Fantasy (Chasing a) (2) 12:11; 29:19

Folly (4) 15:21a; 19:3 (Blames God for the outcome of his decisions); 22:15; 27:22

Fool / Fools (General) (40) 1:7b; 1:32b; 3:35; 8:5b; 10:8b; 10:10b; 10:14b; 10:18b; 10:21b; 10:23a; 11:29b; 12:15a; 12:16a; 12:23b; 13:16b;13:19b; 13:20b; 14:7; 14:8b; 14:7; 14:8b;14:9a; 14:14b; 14:24b; 15:2b; 15:5a; 16:22b; 17:21; 17:24b; 18:2; 18:6-7; 19:10*; 19:13a; 19:29b; 21:20b; 23:9; 24:7; 26:1; 29:9; 29:11a

Fool (Relationship with) (4) 26:3-12; 27:3; 27:22; 28:26*

Fools (Responding to) (1) 26:4-5

Friendships / Friends (10) 12:26a; 13:20a; 17:9; 17:17; 18:24; 19:7b; 27:6; 27:9-10; 28:23

-G-

Gain (Ill-gotten) (10) 17:8; 17:23; 20:14; 20:17; 21:6; 22:16; 28:8; 28:16b; 28:20b; 29:4b

Generosity / Compassion (5) 11:24-25; 18:16; 19:6b; 22:9 (Kindness to the poor); 24:11

Gloating Over the Misfortunes of Others (2) 24:17-18; 25:20

Gluttony (1) 28:7

Goals (13) 13:12b; 13:19a; 14:4 (No accomplishment without difficulties); 15:22; 16:1a; 16:3; 16:9; 16:26; 19:21; 20:18; 21:5; 24:27; 29:18a

God (As a Protector) (5) 2:8; 3:6; 3:25-26; 18:10; 22:12* (God is the ultimate guardian of truth.)

God (As a Shield) (2) 2:7; 30:5b

God (Purposes of) (3) 16:4a; 20:22; 20:24

God's Omnipotence (6) 15:3; 16:33; 20:27; 21:30-31; 22:2; 30:2-4

God's Ways vs. Man's Ways (1) 25:2

God's Word (The Perfection of) (1) 30:5a

God's Word (Warning not to add to) (1) 30:6

Good Man (18) 2:20-21; 10:7a; 10:9a; 10:16a; 11:3a; 11:17a; 12:2a; 12:13b; 13:22; 14:14b; 15:27b; 20:6-7; 25:21-22; 28:14a; 28:18a; 28:20a; 28:26b; 28:25

Good Name (2) 3:4; 22:1

Good Path (2) 2:9; 10:29a

Gossip (6) 11:13a; 16:28b; 18:8* (Consequences of being a gossiper); 20:19; 26:20 (Gossip stirs up a quarrel); 26:22

Government Leaders (5) 8:15-16; 17:26; 24:21-22; 25:3; 28:2

Grave (The) (7) 1:12; 8:36b; 9:18; 15:11a; 21:16; 27:20; 30:16a

Greed (8) 11:26; 11:28a; 15:27a; 16:8; 22:22-23; 28:22; 28:25a; 29:4b

Grief (1) 10:10a

Guidance (3) 1:5b; 6:22-23; 20:18

-H-

Hard Headed People (1) 19:16b

Hard Work (Reward of) (9) 12:11a; 12:24a; 12:27b; 13:4b; 14:23a; 21:26; 22:29; 27:23-27; 28:19a

Hatred (4) 10:18a; 15:17b; 26:26; 29:10

Head (The) (2) 1:9a; 4:9.

Health (5) 3:8; 4:22; 5:11; 14:30a; 15:30b

Healthy Self-Love (2) 19:8a; 19:16

Heart (The) (24) 3:1b; 3:3b; 4:21; 4:23; 6:21; 7:3; 14:10; 14:13; 14:30a; 15:11b; 15:13a; 15:14a; 15:15b; 15:28a; 16:5; 17:3; 17:22a; 18:15; 20:5; 20:9; 21:2b; 22:11*; 23:7*; 27:19

Heart (Definition of) (1) 4:23b

Home of the Righteous (2) 12:7b; 24:3-4

Hope (3) 13:12a; 23:18*; 29:18a

Hot Tempered People (7) 14:16b; 14:17a; 14:29b; 15:18a; 19:19*; 22:24-25; 29:22b

Humility (9) 11:2b; 12:9; 13:13b; 14:35; 15:33b; 16:19; 18:12b; 22:4; 29:23b

-I-

Immorality (5) 12:28b; 23:26-28; 28:13a; 29:3b; 29:4b

Impatience (1) 21:5b

Listen / Listening (The Call to) (18) 1:5a; 1:8; 1:33; 2:1; 4:20; 5:1; 5:7; 5:13; 7:24; 8:6; 8:32-34; 12:15b; 13:10b; 18:13; 18:17; 19:20; 19:29; 20:12

Lists / Listings (In Proverbs) (9 Lists) 6:16-19 (Seven Things God Hates / Attitudes); 8:13 (Four Actions God Hates); 30:7-8 (Three Things Asked of God); 30:11-14 (Four Kinds of Evil People); 30:15b-17 (Four Things That Are Never Satisfied); 30:18-19 (Four Things Too Amazing to Understand); 30:21-23 (Four Absurd Things); 30:24-29 (Four Things That Are Small But Wise); 30:20-31 (Four Creatures That Manifest Dignity When They Walk)

Longevity (4) 4:10; 9:11; 10:27a; 20:29b

Love (7) 3:3a; 8:17; 14:22b; 15:17a; 16:6a; 19:22a; 27:5

-M-

Marriage / Fidelity (3) 5:15; 5:17-20; 14:22b

Mocker / Mockers (16) 1:22b; 3:34; 9:7; 9:8a; 9:12b; 13:1b; 14:6; 15:12; 19:25a; 19:29a; 21:11a; 21:24; 22:10 (Mockers & strife go hand in hand); 24:9; 29:8a; 30:17

Murder (4) 1:11; 1:16; 28:17; 29:10

-N-

National Security (3) 11:14; 28:2; 28:4

Neck (3) 1:9b; 3:22; 6:21

Pretentiousness (7) 13:7 (Both actions are foolish & self-rejecting); 13:8a (Poor man is never truly threatened, with the loss of riches); 23:6-8 (Caution is given in the acceptance of the hospitality of a two-faced individual); 26:24; 27:14 (Warning in patronizing a neighbor); 28:11; 29:5

Pride (10) 8:13b; 11:2a; 13:10a; 15:25a; 16:5; 16:18*; 1:7a; 18:12a; 21:24; 29:23a

Promises to the Righteous (12) 10:3a; 10:25b; 10:28a; 10:29a; 10:30a; 11:4b; 11:6a; 11:8a; 16:20b; 22:6; 28:10b; 29:16b

Prosperity (14) 3:2; 10:4b; 10:5a; 10:6a; 10:15a; 10:22a; 11:4a; 11:10a; 11:11a; 11:16b; 13:21b; 15:30a; 21:21; 28:28b

Prudence / Prudent Life (11) 1:3-4; 8:12a; 12:16b; 12:23a; 13:16a; 14:8a; 14:15b; 14:18b; 15:5b; 22:3a; 27:12a

-Q-

Quarrels (6) 17:19a; 18:6; 18:18-19; 20:3; 26:17; 26:21

-R-

Reputation (1) 3:15 (Two daughters whose names are "Give" and "Give More")

Revenge (1) 24:28-29

Reverence / Respect for God (18) 1:7a; 1:29; 2:5; 3:7; 8:13; 9:10; 10:27a; 14:2a; 14:16a; 14:26-27; 15:16a; 15:33a; 16:6b; 19:23; 22:4; 23:17; 24:21-22; 28:14a

Riches (The Pursuit of) (3) 23:4-5; 28:8; 28:25

-S-

Simple (The) (12) 1:22a; 1:32; 7:7-9; 8:5; 9:6a; 9:16; 14:15a; 14:18a; 19:25a; 21:11a; 22:3b; 27:12b

Sin (Enticement to) (3) 1:10; 1:14; 9:18

Sin (Entrapment of/into) (4) 1:18-19; 1:31; 21:17a; 28:21b

Sin (Turning from) (2) 1:15; 20:22

Slander (1) 30:10

Soul (Value of) (1) 11:30b

Speech (Reckless) (8) 12:18a; 15:28b; 18:6-7; 20:14; 26:18-19 (This scripture speaks of making a joke of your thoughtlessness); 26:23; 26:28; 29:20

Spirit of Man (3) 15:13b; 17:22b; 18:14

Stupidity (3) 1:17; 12:1b; 15:21a

Success (Desire for) (5) 10:24b; 11:27a; 16:7; 21:20a; 29:25b

-T-

Tithing (1) 3:9-10

Thievery (5) 6:30-31; 11:1; 20:10; 20:23; 22:28 (This is like stealing.)

Trickery (Manipulative Behavior) (7) 6:13; 12:2b; 12:5b; 12:10b; 25:23; 26:23; 26:24

Truth (Speaking of/the) (11) 12:17a; 12:19a; 12:22b; 14:5a; 14:25a; 18:4; 18:20; 22:16; 23:23; 24:26; 28:23

-U-

Understanding (The Pursuing & Achievement of) (26) 1:6; 2:2; 2:5b; 2:6; 2:9; 2:11b; 3:13b; 4:1; 4:5; 4:7; 8:1; 8:5; 8:14b; 9:6b; 9:10b; 10:23b; 13:15a; 15:21b; 16:16b; 16:22a; 17:27b; 18:2a; 19:8b; 20:5; 21:16; 28:2

Un-self-disciplined People (8) (Characteristics) 9:13-18; 10:17b; 15:32a; 19:2; 19:19; 29:15b; 29:19 (Cannot be disciplined with words.); 29:21

-V-

Violence (2) 13:2b; 21:7

Vows (2) 20:25; 30:2

-W-

Wealthy (The Rich) (10) 14:20b; 14:24a; 15:16b; 18:11; 19:4a; 19:14a; 22:7; 28:6; 28:18b; 29:3b

Wicked Against the Wicked (2) 12:12a; 29:24

Wicked Behavior (Consequences of) (22) 5:22; 10:9b; 10:24a; 10:25a; 10:30b; 11:5b; 11:7a; 11:8b; 11:19b; 11:21a*; 11:23b; 11:27b; 11:31; 12:7a; 12:21b; 13:21a; 13:25b; 21:7; 22:8; 26:27; 28:13a; 28:27b

The Wicked / General (41) 2:13-15; 2:22; 3:33; 4:15-17; 5:23; 6:15; 9:7b; 10:6b; 10:7b; 10:9b; 10:16b; 10:20b; 10:26b; 10:28b; 10:29b; 10:30b; 11:5b; 11:7; 11:8b; 11:17b; 11:18a; 11:23b; 14:22a; 14:32a; 15:8a; 15:9a; 15:26a; 15:29a; 21:10; 21:18;

21:27; 21:29a; 24:1-2; 24:8; 25:19; 28:5; 28:12b; 28:15; 29:2b; 29:7b; 29:27b

Wicked Intent (12) 13:17a, 16:2b, 16:27a, 16:29, 17:4, 17:11, 21:27, 26:2, 26:23, 26:24, 28:10a, 29:16a.

Wicked (The Way of) (23) 4:19; 10:3b; 10:9b; 11:3b; 12:26b; 13:5b; 13:9b; 13:15b; 14:11a; 14:14a; 14:19; 14:34b; 16:4b; 17:15; 18:3; 21:8a; 21:12; 22:5a; 24:1-2; 24:19-20; 28:12b; 28:28a; 29:10

Wickedness (14) 13:6b, 17:13; 18:5; 19:28b; 21:18; 22:8; 24:15-16; 25:4-5; 26:26-27; 28:4; 28:10a; 29:6a; 29:12; 31:3

Widows (1) 15:25b

Wisdom (Attainment of) (7) 1:2; 2:12; 4:4-9; 5:2; 8:1-31; 9:1-6 (Wisdom has seven pillars); 24:3-4

Wisdom (Call to) (3) 1:20-33; 8:1-4; 22:17-21

Wisdom (The Embracing of) (15) 2:4-5; 2:10; 3:13a; 4:2; 4:4; 4:6-7a; 4:8; 4:11-12; 7:2b; 8:35; 9:12a; 10:1a; 24:13-14; 28:26b; 29:3a

Wisdom (In Creation) (1) 3:19-20

Wisdom (Life of) (2) 24:3-4; 28:1

Wisdom (Origin of) (1) 8:22-31

Wisdom (Rejection of) (5) 1:24-28; 1:30; 4:6; 8:36; 10:1b

Wisdom (Sign of) (2) 16:31; 18:17 (Listen to both sides.)

Wisdom (Speech of the Person of) (3) 8:6-8; 12:6b; 14:3b

-Y-

Total References: 1,151

ABOUT THE AUTHOR

Donn Poole received his undergraduate and graduate education at East Texas Baptist University and Southwestern Baptist Theological Seminary, respectively. He embraced his call to the ministry in college and served in churches throughout the southeast and southwest. Donn has already completed volume two, of his *Proverbial Wisdom for a Fully-Functioning Life Series.* He is currently working on volume three. The subject in this third volume is an individual's spiritual development.

Donn's first book, *What a Man Needs to Know about Himself and a Woman Prior to Entering into a Permanent Relationship* targeted young and middle-aged men. Donn is currently pastor of a Cooperative Baptist Fellowship, new church start, in The Villages, Florida. His personal website is scheduled to be launched in 2016. It will be called: *Proverbial Wisdom for Personal and Spiritual Development.*

Donn has two grown children; Angela Dawn and Jason Spencer. He and his wife Katherine live in The Villages, FL.

CPSIA information can be obtained
at www.ICGtesting.com
Printed in the USA
LVOW10s2258220418
574486LV00036B/503/P